T0245532

MORE PRAISE FOR *THE OSWALDS*
BY PAUL R. GREGORY

"Paul Gregory's compulsively readable memoir is filled with shocking revelations, among them that when the twenty-one-year-old University of Oklahoma student Paul Gregory first started taking Russian language lessons from the twenty-one-year-old Marina Oswald, there was always the same six-month-old *Time* magazine on prominent display in the extremely modest duplex. The cover photo was *Time*'s Man of the Year for 1962: President John F. Kennedy. Paul Gregory relates that Lee Harvey Oswald had carried this old copy with him when he and Marina emigrated from the Soviet Union to Dallas. No novelist would construct such a scene. History is unbelievable."

—JOHN BATCHELOR, host of *CBS Eye on the World*

"Some sixty years ago, an insignificant school dropout who had failed at almost everything he had tried to do, Lee Harvey Oswald, brought his Carcano rifle to the Texas School Book Depository in Dallas and became one of the most infamous criminals in history. Ever since then, the assassination of President John F. Kennedy in November 1963 has been engulfed in a morass of false-hoods and ludicrous conspiracy theories. This book finally sets the record straight about Oswald, building on the earlier seminal work of Priscilla Johnson McMillan. . . . Paul Gregory, who later became one of the world's leading experts on the economy of the former Soviet Union, happened to know Oswald (and Oswald's Soviet-born wife, Marina) exceedingly well. In this book, Gregory brings to bear his authorial skills and academic expertise in showing how the pathetic young man he had known in Texas could have committed such a monstrous crime. Gregory's book offers a definitive personality sketch of Oswald and a great deal of evidence that should put an end, once and for all, to the notion that shadowy forces intent on murdering the president would have enlisted such an unreliable and tempestuous loser. . . . Gregory's book will stand the test of time."

—MARK KRAMER, Director of Cold War Studies, Harvard University

ALSO BY PAUL R. GREGORY

Women of the Gulag: Portraits of Five Remarkable Lives

Politics, Murder, and Love in Stalin's Kremlin:
The Story of Nikolai Bukharin and Anna Larina

Lenin's Brain and Other Tales
from the Secret Soviet Archives

Terror by Quota

The Political Economy of Stalinism

THE OSWALDS

AN UNTOLD ACCOUNT OF MARINA AND LEE

PAUL R. GREGORY

DIVERSION
BOOKS

For more information, email info@diversionbooks.com

Diversion Books
A division of Diversion Publishing Corp.
www.diversionbooks.com

First Diversion Books edition, November 2022
Hardcover ISBN: 9781635768213
eBook ISBN: 9781635767926

Printed in The United States of America
10 9 8 7 6 5 4 3 2 1

Library of Congress cataloging-in-publication data is available on file

To Pete Gregory

CONTENTS

CONTENTS

PART I

THE
ASSASSINATION

Dallas Tx. (AP bulletin) President Kennedy was shot as
his motorcade left downtown Dallas.

1

I KNOW THAT GUY

In the early afternoon of Friday, November 22, 1963, I joined the handful of University of Oklahoma Russian-language students trickling into class. The launch of Sputnik, a short five years in the past, had taught us that the USSR was a credible Cold War threat. And Robert Vlach, our charismatic, chain-smoking professor, had assured us that those who knew Russian would be able to name their own terms in life. While his assertion was somewhat exaggerated, speaking and reading Russian served me well in later life.

Our class met in a small corner room of the university's Gothic Bissell Library. On the way in that Friday, I noticed my economics professor, Jim Hibdon, hunched over a book, sitting at a large table just outside the classroom.

The session was about to begin as classmate Ken Studebaker rushed in with news that was already shaking the world: "The president has been shot in Dallas! All classes are canceled." We all hurried from the classroom without exchanging a word. On the way out, I told Hibdon the news: "The president has been shot." Usually expressionless, he looked at me in shock and perhaps disbelief, and hurried away to find out for himself.*

Earlier that Friday morning in 1963 as I prepared for classes, I vaguely registered the fact that the president had visited my hometown of Fort Worth the day before and was due in Dallas today. I had given some thought to cutting classes to go see him. Had I done so, I would have perhaps witnessed the motorcade, and the public murder of a president. As it was, I avoided that trauma but settled for learning about it at a distance. Not much of a distance at that: Dallas and Norman, Oklahoma, are close enough to each other that I could almost feel the shock waves emanating.

On that November day, I was certainly the only person at the University of Oklahoma, and one of the very few Texans, to know both Lee and Marina Oswald. But I had no inkling that either was or might be even remotely involved in the horrific act taking place at Dealey Plaza.

. . .

When the Pew Research Center asked Americans in 2019 to name the most important historical event of their lifetimes, the top results were not surprising. In first place came September 11, followed by the election of Barack Obama as the country's first Black president, and then the tech revolution led by companies like Google and Apple. But, in fourth place, ahead of the Vietnam War and man landing on the Moon, was the assassination of President John F. Kennedy on November 22, 1963.

Like 9/11, the Kennedy assassination left a deep scar on the American psyche. As of this writing, most Americans of a certain age can still remember where they were when the news flash came in from Dallas.

* Coincidentally, I would meet Professor Hibdon seven years later at a job interview at the University of Oklahoma—on the very day Robert Kennedy lay dying from an assassin's bullet. The RFK tragedy reminded both of us of our fleeting interaction outside my Russian class on November 22, 1963.

The Kennedy assassination also fostered a distrust in government. By appointing distinguished and trusted public figures to investigate the crime as members of a non-partisan commission, headed by the chief justice of the Supreme Court, Earl Warren, politicians and government officials thought that Americans would accept the verdict delivered in a comprehensive report in September 1964: that the president was murdered by a sole gunman—Lee Harvey Oswald—acting alone without the assistance of others.

Decades later, only a third of Americans believe the Warren Commission's conclusion that "one man killed JFK." Instead, two-thirds believe "others were involved." Remarkably in this age of extreme partisanship, there is agreement across age, gender, race, education, and party affiliation that our thirty-fifth president was gunned down by a conspiracy. Most people believe it, but no one can prove it.

That the Warren Commission's lone assassin—Lee Harvey Oswald—was an unaccomplished, poorly educated misfit continues to feed the public's skepticism. *Nonentities do not change history.* By this line of reasoning, we should be leery of the lone gunman conclusion unless we can explain with firsthand detail and confidence how Oswald could gun down the world's most heavily guarded figure using only his own meager devices.

And that's what this book is about. It asks whether our "intimate" portrait of Oswald conveys in him the motive, resources, cunning, and killer instinct to have indeed changed our history as he fired on the president's motorcade passing below him.

I would not be writing this book had I not known Lee Harvey Oswald personally. From June through mid-September of 1962, I was the sole companion of Lee Harvey and Marina Oswald outside of Lee's immediate family. I visited this young married couple often in the duplex where they settled after Lee's return from his defection to the USSR. I drove them around Fort Worth in my family's yellow Buick as we talked, shopped, and explored the city. This was Marina's first taste of her new world.

. . .

During the presidential campaign of 1960, I had supported Richard Nixon. But then Kennedy pulled us through the Cuban Missile Crisis. My friends and I at school in Oklahoma all remembered those tense thirteen days, huddled around a flickering black-and-white television screen at 1318½ Garfield Street. We all pondered whether we would live to see the next day. I became a Kennedy admirer in that very difficult time.

In those days, televisions were not ubiquitous. I hurried the few steps to the student union where I knew there was a TV, large by the standards of the day. About fifty students already sat on the carpet in front of the set (see my photograph in the photo section). It was tuned to CBS. I watched as a familiar Dallas-Fort Worth newscaster, KRLD's Eddie Barker, struggled to handle the biggest story of his professional life. I had grown up with KRLD's reporting of local news, weather, and sports.

Periodically, Walter Cronkite, not yet the venerable "Uncle Walter" of American newsmen, appeared on screen to speak in his deep, reassuring voice. But the main fare was local programming of interviews with motorcycle policemen, eyewitnesses at Dallas's Dealey Plaza, where the shooting occurred, and with officials from the sheriff's office. In the wild confusion, the eyewitnesses told wildly contradictory stories that quickly gave rise to countless conspiracy theories.

We saw pictures of weeping crowds at the assassination site and outside Parkland Hospital, where Kennedy had been taken. KRLD played, over and over again, a smiling President Kennedy in sporty sunglasses waving to the enthusiastic crowds along the motorcade's route. Jackie sat next to him in a pink outfit that would soon be covered in her husband's blood. There was also film of people at Dealey

Plaza, fearing more bullets, protectively covering their children as they crouched on the grass at the plaza. One man, on the verge of tears, told of seeing a massive wound on the president's scalp. Nonetheless, we TV watchers continued to hope that he had not been mortally wounded.

Yet many, if not most, of us knew what Cronkite was about to say when he was handed a bulletin at 1:32 p.m. We watched as he put on his glasses, silently read from the single sheet of paper, took off his glasses, and said in a choking voice:

"From Dallas, Texas, the flash, apparently official: President Kennedy died at 1:00 p.m. Central Standard Time"—glancing up at the clock—"two Eastern Standard Time, some thirty-eight minutes ago."

The old pro newsman paused, overcome by emotion, swallowed hard, put his glasses back on, and continued to read:

"Vice President Johnson has left the hospital in Dallas, but we do not know to where he has proceeded; presumably he will be taking the oath of office shortly and becomes the thirty-sixth president of the United States."

After recapping that the president was dead, Cronkite passed coverage to a CBS colleague and left the studio sound stage to regain his composure.

Back in Norman, Oklahoma, there was no sobbing among the assembled students. Only stunned silence. What could anyone say at a time like this? I did not see anyone I knew among the crowd. We sat there as strangers yet all partners in grief, as we numbly watched KRLD broadcasters continue their coverage, waiting for interruptions from the CBS network.

Vague reports came in that a police officer had been shot dead and that the shooter had been apprehended and was being brought to the police station. There was no information linking the two events.

At 2:01, an excited reporter, located at Dallas police headquarters, shouted out on camera: "They are bringing in a suspect!" The TV showed a short man, disheveled in a white, V-neck tee shirt and dark trousers. He was surrounded by police officers. His face was bruised, and one eye was black.

I stared in utter and stunned disbelief. It was clearly Lee Harvey Oswald! I muttered mainly to myself in shock: "I know that man."

. . .

The late Priscilla McMillan, author of the memorable book *Marina and Lee*, urged me for years to write my recollections as the one "who knew Lee best." Almost sixty years later, I am finally following her advice. Shortly before her death at the age of ninety-two, Priscilla read the first draft of this account, and judged it "authentic."

When I chose to characterize Lee Harvey Oswald as my "friend" in an essay I wrote for the *New York Times* marking the assassination's fiftieth anniversary, I used the fourth dictionary definition: "A person one knows; an acquaintance," not the more common "a person whom one knows, likes, and trusts." I would say that Marina and I *did* become friends in this stricter sense, since she refused to accept payment for the language lessons she gave me, stating that "friends don't take money from friends."

I doubt that Lee had any friends with the possible exception of his two buddies in Minsk, Pavel and Erik. Pavel was assigned to Lee by the KGB, so he really doesn't count. Erik hung out with Lee to improve his English, but he forged as close to a real friendship as anyone in Lee's life did.

Lee's aversion to people was already evident as a teen. When asked by a school psychiatrist whether he preferred the company of girls or boys, Lee's response was terse: "I dislike everybody." As Lee and Marina began to circulate in the Dallas Russian community, the story was always the same: people liked Marina but disliked her boorish husband.

It was not until I read testimony before the Warren Commission from Lee's brother Robert Oswald that I fully appreciated my standing in being able to speak of Lee and Marina as they began a new life in their young marriage:

MR. JENNER (Warren Commission Deputy Counsel): Now, you were seeking to report to us the friends and acquaintances of your brother and your sister-in-law subsequent to their return to the United States in June of 1962. Now, who next in addition to Paul and Peter Gregory?
MR. OSWALD: None, sir.
MR. JENNER: None?
MR. OSWALD: None.

The "Peter Gregory" (Pete) in Robert's statement was my father. It was through his Russian background (his name at birth was Pyotr Grigoriev) that the connection with Lee and Marina was made. Pete, however, developed an immediate aversion to Lee and kept his distance. He would later testify that he disliked Oswald "as arrogant, stubborn, and would not discuss anything but his particular type of politics, which was definitely radical."

This left me as the only friend of Lee and Marina Oswald as they settled into a run-down duplex on Mercedes Street in the looming shadow of the giant Montgomery Ward mail-order headquarters, and Lee began his work as a manual laborer at Leslie Welding Company.

Lee Oswald's address book confirms his limited world. Upon checking the entries, among the very few "social" addresses, Oswald had both my Fort Worth and Norman addresses as well as our Fort Worth telephone number (Pershing 1 1639).

In this book, I use my experience with Oswald and his wife, Marina, to create a portrait that offers a key to the national trauma of November 1963 when a high-school dropout, undesirably discharged Marine, defector to the Soviet Union, and down-and-out welder gunned down JFK. The army of assassination buffs are wasting their time on missing bullets, Oswald doppelgangers, and Soviet, Cuban, or Mafia assassinations. We need to look no further than Oswald himself. We must ask how this "little man" with megalomaniacal ambitions mustered the wherewithal to kill the ideal target for someone who wanted to go down in history books.

. . .

No one around me reacted when I muttered "I know that man," which was no surprise: anyone who'd heard me would have thought I was befuddled by the events playing out on television that day. My first real thought was that they probably picked Lee up because of his suspicious background, which would have been known to the Dallas authorities. But how could they have worked so fast? And why was his face bruised?

Lee spoke up in a voice familiar to me. He declared himself innocent, a patsy. He said he had no idea why he was in custody. Surrounded by a mob of reporters, he pleaded for a lawyer.

We sat glued to the television until dusk. As I walked home across the campus, nothing moved on the streets. The silence and stillness were eerie, as Americans everywhere watched the president's casket being hoisted aboard Air Force One and the ensuing takeoff from Dallas's Love Field.

We waited the two and a half hours for the president's plane to land at Andrews Air Force Base. We watched as the solemn new president, Lyndon Baines Johnson, vowed, in a lackluster Texas-twanged speech, that "I will do my best. That is all I can do. I ask for your help and God's."

The new president was then escorted to greet top congressional figures assembled on the tarmac. Shaking hands and mingling brought LBJ back to familiar ground, but, at least in my view, the new president had failed to comfort a grieving American people.

Returning from the student union, I walked up the makeshift wooden staircase to my second-floor student apartment at 1318½ Garfield Street. My roommate, Jerry Guymon, was away for the weekend. I was alone. Struggling to come to terms with the day's events, I telephoned my parents in Fort Worth.

My mother answered, her voice subdued and troubled.

Me: "Did you see it too?"

Mother: "Yes."

Me: "It is Lee Oswald."

Mother: "Yes."

Me: "Any calls yet?"

My mother: "No. We are waiting."

There was nothing more to say. We hung up.

. . .

There was another call that my mother had to make. It was supposed to be one of congratulation. It had become a call of grim tidings.

My older sister, Edith, began her birthday on November 22 in anticipation of a baby shower being thrown for her by her fellow teachers at Maxie Speer Elementary School in Arlington, Texas. Having adopted two children, Edith and her husband, Joe, were expecting the birth of their first child. Edith looked forward to that Friday as a rare happy weekday in the harried life of a special-ed teacher.

As word came in that the president had been shot in nearby Dallas, classes were canceled. Parents hurried to pick up their children. Teachers assembled before the office television screen as they joined in spirit those holding a vigil in front of Parkland Hospital just a few miles away.

The shower presents were long forgotten as were any thoughts of joy and celebration. Each teacher left Edith's party to grieve in his or her own way.

The phone rang inside my sister's Arlington home as she returned. In a shaking voice, our mother told her that the suspected assassin was someone we knew: Lee Harvey Oswald. She gave Edith a brief sketch of how the Gregory family came to know the man now in custody in Dallas.

Edith was not only surprised, but she was also confused. She had never heard of Lee Harvey Oswald or his Russian wife. Oddly, although the Gregory family met at least once a week for dinner and cards, their connection with the young Russian couple was not something my father, Pete, or my mother, Elizabeth, felt important enough to mention.

The combination of Edith's pregnancy, the president's death, and now a family connection to the accused assassin proved too much for my sister. Alone in her house, she began to experience what she feared were premature labor pains. Joe rushed home to drive her to the hospital, where she spent the night. The baby was safe.

. . .

As I conjure up memories of sixty years past, I can picture myself as a slender, six-foot-tall tennis player with an athletic scholarship at the University of Oklahoma. I was majoring in economics with a minor in Russian. People who knew me then might have regarded me as handsome, though it would have been news to me.

By extreme contrast to the crazy-quilt life of Lee Harvey Oswald, I hailed from a stable, loving American home. I was acquiring the higher education that Lee longed for. I had a mother and father who were living the dream of first-generation Americans. My father, born on the trans-Siberian railroad, immigrated to this country via Manchuria and Japan. My mother was born in the North German city of Bremen. Her father moved to New Orleans as a steel and cotton merchant. She spent World War I in Germany because of an ill-timed visit to German relatives as the war broke out.

My 1950s childhood was a *Leave It to Beaver* one. We relished the mild mischief that the rascally Eddie Haskell conjured up for the upright Beaver and brother Wally on television. Our family grew up on books. Sunday evenings were set aside for radio shows: *The Jack Benny Program*, Ted Mack's *Original Amateur Hour*, and *The Edgar Bergen and Charlie McCarthy Show*.

For a short time, Lee attended the same high school as I did. On employment applications, Lee listed our Arlington Heights as his high school, although he spent less than two months there. Oswald's lack of a high-school diploma was not the result of a low IQ. In middle school, Lee scored well on achievement tests, except in writing and spelling. Had he taken advantage of the educational opportunities the Marine Corps offered, he would have had a second chance at higher education. Instead, Lee left the Marines with a flawed record that hampered his chances when he returned to the United States.

· · ·

What I remember most about returning to my apartment that evening of the assassination was the haunting sense of loneliness and isolation. There was no one with whom to share the burden that I knew the person suspected of killing the president of the United States.

I returned to the mind-numbing television coverage. This was unprecedented television with no commercial interruptions. I had never seen it before. We have since grown accustomed to such things. After major disasters—9/11, the *Challenger* explosion, and the Boston Marathon massacre, the early days of Covid-19—we have come to expect round-the-clock-coverage until viewers tired. The Kennedy assassination was the first such case. It went on and on and on, repeating the same things over and over.

Finally, I retired for a fitful night of sleep.

· · ·

My parents in Fort Worth had even less sleep. Their doorbell rang insistently at three in the morning. When my father, Pete Gregory, opened the door, two men dressed in dark suits identified themselves as Secret Service agents. One identified himself as Agent Mike Howard, the other as Charles Kunkel. It was clear that Howard was calling the shots.

Pete knew instantly why they had come. They peppered him with questions about one Lee Harvey Oswald. How did he meet Oswald? When was the last time he saw him? Did Oswald associate with suspicious people? Pete explained how he knew Oswald and that he had not seen him for over a year. He also mentioned that I knew Lee and Marina better than he. Agent Howard asked for my address in Norman, Oklahoma. He sent word to the Oklahoma City office to check out one Paul Gregory, a "known associate" of Lee Harvey Oswald.

Mike Howard sized Pete up as a reputable person unlikely to be involved in an assassination of the president. He also noted that Pete was a native Russian speaker. Howard left his telephone number in case Pete needed to call him.

The agents left Pete's home as quickly as they had come. The Secret Service had suffered its biggest failure ever, and Agents Howard and Kunkel had much to do that night. They had other doorbells to ring, probably lots of them. Presidential trips under normal circumstances meant a constant flurry of activity. Agent Howard had been at JFK's side during his speeches in Fort Worth and had been in the fatal Dallas motorcade. In the last two days, Howard and Kunkel had gotten only a few hours of sleep.

There would be little opportunity to rest in the days to follow. For all the agents knew, Oswald was only the tip of an iceberg, the trigger man in an assassination ring. Chilling thoughts coursed through their minds. Oswald, an ex-Marine and a deserter to the USSR, and his Russian wife could have been following Kremlin orders to strike the most devastating blow of the Cold War.

The agents also knew of Oswald's work on behalf of the Fair Play for Cuba organization. Could this shocking murder have been retribution for the Bay of Pigs? Did the conspirators target other members of government—or were they about to? Howard and Kunkel, as well as their countless colleagues in the Secret Service and FBI, had begun putting together a complex jigsaw puzzle, and they had precious little time to gather its pieces.

But the first step was to locate the other two female Oswalds, Marina and Lee's mother, Marguerite. It was Pete Gregory who would help provide them with their whereabouts.

2

MY TURN
FOR QUESTIONING

Saturday morning, the day after Kennedy was killed. Virtually no traffic on the streets; everyone was at home, following events on television. I heard a car door slam shut and peered down as two men climbed out of their car parked in front of our place on Garfield Street, a block from the campus. They consulted the street numbers, found 1318½, and headed up the wooden outside staircase.

They knocked at the door. I greeted them with the words: "You found me pretty quickly." We all understood what I meant. At the door, the men politely identified themselves as Special Agent Jack Nielson of the Secret Service and Norman's chief of police, Sid Wilson. They invited me to accompany them to Oklahoma City, some twenty miles down Interstate 35. They had some questions to ask me. Agent Nielson had been alerted by a phone call from Dallas. At this early stage of the investigation, no theory could be ruled out—including an organized conspiracy. As a "known associate" of Oswald, I could have been a part of the gang that had orchestrated the murder of the president.

In the year and a half from his return from Russia to the assassination, Lee Harvey Oswald relocated *eight* times, leaving behind, at one point or another, almost everyone who'd crossed his path. So, my many hours spent with Lee and his wife, Marina, made me a consequential eyewitness.

Branded as a "Known Associate" of Lee Harvey Oswald, I was picked up by the Secret Service less than twenty-four hours after the shots were fired. The agents posed the questions that must be asked: Had Oswald shown animosity toward JFK or other political leaders? Did he reveal a violent streak? Did he have political views that could lead to a political assassination? Did I know of colleagues or friends with whom Oswald could have conspired to kill the president? Should I and others who knew him have seen this coming, as Robert Oswald once asked out loud?

These questions remain relevant today. My answer then and now: with the exception of violence toward Marina, I detected none of the trademarks of a future assassin. Yes, he was an avowed Marxist but no hint of an advocate of political assassination. Yet, remarkably, Lee's actions on November 22, 1963, did not surprise me. Rather, it was as if the pieces of a puzzle were falling in place as I saw him brought hand-cuffed and bruised into the Dallas police station.

Only one person did see the possibility of a political murder, and that was Marina after Lee confessed to her that he had attempted to shoot General Edwin Walker, the leader of Dallas's right-wing community. Had she come forward, history could have changed its course.

The assassination of President Kennedy unleashed perhaps the most comprehensive governmental investigation in history. It was carried out by the President's Commission on the Assassination of President John F. Kennedy, otherwise known as the Warren Commission. Its reports are measured not in page count, but in meters of shelf space. Its comprehensive twenty-seven-volume report was issued in September 1964. Since then, further releases of documents occurred in 2017, 2018, and 2021. Many items have yet to see the light of day.

As just one example of the thoroughness and care of the Warren Commission, virtually all American passengers on the bus that Oswald took to Mexico City in September 1963 were tracked down and interviewed. Former neighbors and landlords gave depositions. In the end, almost anyone who had had some contact with Oswald told their stories to commission investigators.

As I worked my way through the Warren Commission files, new information continued to pop up, some highly personal: I had no inkling that my mother, Elizabeth Gregory, had testified. Yet, there it was, dated November 25, 1963, the transcript of FBI agent S. A. Haley, questioning Elizabeth Gregory about Oswald. I can imagine my mother in our living room, sitting in front of a tape recorder as she answered the agent's questions. My mother stated that she was leery of Lee Oswald from the beginning and had advised Pete against further contacts. She then softened her stance and agreed to host Lee and Marina for a fateful dinner.

■ ■ ■

Agent Nielson, who picked me up the day after the assassination, described his first impression of me in a report he sent to Dallas the next day. I was, in his words, a "white male, brown eyes, slender build" who "speaks with a noticeable lisp." (Only after reading the transcript of the November 23 proceedings fifty years later did I learn that I have a lisp!) Nielson went on to write: "He has a degree in economics and is pursuing a master's degree in economics. He expects to obtain his PhD and then enter the teaching profession at Oklahoma University [sic]." (I doubt that I said that.) "He admits to being a member of the Russian Club, the economics club, and the O Club, which is the varsity letter club. Gregory stated that he is a three-year letter man in varsity tennis and while an undergraduate was on a tennis scholarship at Oklahoma University. He is also Phi Beta Kappa."

These credentials hardly matched those of a co-conspirator to kill the president of the United States.

The three of us climbed into the car and made our way the short distance to Oklahoma City. As we drove, we made small talk. Periodically, reports came in on a special radio frequency. I heard dispatches blaring through the static: "They have the rifle. We're pretty sure we have the right guy."

Knowing the agents wanted me to tell them about Lee Harvey Oswald, I launched into an extended monologue on how we met, my evenings with Lee and Marina, and the Dallas Russians. They listened, not interrupting. I did not realize that I was jumping the gun. They would ask questions when we got to their office where our session could be recorded and transcribed.

Politely, they turned the conversation to my studies, what I thought about the economy (as an economics major I was supposed to know something), and my impressions of my fellow students at the University of Oklahoma. They were simply trying to make small talk to fill the silence. These topics were not exactly on my mind at the time, but I got the impression that they were taking the opportunity to check out "subversive" elements at the university and, if so, whether I knew any of them. The conservative University of Oklahoma was far from a refuge for radical students, so this conversation petered out.

We drove down into the basement garage of a nondescript building in downtown Oklahoma City and made our way to a large office. I remember being surprised that it was a field office of the Secret Service. I had thought its agents were all based in Washington to protect the president and other high government officials.

We three sat down at a large conference table. A stenographer joined us. I turned down their offer of coffee, which I still do not drink, and we began the interrogation with a tape recorder softly whirring and the stenographer typing away. When the session was over, she would prepare an affidavit for me to sign and for Special Agent Nielson and Sheriff Wilson to witness.

Nielson conducted the questioning. In the car, we had already gone over the first order of business: establishing where I was at the time of the shooting. (I was in class—easily verifiable.) I stated that I had not seen Lee or Marina for a year. I last saw them on November 22, 1962, exactly one year before the assassination.

• • •

Just who were Lee and Marina Oswald?

My mind readily conjures up visions and impressions of Lee and Marina as we sat together in the summer of 1962 in their threadbare living room, baby June sleeping on a bed improvised from two open suitcases. Lee came across as medium height, wiry, receding hairline, and powerful in his way. Even fresh from work, he dressed neatly in slacks and a long-sleeved shirt with the sleeves rolled up to his elbows. Lee exuded high energy even after eight hours of welding.

Lee had a distinctive coldness or, rather, a blankness about him. With most people I meet, I register something from them: like or dislike or a more subtle reaction. With Lee, I picked up no vibes, either positive or negative. This did not mean he was without emotion. His voice rose when he got mad or felt himself on the defensive. But for the most part in our relationship, he remained a blank slate. When Lee and Marina later came under the mentorship of the "Dallas Russians" (as we called the Dallas émigré community), Lee did not disguise his dislike of them. At best I was an object of his indifference. What I interpreted as indifference could have been hatred for someone like me, who had had it easy in life.

Marina came across as a shy, natural beauty. She dressed in frumpy clothes of Soviet origin or hand-me-downs, usually a simple dress but sometimes Bermuda shorts, a gift from her sister-in-law. She smoked, as did most Russians of her generation. Marina was very thin, almost emaciated. She had a "lost kitten" air about her that made people want to help her. She spoke little and in a hushed voice. She smiled even less to cover a rotting tooth. Marina was breastfeeding June and had brought a breast pump with her from Minsk. She packed a milk bottle prior to each of our excursions.

Lee and Marina had an established household routine. Lee left early for work, walking to the bus stop on West Seventh. Marina slept late and tended baby June. She had dinner ready when Lee returned. (If not, she risked catching hell from her mother-in-law, Marguerite.) Marina often sat on the front porch awaiting his return. Lee would tease her about whether she had been to nearby Montgomery Ward to "window shop." Unlike Russian husbands, Lee was willing to do household chores. Like Russian husbands, Lee beat Marina on occasion in the privacy of their home. Only later did he strike her in public. The couple received an occasional visit from Robert. Once they had to scurry Robert out of the house with the explanation that I was coming.

Lee discouraged visits from his mother, Marguerite, whom he despised. When he forbade Marina to allow his mother into the house, Marina objected. She wanted to be a good daughter-in-law, and she had lost her own mother at age fifteen. Neither Lee nor Marina knew that Marguerite was staking out their duplex from the Montgomery Ward parking lot. She felt compelled to check on Marina's comings and goings.

In all our time together, the young couple never exchanged any gestures of endearment. I had to learn from the Warren Report that Marina called Lee by his Minsk nickname of Alik or its diminutive Alka. I never heard Marina use these endearments when we were together. Both of them clearly loved infant June. They worried for her health and gave every impression of being devoted parents; though poor, they did the best they could.

. . .

Agent Nielson's questions, less than one day after the shooting, showed that the Secret Service's main concern was an organized conspiracy. If there was one, was I a part of it? If not, could I give them names of individuals who might have conspired with Oswald to pull this off? Agent Nielson ran through a number of names, such as those of the Dallas Russians, which I knew. He asked whether I recognized numerous other names, which I assumed identified people associated in some way with the Oswalds. Other than Robert Oswald, I did not recognize any of them, and when asked directly, I realized I was not sure whether I had met Lee's half-brother, a man by the name of John Pic.

Nielson walked me through my meetings with Lee Harvey Oswald and Marina. He wanted to know whether Oswald expressed animosity toward President Kennedy, Catholics, millionaires as a group, or any particular race. I told him I had not seen any firearms in the Oswald home or discussed hunting or target practice with him. Nor was I aware of any particular organization that Oswald associated with. I related what little I knew about Oswald's life in Russia.

· · ·

The Warren Report covers Lee's defection to the Soviet Union largely through the reports of American diplomats who dealt with him during his three years behind the Iron Curtain. We knew little about this period of his life until outgoing Russian president Boris Yeltsin turned over Oswald's Russian KGB files in 1999. Labeled as top secret in a country that expected to keep its secrets forever, the KGB file captures the USSR leadership's handling of Oswald's annoying defection. What were they to do with this obvious oddball? If he were to commit suicide, as he threatened, this would be a blow to the Soviet image.

As someone who has worked professionally with Soviet state and party documents for over a decade, the Yeltsin documents appear authentic to me. We learn that Oswald's case was dealt with at the highest levels of the Politburo and KGB—not by the local passport office as I had previously thought. The file follows Oswald from his Moscow sojourn to his three years in Minsk under constant surveillance. The

Oswald file then skips to the November 22, 1963, account of their panic upon learning that U.S. headlines were screaming that Oswald had defected to the USSR and was an active Castro supporter. To make matters worse, the Embassy had received a visa request for both Lee and Marina and knew that Oswald had recently visited the Mexico City Embassy.

Within two days of the assassination, the Politburo launched a disinformation campaign to shift blame from the USSR, Castro, and leftists to right-wing extremists or Mafia. The original USSR counterattack eventually implicated the Gregorys in a "White Russian Conspiracy." This Soviet version remains an active thread in the JFK conspiracy portfolio. I guess Pete and Paul Gregory are still under suspicion of some kind in some quarters.

. . .

Back under questioning the day after the assassination, I was coming off watching nonstop television coverage for almost twenty-four hours. I had seen the evidence piling up against Lee. That he had worked at the Texas School Book Depository, where the fatal shots had been fired, was a fact. That he had shot Police Officer J.D. Tippit dead seemed pretty certain. The news bursts I heard on the way from Norman to Oklahoma City added to the incriminating evidence. Then, in this nondescript office building, the agents asked me the question that I finally had to answer: "Do you think that Lee Harvey Oswald was capable of killing the president of the United States?"

In response to this probing question, I said aloud, for the first time, what I had been pondering since I saw Lee being brought into the Dallas police station the day before: yes, Lee Harvey Oswald was entirely capable of attempting to assassinate the president of the United States.

Agent Nielson probed further: "Did he have a motive that you know of?"

My answer came without hesitation. Yes, he had a motive: He dreamed, I strongly suspected, of becoming a part of history. He wanted the world to understand that he was not an insignificant figure.

Agent Nielson bored in on whether Lee could have been part of an organized conspiracy. I answered that I had no evidence pro or con, but I volunteered that if I were to organize such a heinous crime, the last person on earth I would include in the conspiracy would be Lee Harvey Oswald. I stated that Oswald marched to his own drummer. He could not be relied upon, and he would not take kindly to orders from others. This personal opinion somehow did not make it into the official transcript of my remarks, but I am sure I said it.

The interview over, we waited for the stenographer to prepare the affidavit for my signature. The text was not a verbatim transcription. Rather it was a summary of what the stenographer had heard. The choice of words and expressions were not my own, but it did summarize my answers, by and large, correctly.

Here is my summary of Lee Harvey Oswald as recorded in the transcript:

"As far as my opinion of Lee Oswald goes, I believe he was not a particularly intelligent person, he was dissatisfied with his lot in life, but he at no time indicated to me that he was so dissatisfied with his lot in life that he would seek to change it by murder, assassination, or any such act. While we discussed comparative government and political philosophy, Oswald at no time indicated a rabid [I would not have used that adjective] preference for any type of governmental system and at no time tried to propagandize me toward any particular system of government. I feel now, that because of Oswald's mental outlook, he could potentially be capable of the act with which he is charged, but at the time of my association with him, I would not have believed so."

At the bottom of the fifth and final page of the transcript, I wrote in my own hand: "I have read this statement and it is true." To the right of that is my signature.

Recognizing that Lee Harvey Oswald was capable of shooting the president does not mean that I had some inkling this would happen. At most, I pictured him as a leftist foot soldier on some street corner, peddling radical literature to disinterested passersby. That he could order a rifle, practice with it, and use it to kill the most powerful and closely protected person in the world would have struck me as the most peculiar of propositions. Anyone who suggested such things would need his head examined.

. . .

I have no illusions of psychiatric acumen, but some of Oswald's behavioral patterns stood out, even back then to a naïve kid like me.

First, whenever I innocently brought up Marina's learning English, Lee would become angry, fidget, or show his discomfort in other ways. Marina knew that her learning English was a sore point with Lee. When I offered her English-Russian flash cards, she knew to turn down the offer. Fortune was on Lee's side in this case. Marina exhibited little interest in learning English. She preferred leisure and sleeping late to toiling over English vocabulary and grammar.

Lee's fear was that he would be exposed as a loser. The image he promoted to Marina was that of a dashing, radical intellectual who would make the world a better place if the world only paid attention to him. Surely major publishers would compete for his *Historic Diary*. Such thoughts moved Marina, not to admiration, but to derision and then to fear when she gained some insight into the possible consequences of his vainglory. Lee must have feared that I, as an outsider, could let slip that they were impoverished in a land of plenty. And Lee was right to worry. Although I assumed a nonjudgmental stance toward Lee, it was an inadvertent blunder on my part in November 1962 that exposed who Lee actually was.

Second, as a frequent visitor to the Oswalds, it was hard to miss Lee's physical abuse of Marina. I witnessed facial bruises and black eyes. On the first such occasion, Marina was sporting a prominent blue bruise under her eye. I was about to ask what had happened when Marina gave me a warning glance that signaled "none of your business." I would later learn that Lee's abuse became more frequent and even public.

Spousal abuse was not just something Lee picked up in Russia. His American mother believed that "there may be times that a woman needs to have a black eye." I doubt that four-times-married Marguerite applied this principle to herself. For his part, Lee played the typical role of abusive husband well, swearing that he would not do this ever again. And Marina stayed with him.

Third, I found it odd that Lee prudishly objected when Marina let infant June sleep naked in my presence, stating *"eto ne krasivo"* (this isn't proper). After all, these were the hot days of Fort Worth summer. Admonished, Marina dutifully followed Lee's order and wrapped June in diapers. Was Lee's prudishness a sign of sexual repression? We do know that Lee's biggest objection to middle school was having to shower naked with other boys.

Thanks to Priscilla McMillan's extensive post-assassination interviews with Marina, we have an intimate firsthand account of Marina and Lee's sex lives. We know that Marina had an extramarital affair shortly after they were married, and she played on Lee's jealousy by staying in touch with an old flame. Worse still were Marina's complaints about Lee's love-making. From FBI surveillance and wiretaps, we also have information on Marina's post-assassination sex life, which belies her image as a shy shrinking violet.

McMillan's interviews establish Marina as a sexual creature, at times demanding of a husband worn out from eight straight hours of phys-ical labor. Post-assassination FBI wiretaps and Warren Commission testimony revealed Marina's strong sexual drive after the assassination. She carried on an open affair with her married and handsome "busi-ness manager," James Martin. Their liaisons included a night together at the exclusive Willard Hotel in Washington, DC, with FBI agents monitoring from the next room. After Robert suggested that the Secret Service had allowed a rape under their watch, Marina tempered his claim with a statement that what had happened was consensual.

After the public attention tapered off, Marina went off the deep end, spending nights at strip clubs and neglecting her two daughters. She was ultimately rescued by her second husband, a rancher by the name of Ken Porter. She and Porter divorced but they continued to live together. Their marriage produced a son.

Not only did Marina belittle Lee's political views and aspirations. She humiliated him, saying he was sexually inadequate—a hard blow for someone with Lee's tenuous grasp on reality.

. . .

When my November 23 interview with the Secret Service concluded, my questioners asked whether we had left anything out. I could think of nothing.

Special Agent Nielson then excused himself. He left to telephone Dallas the summary of our conversation, which he had prepared:

"Special SYNOPSIS: Associate of suspect assassinator of President Kennedy interviewed regarding his association with suspect. Details provided Chief's Office and Dallas Office by telephone.

"Paul Gregory stated that at no time did Oswald indicate any animosity towards President Kennedy, Catholics, millionaires as a group or any particular race. All of these areas were discussed as well as political philosophies of America and Russia but never with any undue excitement on the part of Oswald. Paul Gregory stated he did not see any firearms in the possession of Oswald, nor did Oswald ever discuss marksmanship, target practices, an interest in hunting, and so forth. Gregory knew of no organizational affiliations of Oswald but rather stated during his association with Oswald he did not believe Oswald's associating with any organization."

Agent Nielson's summary continued:

"Concerning Oswald's residence in Russia, Gregory stated Oswald did not mention any official governmental interests in him when Oswald was a resident of Russia and the only possible governmental association indicated by Oswald was when he was sought out by a Russian Army general's son. Gregory stated Oswald related that the association presumably started because of the general's son's interest in learning the English language. A signed, sworn statement was obtained from Gregory and is attached to this report."

Agent Nielson concluded with an assessment of my testimony: "Gregory seemed to be straight forward and truthful in his answers. He did not seem evasive or in any way offensive. He was somewhat nervous but considering the issue involved, not unusually so."

Our business finished, Sheriff Wilson and I proceeded down the elevator to the waiting car and drove back to Norman, trying to keep the conversation on other subjects. I returned to an empty apartment. There was no one with whom to share this momentous secret. I sat glued to the television, alone with my own thoughts, not even suspecting the unimaginable events that would follow the next day.

My interlude in Oklahoma City apparently removed me from the list of suspected co-conspirators in the absence of further evidence. As Agent Nielson wrote under "disposition of the case": "This matter is considered closed in Oklahoma, to be re-opened should circumstances warrant."

3

LEE IS DEAD

Sunday, November 24, began with mind-numbing repeats of the tragic events of the previous day. Viewers were told that Jackie Kennedy was consulting with historians of the Civil War. She had decided to pattern her husband's funeral after that of Abraham Lincoln.

Periodically, television coverage gave way to dispatches from the Dallas police headquarters, where the accused assassin was being questioned. The interior of the police station was now familiar to all Americans. Although few noticed, there appeared to be no security to the unpracticed eye. Reporters swarmed the corridors and jockeyed to get close to Lee as he was led from one room to another. En route, he kept protesting his innocence in impromptu press conferences. He insisted that he had no idea why he was being held. He knew nothing about the assassination of President Kennedy. He appealed for legal representation as camera flashbulbs went off all around him. It really seemed as if no one was in charge.

The Dallas police, under Sheriff Jesse Curry, were concerned about the transfer of Oswald to a new location. Originally, they sent out word that Oswald would be moved around 11:00 a.m. to the city jail. They then considered a night transfer but decided they should "play straight" with the press and public. Off-duty police officers were called in and issued locational assignments so that virtually all nooks and crannies were covered. The police even inspected the elevator shaft to make sure a gunman was not hiding there. The police arranged to transport Oswald in an armored vehicle that was standing by in the basement garage.

The police headquarters building was filled with a number of unfamiliar faces. But some were familiar, one being that of a short, stocky man, dressed in black. Jack Ruby was a frequent visitor to the police station. His face was known, and he knew several of the detectives. Wanting to be helpful, he had volunteered to bring in sandwiches earlier in the day.

As the time for the transfer approached, reporters and TV crews formed a gauntlet along the basement path Oswald would take to the waiting vehicle. Their jostling for favorable positions made an unruly situation even worse. And then they settled in a hushed silence, waiting for the infamous Lee Harvey Oswald to appear.

At 11:21, the black-and-white TV images showed the elevator door opening and Lee, dressed in a sweater, standing between police detectives—a short man in the company of giants. The officers surrounding him all wore wide-brimmed Texas hats, almost a caricature of a low-budget Hollywood Western. The print and TV reporters were identifiable by their bare heads. The camera focused on Lee as he surveyed his surroundings, somewhat bewildered. Some said he had a smirk on his face. (See photo of Lee surrounded by Dallas detectives in cowboy hats).

His escorts led him through the crowded basement toward the armored car. About five steps before they reached the car, a single firecracker sound rang out at the same time as a man in a black hat lunged forward from the crowd. Lee hunched forward, his face distorted, and fell forward to the cement ground.

Panic and chaos broke out as the police wrestled the shooter to the floor and hustled him back to the elevator from which Lee had just emerged. Shouts of "he's been shot" could be heard from the crowd in the basement parking lot. The police cleared a path from Lee lying on the concrete to an ambulance that raced to the scene as the waiting armored car moved to make way. One of the detectives tried to stanch the bleeding. The next camera shots showed Lee Harvey Oswald, his face clearly visible, apparently unconscious, being shoved into the ambulance on a stretcher. An excited TV reporter, his voice shaking, tried to control himself as exclamations of "Unbelievable!" and "Incredible!" rang out.

Along with an entire nation, I witnessed the shooting of the suspected assassin of President Kennedy on live TV. No one could believe what they had seen.

At exactly the same time in Arlington, Texas, Pete Gregory, Robert Oswald, and the Secret Service were preparing to drive Marina and Marguerite to a hiding place outside Forth Worth. A Secret Service agent whispered to Robert and Pete that Lee had been shot. As Robert Oswald rushed off to Parkland Hospital, Pete and the rest of the Oswald family got into the car, as the Secret Service agents considered where to take Marina and Marguerite and whether to tell them that Lee had been shot.

A short time after the shooting, the media reported that the man who shot Oswald had been identified as Jack Ruby, the owner of a Dallas strip joint. Ruby was purported to have underworld ties. According to those who knew him, Ruby, like Oswald, was a "loner." He had few friends. He was known to fly off the handle, once beating up a bar patron for a racial slur. Ruby was clearly distraught over the murder of JFK. Witnesses reported seeing a sobbing Ruby outside police headquarters.

Ruby was hustled upstairs for interrogation in the same room that had been used to question Lee Harvey Oswald. The head of the Dallas

Secret Service, Forrest Sorrels, misheard Ruby's name. He sent orders to DC to investigate one Jack *Rubin*. Back in Norman, watching repeated TV images over and over, I looked for details that I had missed in the live version: Lee's face as he exited the elevator, almost expressionless . . . Lee looking from side to side as his escort led him toward the waiting armored car . . . Ruby, hand extended, rushing forward so fast that it seemed Lee did not see him. If you looked closely you could see the revolver . . . Lee grimacing as if the air was sucked out of him, feeling the bullet enter his abdomen. Lee's hands reflexively jerking upward to the point of entry.

After police officers forced the crowd to make way for a stretcher to carry Lee, I saw him disappear into the ambulance. I hoped that he was not mortally wounded. A body wound shouldn't be fatal. He would be in the hands of the best physicians at Parkland. The worst thing that could happen, I thought, would be for Lee Harvey Oswald to die and leave too many questions unanswered.

The shooter was in the hands of the Dallas Police and Secret Service Dallas office, where Forrest Sorrels, the head of the Dallas Secret Service, asked him why he did it. The dazed Ruby declared that he wanted to spare Jackie the trauma of a trial and that "he wanted to show the world that a Jew had guts."

Meanwhile, as the scene of Jack Ruby shooting Oswald replayed on the small screen, I became more and more incredulous. We must, I thought, be living in a world that has gone mad; things like this simply do not happen.

4

MOSCOW PANICS

As news flashes reached the Kremlin that Kennedy's likely killer was an ex-Marine who had deserted to the USSR, the ruling Politburo frantically called for the records of Lee Harvey Oswald. Then called the Praesidium of the Central Committee—consisting of Nikita Khrushchev, Leonid Brezhnev, Andrei Gromyko, Anastas Mikoyan, Nikolai Bulganin, and Alexei Kosygin—the group met nonstop to plan strategy.

In its official actions, the Politburo approved an elaborate mourning and condolence campaign. A somber Khrushchev visited the U.S. Embassy. The experienced Mikoyan headed a delegation to the funeral and exchanged tearful words in English with Jackie Kennedy. Khrushchev's wife, Nina, wrote a personal note to Jackie Kennedy. This carefully crafted campaign emphasized the heinous nature of the crime, personal grief over the loss of a friend, and the hope of the Soviet Union that peace negotiations would continue.

The Politburo's secret records show that their real concerns lay elsewhere. Ambassador Anatoly Dobrynin in Washington understood that U.S. authorities would demand information on Oswald. Of concern was that Oswald had written the Soviet Embassy with a request for a visa just two weeks before November 22. Oswald used regular mail; hence, the FBI would know of the letter.

When ultimately asked for Oswald's letter to the Washington Embassy, Soviet authorities declared it a forgery, a "clear provocation: it gives the impression we had close ties with Oswald and were using him for some purposes of our own."

Then there was the problem of Oswald's leftist beliefs.

The Soviet leadership had initially counted on the JFK assassin or assassins being anti-Soviet right wingers, such as those inspired by General Edwin Walker, who resided in Dallas. That the likely suspect turned out to be a communist defector to the Soviet Union cast suspicion on Cuba and the Soviet Union. Even worse, Lee Harvey Oswald had recently visited the Cuban and Soviet Embassies in Mexico City. The Soviets, who had been hoping that the American right was guilty, now had to avoid blame themselves. Perhaps they could scapegoat the local Russian community, whose ties with Oswald and his wife ran deep.

The declassified Soviet Oswald file shows that the Politburo worried from Day 1 that the American press "has disseminated various slanderous fabrications regarding some Soviet and Cuban 'connections' of Lee Harvey Oswald, who was charged with the assassination and himself killed 'under mysterious circumstances.'" The Politburo complained that the U.S. press refers "to the fact that Oswald lived in the Soviet Union from October 1959 through June 1962." To counter such "slander," the Politburo ordered the Ministry of Foreign Affairs and the KGB to prepare a press briefing stating that the murder of Oswald himself [by Jack Ruby] reveals now even more clearly the identity of the groups behind the assassination as they cover up their tracks. "Such fabrications cannot but elicit a bitter smile and understandable indignation not only outside the United States but among all decent Americans, who have the right to expect that justice will be meted out to the real murderers and organizers of this shameful crime."

The Soviet's Mexican Embassy was instructed to say that they had no further contact with Oswald after turning down his request for a visa.

Despite their stated intent at openness, the Politburo on November 28 refused the request of the *New York Times* to send a reporter to Minsk. The Politburo instructed the Ministry of Foreign Affairs to respond that the facts relating to Oswald's temporary stay in and departure from the Soviet Union are known to the U.S. government; thus there is no need to travel to Minsk to collect information about Oswald.

• • •

J. Edgar Hoover's FBI had its own informant at a high level in Soviet intelligence. The informant reported that the Soviet leadership feared a right-wing coup that might target Cuba or even the Soviet Union itself in retaliation for JFK's murder. Like many others, Soviet authorities could not accept the notion of a lone gunman assassination.

The reams of material declassified in 2017 and thereafter are rich with nuggets of new information drawn from the FBI and CIA.

The FBI surveilled and wiretapped Marina, Robert, and the fleet of opportunists who glommed on to Marina. I was surprised to learn that I remained on the FBI's radar. When the FBI learned that Marina's business manager had bought an air ticket to Oklahoma City, their agents checked whether he had come to Oklahoma to see me. (No.) On the more lascivious side, FBI wiretaps caught Marina gossiping about her dreams and sexual obsession for her business manager and inquiring about medications to dampen her sex drive.

These are all fascinating tidbits, but, most important, the Warren Commission archives offered the opportunity to test my own memory against that of other key figures, including Marina Oswald herself.

As I revisited events witnessed by others, I discovered that my own memories generally held true. My faint recollection of a letter from "Pavel" in Minsk referring to me was confirmed when I found his letter in the Warren files. In some cases I found errors in official documents, such as a Secret Service report that did not include me as being present at the dinner with the Oswalds and Dallas Russians.

The Warren Report provides five independent accounts of the August 1962 dinner party attended by Pete, two Dallas Russians, my mother, Marina, Lee, and me. Like the classic Japanese film *Rashomon*, we each told slightly different versions. Neither of the Dallas attendees mention Oswald's agitation when asked to explain why he went to Russia. For me, sitting to the right of Lee, his discomfort was palpable as his voice rose in exasperation. It was a good example of how people view things differently.

■ ■ ■

Among those most relieved when on September 27, 1964, the Warren Commission announced its conclusion that Oswald acted alone, was the Soviet leadership. The Warren Commission, in effect, had absolved the KGB and its Cuban proxy of involvement in the assassination. The Politburo did not know then that a whole conspiracy-theory industry would arise to counter the Warren Commission's conclusions. Among the latest is an account co-authored by a former U.S. director of intelligence accusing the USSR general secretary, Nikita Khrushchev himself, of ordering Oswald to assassinate Kennedy.

■ ■ ■

More books and articles have been written about the assassination of President John F. Kennedy than any other single event in the history of the country. Of these, a majority fall in what I call the "forensics" category. They bear down on details like missing bullets, a "second" Oswald, Pete Gregory's "sinister" insistence on translating for Marina, the impossibility of the sequence of shots that killed JFK, and the remarkable coincidences that led Oswald to the Texas School Book Depository on November 22, 1963. Their forensic conclusion: Oswald was either not the shooter or else he did not act alone. President John F. Kennedy was therefore assassinated by a conspiracy, of which

Oswald was a part. As Oswald himself claimed from the Dallas police station: "I am a patsy."

I cannot consider the hundreds of theories that reject Lee Harvey Oswald as the sole gunman. To get embroiled in them would be like falling into a vast sinkhole of bullet trajectories, purported conversations, conjecture, and complex conspiracies. Let others debate them. It is my firsthand knowledge of Lee Harvey Oswald that convinces me they will come up empty-handed.

At the end of their official inquiry into the assassination, the Warren Commission came to a definite conclusion: Lee Harvey Oswald pulled the trigger, and he acted alone. This presidential commission did not pull its findings out of thin air. The Warren Commission Report rests upon hundreds of thousands of documents, testimonies, administrative folders, and technical reports to back up its "lone gunman" conclusion.

The notion of Oswald acting alone fails to satisfy those seeking excitement, mystery, and intrigue. The story is too pedestrian: A misfit-deserter to the USSR fails to find the communist society he expects. He returns to the U.S. with his wife, works various menial jobs, and tries to ingratiate himself in radical circles. He orders a mail-order rifle and fails to kill a local leader of the conservative community. Shortly thereafter he shoots to death the president of the United States, whose motorcade passes under the window where he works.

This account cannot compete with smoke-filled rooms teeming with clandestine Cuban, Russian, Mafia, or oil miscreants plotting to kill the president of the United States and pin it on an unsuspecting little guy. A perfect screenplay for a Hollywood thriller.

But "forensic" accounts lack the most essential ingredient—an understanding of the little guy's life, marriage, hopes, dreams, his view of himself and of his surroundings, and oddly (in the case of Oswald) his peculiar sense that he was destined for a place in history.

Now is the time to relive these events and to add what I can to the historical record.

PART II

OSWALD IN A WORKER'S PARADISE

Lee Harvey Oswald considered himself a writer, and he wrote prolifically—and badly. His favorite subjects were his own life experiences and his musings on political philosophy. He feared that potential readers would be turned off by his scribbled handwriting, misspellings, and grammatical errors, and so, upon returning to Fort Worth from the Soviet Union, he hired a typist to turn his drafts—*Historic Diary* and *The Collective*—into a more readable form. Later, in Dallas, he enrolled in typing classes. Despite dyslexia, he began to type his own letters, often going through ten attempts to get a clean script.

He left behind a record in his own words; namely, the story of his life and his thoughts about the world around him—a world that, in his opinion, needed to change. Although Lee had much to write about—vagabond life with an unstable mother, failure and truancy at school, bullying in the Marines—he wanted to live a new life worth writing about as he boarded a train in Helsinki in 1959 bound for a socialist state.

5

A SUICIDE ATTEMPT

Lee Harvey Oswald's *Historic Diary* tells of a disillusioned young ex-Marine, convinced that capitalism unjustly oppresses the little guy. It tells how he scrapes his money together. In Finland, he obtains an Intourist visitor's visa to the Soviet Union. He arrives at Moscow's Oktyabrsky train station on October 16, 1959, ready for a new life in a real-life Marxist state.

An eventful two weeks later (Saturday, October 31, 1959), U.S. Embassy consul Richard Snyder's anticipation of a quiet Saturday was broken by an unscheduled visit from a young American. A neatly dressed but clearly agitated Lee Harvey Oswald announced that he had come to renounce his U.S. citizenship. Seeking to take control of the conversation right from the beginning, Oswald declared that his allegiance was to the Soviet Union. He had already applied for Soviet citizenship. He declined to listen to any comment from Snyder. He claimed already to know American law on revoking citizenship. Oswald left his passport on Snyder's desk along with a prepared statement requesting his citizenship be revoked, stating that he had applied for USSR citizenship, and that he had reached this decision for political reasons after careful consideration.

In his meeting report to Washington, Snyder wrote that he noticed from the passport that Oswald's tourist visa had already expired. As to the reasons for his action, Oswald stated that he is a Marxist, he admires the Soviet system, and wishes to serve the Soviet state.

Snyder observed that the "obnoxious" Oswald had "displayed all the airs of a new sophomore party liner." At one point, Oswald alluded to hardships endured by his mother as a "worker." He declared that his Marine service had given him a chance "to observe American imperialism." He added that he had voluntarily told Soviet officials that he would make known to them all information concerning the Marine Corps and his specialty therein, radar operations.

Snyder did not permit Oswald to renounce his citizenship, saying such matters cannot be carried out on Saturdays. He also extracted Oswald's mother's address. He kept Oswald's passport.

Oswald describes his feeling in his *Historic Diary* as he left the Embassy (his text uncorrected): "I leave Embassy, elated at this showdown, returning to my hotel I feel now my enorgies are not spent in vain. I'm sure Russians will except me after this sign of my faith in them."

That same day, Snyder sent a telegram advising the Department of State of Oswald's visit. Copies were immediately furnished to the FBI and the CIA. The telegram was followed on November 2, 1959, by an Embassy report that Oswald's request should be subject to "delay action." Snyder wanted to avoid precipitous action in case Oswald was mentally ill.

Snyder would not have known at the time that this would be his first of many dealings with Lee Harvey Oswald as the ex-Marine's demands turned from revocation of citizenship to discussions of return to the United States, and then negotiations for a loan to return him and his new wife and infant daughter back to Texas.

Contrary to the usual practice of American visitors checking in with the embassy upon arrival, Oswald hadn't made contact until his meeting with Snyder. Consular officials had no idea that tourist Lee Harvey Oswald had already been in Moscow for an eventful two weeks.

Oswald's Soviet adventure had begun when his train pulled into Oktyabrsky station from Helsinki. Tourist visas in those days included a guide who constantly monitored the "guest" of the USSR. Oswald's guide, Rimma Shirokova, took him to register at Hotel Berlin, the Intourist hotel used for foreigners at the time. After some obligatory sightseeing, Oswald informed Rimma of the true purpose of his visit: he wished to become a citizen of the USSR.

Rimma swung into action, informing the necessary authorities about her odd charge. She helped Oswald prepare the petitions for Soviet authorities and followed orders to stay close to the would-be defector and make him think of her as a friend and confidante.

Six days after his arrival, the Soviet foreign office appeared to dash his hopes for a new life: the visa office informed Lee that he must leave; his tourist visa had expired. As Lee described the meeting in his *Historic Diary* (text uncorrected): "Oct. 21. (mor) Meeting with single offial . Balding stout, black suit fairly. good English, askes what do I want?, I say Soviee citizenship, he ask why I give vague answers about 'Great Soviet Union'. He tells me 'USSR only great in Literature wants me to go back home' I am stunned I reiterate, he says he shall check and let me know weather my visa will be (extended it exipiers today) Eve. 6.00 Revive word from police official . I must leave country tonight at. 8 .00 as visa expire."

Little did Soviet visa officials know the determination of the young man. To thwart being kicked out of the USSR, Oswald staged a bathtub-cut-your-wrists suicide attempt timed to coincide with Rimma's arrival to pick him up. As Lee described melodramatically in his *Historic Diary* (uncorrected): "somewhere, a violin plays, as I watch my life whirl away. I think to myself. 'how easy to die' and 'a sweet death, (to violins) about 8.00 Rimma finds my unconscious (bathtub water a rich red color) she screams (I remember that) and runs for help."

Alarmed Soviet authorities confined Oswald to a mental hospital and then to a regular hospital. Upon release from the facility and its bad food, Lee transferred to the Metropole Hotel, a few steps from Red Square. He worried about his dwindling funds as he waited for word: Would he be allowed to stay?

Lee Harvey Oswald was to spend nearly three months in Moscow, while his fate was being decided. Most of his time was spent in the historic Metropole that had served as home to the Bolshevik leadership while they began the building of socialism. Although not expensive by tourism standards of the day, Oswald's finances would not have come close to covering the cost of such a long stay.

Complaining of boredom in his diary writing, Oswald spent his time in limbo—studying Russian on his own, eating in his room, not going out because of the cold, and getting down to $28 in cash.

Thus proceeded a protracted battle of wits involving the Soviet foreign ministry, the U.S. Embassy, and Lee Harvey Oswald. For his part, Lee kept on pestering the U.S. Embassy with written requests to revoke his U.S. citizenship. He wrote to his brother Robert, cutting off any future correspondence. His strategy: convince Soviet authorities that he was dead serious about becoming a citizen of the mighty Soviet Union.

From his hotel room, Lee made plans for a life in Moscow. He applied to Moscow's Patrice Lumumba University, where he could associate with serious young Marxists from the four corners of the globe. He could also be of benefit to the Soviet military by recounting his work with radar in the Marines. He would finally be in a place where good people thought as he did—where all are equal. As he had told Consul Snyder in the Embassy: he was not going to share the fate of his mother as an exploited worker.

Little did Lee Harvey Oswald know that his application for Soviet citizenship had made it to the very pinnacle of Soviet power—the

Politburo of the Central Committee of the Communist Party. In their December 1, 1959, meeting, they agreed with the November 27, 1959, proposal by the Ministry of Foreign Affairs and the Committee for State Security (KGB) that "U.S. national Lee Harvey Oswald, who has applied for Soviet citizenship, be granted the right of temporary sojourn in the Soviet Union for one year, and that the question of his permanent residency in the USSR and of his receiving Soviet citizenship be resolved upon the expiration of this period." The Politburo cautioned that Oswald's state of mind "has not been sufficiently examined" in light of his suicide attempt. The Belorussian party secretary was instructed to find employment for Oswald in Minsk as an electrician and to assign him a separate small apartment. The Red Cross of the USSR was ordered to appropriate 5,000 rubles to furnish the apartment for Oswald and to provide an allowance of 700 rubles monthly for one year.

The Politburo had come up with a predictable compromise. This Lee Harvey Oswald fellow is trouble. Better to get him out of the way, but we cannot afford to have a dead Marine defector on our hands. Let's send this young guy into "isolation" in "the sticks" of provincial Minsk. There he could be monitored by the KGB. Local authorities could arrange a kind of Potemkin village for the disgruntled defector— friends, particularly female, and an apartment. True, Minsk did not have much of a nightlife or forums for intellectual discussion, but the young newcomer could not expect everything.

Priscilla McMillan, who would later write a book about Lee and Marina, interviewed Oswald in his hotel room at the Metropole. Fluent in Russian and previously a Kennedy White House employee, she was working in Moscow as a freelance journalist. She spent several hours interviewing this "pale and sparse young man with a trace of Southern accent" only to realize that he had not revealed any of himself to her. Lee was willing to talk to reporters, but his personal space was to remain private.

Lee's plans for a Moscow life went up in smoke when the foreign office informed him on January 4, 1960, that he would be granted residency, not Soviet citizenship, in the Belorussian capital of Minsk. There he would have a job and an apartment. It was in sleepy Minsk that Lee Harvey Oswald was to begin his service to the Soviet state.

Lee recounts the meeting that resolved his fate (text uncorrected):

"Jan 4. I am called to passport office and finilly given a Soviet document not the soviet citizenship as I so wanted, only a Residence document, not even for foringners but a paper called for those without citizenship. Still I am happy. The offial says they only are sending me to the city of 'Minsk' I ask 'is that in Siberia?' He / laughes."

The January 4 meeting also straightened out Lee's tenuous finances. He was instructed to pick up the incredible sum of 5,000 rubles from the office of the Soviet Red Cross. In his words: "Jan. 5. I go to Red Cross in Moscow for money with Interrupter (a new one) I recive 5000. rubles a huge sum!! Later in Mink I am to earn 700 rubles a month at the factory. Jan. 7. I leave Moscow by train for Minsk, Belorussia."

Oswald would later reveal that he continued to receive money from the Soviet Red Cross, funds he had characterized as the price of "selling his soul" for his denunciation of the United States. He swore never to repeat such a demeaning act. But, after the initial 5,000-ruble payment, Lee continued to receive in Minsk the equivalent of his monthly salary, which was already envied by his fellow workers. Oswald confessed to his diary that he never told anyone of the Red Cross payments. Oswald found himself awash in money but with little to buy.

On January 7, Lee Harvey Oswald arrived at the Minsk train station ready to begin his service to the Soviet communist state.

6

SEEKING A WIFE

Lee Harvey Oswald arrived in Minsk on January 7, 1960. A week later he began work as a machinist in the experimental shop of the Minsk Radio and Television Factory. One of the biggest companies in a city of a half million, Lee's new employer listed more than five thousand workers on its payroll—one thousand of whom were members of the communist party. Among the workers also were military personnel who managed the company's defense production.

Lee was met at the train station by two women from the Red Cross. One, named Rosa, Lee found attractive. He wrote that she seemed to reciprocate his feelings. Lee likely did not understand that attractive women who come on to him may be just doing their jobs as spies. In any case, Rosa became Oswald's first Russian girlfriend.

No ordinary newcomer, Oswald was taken by the Red Cross women to meet the mayor, who promised him an apartment "soon." In the meantime, he was to stay in Hotel Minsk. He began his job on

January 10. He had to wait until March for the apartment—his first taste of living in a scarcity economy.

With Lee speaking little Russian, the factory management assigned a couple of experienced workers to show him the ropes. One of them, Stanislav Suskevich, would later serve as Belarus's first head of state. The Experimental Shop where Lee worked was a nondescript red-brick structure with a corrugated metal roof. Lee described his work as a "checker" being an easy gig. He turned down an invitation to speak to the assembly of workers—a ready audience, but his Russian was not ready for public speaking.

His Russian improved quickly. He characterized his fellow workers as friendly and cooperative, that is, until they learned that he had his own apartment and earned more than they. Lee's "blood money" from the Red Cross continued as a monthly payment. Combined with his monthly wage, Oswald earned, by his calculation, about as much as the director of the factory.

On March 16, the mayor delivered on his promise—a one-bedroom flat, an eight-minute walk to the factory, with a splendid view of the river from its two balconies, almost rent free. It is, in Lee's words, "a Russian's dream."

Lee gradually accumulated a circle of friends. Pavel Golachev, the ne'er-do-well son of a general, was among the first. He spoke good English. Most likely Pavel had been "encouraged" to befriend Lee. A handsome blond Adonis, Pavel introduced Lee to girls at the language academy, and Lee recorded in detail their physical attributes in his *Historic Diary*. (See the photo of Pavel, Lee, Marina, and another woman in the photo section.) Pavel and Lee would drop in on the ladies' crowded dorm room at will, convenient or not. On their part, the girls welcomed practicing their English with a real-live American, and they even arranged for Lee to tape-record his voice as an example of southern speech.

Lee took on the nickname of "Alik," and that moniker is what he's known as during his Minsk years. His future wife (Marina) will address him as Alik.

Ernst (Erik) Titovets, a medical student, sought out Lee to practice his English. In the course of their English conversations, they tackled weighty subjects such as political philosophy and Marxism. At first, Ernst took Lee for a highly educated person, an expert on Marxist thought. As Ernst's English improved, he had second thoughts about the depth of Oswald's knowledge.

Ernst became Lee's best friend, along with Pavel. Together they hung out in Lee's apartment, played practical jokes, and chased girls. The two searched for KGB bugs in his apartment. They engaged in hijinks that included recording mock TV interviews, in which Lee affected a credible Shakespearean voice.

. . .

Lee, with time and money on his hands, partook of Russian culture. Neatly dressed, he attended opera, ballet, and folk music concerts. Apparently impressed, he wrote out by hand the lyrics of folk songs that he liked. He was particularly enamored with Tchaikovsky's opera *The Queen of Spades*. He even tried to mimic its style in a love letter to Marina.

Lee's main activities seemed directed at finding a Russian mate. The most frequent entries in his *Historic Diary* concerned women he met, dates, and seductions. He brags about a female conquest whom he dumps after several dates.

With respect to Minsk women, Oswald was pretty much the proverbial "kid in a candy store." In his pre-defection life, girls had ignored him—average height with premature receding hairline, a pronounced overbite that earned him the Marine nickname of "Ozzie Bugs," and nothing special to offer. In Minsk, he was the exotic "American." He dressed well, had plenty of money, and he had his own flat. His dates, on the other hand, lived either with relatives, in crowded dorms, or in miserable rented rooms. Oswald enjoyed the luxury of hosting parties in his own apartment.

It was not until he settled in Minsk that Oswald's sex life blossomed. As the only American in Minsk with generous pay and his own apartment on Kalinin Street, the neatly dressed and polite Oswald did not lack dates, a number of whom he lured into his bed. Those girls who resisted his advances (a dark Jewish beauty named Ella German and Marina) were awarded marriage proposals. Marina accepted shortly after Ella turned Lee down.

By June of 1960, Lee had fallen madly in love with Ella as she resisted "his more dishonorable advances." In his diary, lady-killer Lee brags about playing Ella off against Rosa at a small party in his apartment. He records that their jealousy brought "a warm feeling to me."

Oswald and Ella dated for a half year, and Lee was a welcome guest in her home. Confident she would accept a proposal of marriage, Lee was stunned when she rejected him on January 2, 1961, shortly after Lee had celebrated the new year with Ella and her family.

Ella related to Lee some facts of Soviet life. Marriage to someone like Lee carried with it certain dangers. They might be living in a period of "thaw" of Soviet-American relations, but things could return to the way they were only a few years earlier. Jews had been saved from a Stalin purge by his March 1953 death, but Ella reminded Lee that Germans, Jews, and Poles had been arrested and worse just for their nationality. Who knows what could happen in a mixed marriage of a Jew with an American ex-Marine?

For Lee, Ella's rejection was probably his first lesson in the Soviet repression that had claimed millions of lives under Stalin. Lee had already been surprised that nationality was printed in all Soviet passports. He now knew that one's nationality alone could mean serious trouble.

Ella's rejection ended the "happy" phase of Oswald's Minsk sojourn. He fell into a depression as he mourned the loss of his love. In his *Historic Diary*, he complained that: "The work is darp [drab], the money I get has nowhere to be spent. No nightclubs or bowling alleys, no places of recreation except the trade union dances. I have had enough."

· · ·

Oswald's personal experiences at work and play in Minsk were casting serious doubt on his expectations of a socialist paradise. From Day 1, he resented the picture of Lenin glaring down from its "place of honor" on the wall of the shop floor. Even bigger irritants were the compulsory morning gymnastics and the endless meetings, timed to the lunch hour so as not to sacrifice production.

As workdays and holidays passed, Lee Harvey Oswald showed himself to be a surprisingly keen observer of Soviet reality. Unbeknownst even to the cerebral Ernst, he wrote by hand a nineteen-thousand-word account of the Minsk Radio and TV Factory, which he entitled *The Collective* (*kollektiv* in Russian).

As described insightfully by Oswald, the *Kollektiv* is the basic unit—the atom—of the Soviet enterprise. Each *Kollektiv* is controlled by a party professional, likely a graduate of a higher party school. At the Minsk factory, these party leaders directed the one thousand party members in the workforce. The party professionals directing the *kollektiv*s ranked higher than the nominal bosses in management. These managers dared not buck the *Kollektiv*.

Oswald's *The Collective* proceeds to describe the various *kollketiv*s and the party professionals who direct their activities. He generally gives high marks to those party leaders, who have advanced from "shock workers." He is less tolerant of the party bureaucrats who call fifteen meetings a month (fourteen compulsory). As described by Oswald (as edited for grammar and spelling by the Warren Commission): "A strange sight indeed is the picture of the local party man delivering a political sermon to a group of usually robust simple working men . . . turned to stone all except the hard faced Communists with roving eyes looking for any bonus-making catch of inattentiveness."

Such observations destroyed any illusions Oswald might have had about a worker state dedicated to communist ideals. The main objective of workers, he wrote, was a "quiet life" of adaptation to all the irritations imposed on them from above. Nor were their private lives any better. The search for an apartment consumed workers and their families while they shared communal apartments, doubled up with relatives, or rented single rooms. Housing officials routinely took bribes. Workers would list nonexistent babies to get a little higher on the housing waiting list.

Nowhere did Oswald encounter genuine enthusiasm for communism. Oswald described in *The Collective* with a jaded eye the staged communist demonstrations and rigged elections with 99.9 percent turnout. Failure to participate in these shows of enthusiasm could lead to police investigations, "the one thing to be avoided in any police state." Lee wrote that Minsk's fifty-eight Agitprop stations were not for party education, but for denouncing colleagues or neighbors.

Nor were Soviet citizens allowed to live where they wanted. Moves from one city to another had to be approved by the authorities. The state restricted travel, and international travelers had to "leave behind close relatives, preferably a wife and children, or mother and father."

· · ·

Oswald's unflattering take on Soviet life explains his January 4, 1961, rejection of the Soviet citizenship that he had requested upon arrival in Moscow. The Soviet-citizenship prize for which he had feigned suicide was his to take, but he no longer wanted it.

On February 13, he notified Richard Snyder in the U.S. Embassy that he wished to return to the States. The Embassy wrote to Oswald that he must come to Moscow. Oswald responded that he could not come at that time.

Lee's courtship of Marina Prusakova accounts for his hesitancy to travel to the Moscow Embassy. He met Marina at a trade union dance on March 17. Marina—a certified pharmacist and an orphan—was living with her aunt and uncle in Minsk. Her uncle held a position with the Ministry of Interior, of which the KGB was a division. (This "spy" uncle would later be used as evidence that Marina herself was a spy.)

At the dance, Marina cut a striking figure. As described in Lee's *Historic Diary* (text uncorrected): "I am introduced to a girl with a French hair-do and red-dress with white slipper I dance with her. than ask to show her home I do, along with 5 other admirers Her name is Marina." For her part, Marina attracted more than her share of suitors and marriage proposals.

Lee and Marina commenced dating, and their relationship deepened when Marina became a frequent visitor during Lee's hospitalization with an ear infection. As Lee's courtship of Marina began, he was getting over Ella's rejection, and Marina was juggling three suitors at once. Unlike most marriage-minded girls in their circle, Marina liked the fact that Lee was a foreigner. Having lived most of her life with relatives, some of whom considered her a "loose woman," Lee's apartment served as a major attraction. Unlike Russian men, Lee was neat and clean. He made sure that his apartment was well furnished and spotless. Whereas Marina concealed from Lee that she was illegitimate, the twenty-one-year-old Lee told Marina he was twenty-four to appear more mature in her eyes. He also told her that he was an orphan. He tried to conceal the fact that he was a manual laborer by washing his work clothes out of Marina's sight. It was only when Lee received a letter from Fort Worth that he admitted that his mother was alive but that they did not get along.

On April 20, 1961, Marina accepted Lee's marriage proposal. At the civil registration office, they were directed to another office that handled foreigners. They had to wait ten days while the Minsk bureaucracy figured out how to register the marriage of a Russian woman to an American. During this waiting period, Marina resisted Lee's pleas for sex, arguing that they were not officially married. She warned that the registry office could easily reject their application.

Marina managed to fend off the advances of her suitors, including Lee, and was a virgin on their wedding night. Lee thanked her for "saving herself."

The civil ceremony was followed by a boisterous wedding party at Marina's uncle's apartment. Marina's uncle and aunt's celebratory mood was also heightened by the freeing up of the room that Marina occupied. With the assistance of friends, they moved Marina's things into Lee's apartment, where KGB bugs recorded their violent arguments and sexual moments.

The newlyweds settled into a routine with Lee making his own breakfast and walking early to work. Marina would awake later and drag herself to the hospital dispensary. Their evenings were spent at a small nearby bistro followed by shopping for items to complement their apartment. Among Lee's hobbies was tending a potted flower garden arranged on their expansive terrace overlooking the river.

. . .

Marina's Alik (Lee) proved to be extremely jealous. He allowed no former boyfriend to set foot in the apartment unless now married. He would not permit Marina to dance with anyone but him. Later in the U.S., he was on the alert for unwanted advances toward Marina, and in one case was convinced that an FBI agent had come on to her.

As a gesture to start with a clean slate, Lee confessed that he'd had five sexual partners during his duty in Japan, none of whom he found attractive. (He could not tolerate chubby women; skinny Marina was his type.) He did not confess to Marina, however, that these encounters left him with gonorrhea.

Marina learned that Lee was, moreover, a Puritan about sex. He hated divorce and infidelity, especially if committed by the woman. Lee disapproved of abortion, asserting that women should pay for their mistakes.

Neither Lee nor Marina were deeply in love as they wed. Lee was getting over his infatuation with Ella, who had rejected his first marriage proposal. Marina matter-of-factly calculated that Lee was her best option among her many suitors.

Marina and Lee had to contend with the fact that Marina was left unsatisfied with intercourse. They experimented with various techniques including oral sex, of which Lee learned through locker-room talk at work. Lee blamed himself for reaching climax too soon, while Marina blamed herself for her inability to reach climax other than through a form of sex of which she felt ashamed. They both enjoyed sex—it was one of the best things in their life together—but because of the form it took, Lee thought that he was less than he should be as a man.

There is no credible evidence that Lee ever cheated on Marina, although some unlikely rumors floated about a marital indiscretion during his trip to Mexico City in August 1963. The same could not be said of Marina. During Lee's absence in Moscow in July of 1961, Marina agreed to meet an old flame from the previous summer. She wanted to test whether she had made a mistake in marrying Lee. Their extramarital tryst ended in fiasco as her boyfriend himself proved a virgin and was overcome by nervousness. Marina insisted on walking home by herself—at two o'clock in the morning.

Later, Marina became vocal with her complaints about Lee's lovemaking. In public, she declared that "Lee is not a real man." Not only was Marina derisive of her husband's politics and philosophy. She shamed him for his deficient performance in the marital bed. We can wonder what effect his wife's cruelty had on a man like Lee with a loose grasp on reality.

The couple disagreed on the topic of children. Lee wanted a child as soon as possible. Marina wanted to wait. After Lee threw out contraceptives that Marina obtained from her pharmacy, Marina fainted, and it was confirmed that she was pregnant. Marina would deliver their daughter, June Lee, in a Minsk maternity ward on February 15, 1962.

The secretive Lee had concealed from his bride that he had begun preparations for a return to the United States. Eventually, Lee told Marina that he wanted her to leave the USSR and come with him to Texas where his brother Robert would host them in his house. Lee regaled Marina with tales of full shelves, private automobiles, and attractive apartments available to all in the American promised land.

Marina's first reaction was one of shock, but Lee whittled away at her resolve, even getting on his knees to plead with her. The birth of daughter June had sealed the deal. Marina, who never knew who her father was, did not want her child to suffer the same fate.

On May 30, 1961, a month into their marriage, Lee swallowed yet another disappointment—one that sealed his resolve to return to America. Patrice Lumumba University in Moscow informed Lee, with regret, that it was reserved for students from developing countries in Africa and Asia. Lee's last hope to jump from manual laborer to intellectual vanished with this letter.

· · ·

Marina would have been aware of the potential dangers of marriage to a foreigner, but it did not seem to faze her as it had Ella. Oswald began his courtship of Marina as his decision to return to America was being finalized. True to Lee's secretive nature, he kept his plans from his fiancée only to tell her after they were married. But as Lee's negotiations with the U.S. Embassy intensified, he had to notify the Embassy that he was married, and that his wife would accompany him. On July 8, Lee boarded a plane to Moscow to meet with U.S. consular officials. Weighing on him was the fear that he would be subject to arrest once he entered the United States. In his answers to consular officials, Lee lied that he had never applied for Soviet citizenship and denied that he was a member of the Minsk Radio Factory trade union.

Notably, Oswald's case fell again to Richard Snyder, the consular official with whom Lee had met upon his entry into the Soviet Union.

Snyder noted a different, "more mature" Oswald. Lee was subdued, his arrogant and abrasive manner a thing of the past. Had Snyder known Oswald better, he would have known that Lee could play the role of chameleon if necessary.

By July 9, a pregnant Marina was definitely aware of Lee's plans as she traveled to the U.S. Moscow Embassy to fill out paperwork. Under Lee's supervision, Marina was instructed not to reveal her pregnancy. Nor should she admit to being a member of the hospital trade union.

Marina got her first taste of American life as she entered the U.S. Embassy. The guards, thinking Lee and Marina were both Americans, saluted as their cab arrived. The consular official who interviewed Marina, with Lee as translator, treated her with courtesy, unlike the typical Soviet bureaucrat. Marina, dressed in her finest, was fascinated by the fashionable shoes that Russian women employed by the Embassy wore. The Embassy washroom was another revelation with a clean smell, real toilet paper, and a device that dispensed fresh linen towels.

The bureaucratic hurdles through which Lee Harvey Oswald had to jump were formidable. From U.S. authorities, Lee needed his passport returned, visas for his new wife, and money for the trip. From the Soviet side, the couple required rare exit visas for the United States. On a personal level, the couple needed to keep up appearances at their work and with their friends as they made preparations to leave. On that score, Lee kept his job almost till departure. Probably no one at the radio factory wanted to be responsible for firing an American defector. Marina, on the other hand, was shunned by her friends and colleagues when word of her impending departure got out. She was fired after a humiliating meeting of her collective. Marina had crossed her own Rubicon. A few friends openly envied her chance to live in the United States, but most advised she was making a serious mistake.

One hurdle proved surprisingly easy. On December 25, 1961, Marina was told by the Soviet passport office that she and her husband were to be granted exit visas, a fact Lee reported to the U.S. Embassy. (Some think that her connected uncle greased the wheels.) With exit visas in hand, Lee negotiated with the Embassy for a loan to cover their travel expenses. He signed a promissory note for the loan of $435 on June 1, 1962—the day of departure by train to Rotterdam and from there by ship to Hoboken, New Jersey. On June 15, 1962, they flew to Dallas's Love Field, ready for their next life adventure.

7

THREE YEARS
BEHIND THE IRON CURTAIN

When Lee Oswald landed on American soil on June 15, 1962, he had lived three years in what he now openly called "a police state." Party officials ran the show. By no means was this a worker's paradise. Any enthusiasm for "building socialism" was feigned under pressure from the ruling class. Soviet socialism left its people huddled in cramped dorms and standing in line for life's basics. The devout Marxist had had his encounter with real-world socialism, and he came away disheartened by what he saw.

Yet by Lee's own account, his three years in Minsk included some of the best experiences of his life. He had friends, parties, camping trips, and hunting excursions. Women accepted his invitations to parties, concerts, and, in some cases, to bed. Perhaps most important: Lee married a beautiful woman and had an infant daughter. In Minsk, he seemed to have the prerequisites for a normal life in the socialist paradise that General Secretary Nikita Khrushchev promised for the near future.

Lee and Marina might have lived thusly until old age, sitting on a park bench like British spy Kim Philby of the "Cambridge Three." By Soviet standards, their life would have been good. They would have had their own apartment. Jobs would not have been a problem. Lee would have reconciled himself with the imperfections of the system he saw around him. He likely would have found some white-collar work due to his knowledge of English. He would have been off the factory floor.

But this alternate life would not do for the restive Lee. He came expecting no less than a worker's paradise. Lee Harvey Oswald's persona had been dictated by his Marxist beliefs, forged from reading about socialism and communism since his teenage years. But three years in the USSR had demonstrated that Lenin, Stalin, and their successors had created a mess. Lee had to create a new persona in a new setting—his hometown of Fort Worth, Texas.

. . .

On board the SS *Maasdam* headed for the East Coast of America, Lee Harvey Oswald sat down with ship stationery to sketch out his alternative to capitalism or socialism in which "constructive and practical people can live in peace."

Covering seven pages of tightly scribbled text, interspersing Marxist jargon (withering away of the state, anti-Duhring, etc.) with everyday language, Oswald rambles on about surplus value, the socialist state, and those who fomented revolution in Russia and in America. He is oddly attracted by the Minutemen of colonial America, who took matters into their own hands. Perhaps patriots like this would be the ones to build an ideal socialist state.

Oswald's tract offers no practical guidance as to what was to be done. Rather than develop the features of his "ideal state," he detours to petty complaints about the Red Cross payments for his denunciation of America and other personal gripes.

Oswald's shipboard ramblings reveal him to be rudderless and anchorless. Those who attempted to bring Marx's vision to life had failed. He realized that, but he had no alternatives to offer. Perhaps Cuba had avoided the mistakes of their Soviet mentors. Maybe he could check that out in person one of these days.

That Lee Harvey Oswald could not put together a coherent vision of the ideal system of government is no surprise. Brilliant minds have consistently failed in this exercise.

. . .

What is surprising in his writings is Oswald's keen power of observation as reflected in *The Collective*. In this long essay written well before his departure, Oswald takes us on an insightful tour of the Minsk Radio and Television Company. Given the time and place in which he wrote, Oswald's *The Collective* could have enhanced our knowledge and understanding of the way Soviet enterprises worked. Instead, it remained among Oswald's papers gathering dust.

As someone who studied the Soviet *kollektiv*—through books at first, then in person—I wondered how Oswald was able to put together such an insightful picture of the Soviet enterprise. It turns out that he used his fairly wide circle of friends and acquaintances to gather the figures and descriptions of the inner workings of the Soviet system as reflected by the Minsk Radio Factory.

. . .

Researching Lee Harvey Oswald's three years in the USSR, I learned a great deal about how the man I would meet in the summer of 1962 had been shaped. American consul Snyder's first impression of Oswald as a "new sophomore party liner" echoed my first impression as well. Snyder was also witness to Oswald's playacting as a repentant prodigal son desiring to return to his homeland. From Priscilla McMillan's Moscow interview of the nineteen-year-old, we learn of Lee's ability to conceal his true self. Indeed, the persona of Lee Harvey Oswald was strictly off limits to others.

Most important for understanding the assassination is Oswald's uncanny ability—already on display in his Russian years—to organize, manipulate, pester, and cajole. Moscow originally wanted to expel him, but he got his way by a staged suicide. Lee Harvey Oswald managed, after renouncing the United States, to get his passport back, acquire a visa for his new wife, and even secure a loan for his travel expenses. Despite his atrocious spelling and punctuation, he managed to fill out the numerous forms and attain the necessary affidavits. If Oswald was determined to get something, he had a way of doing it.

Nothing illustrates the determined Lee Harvey Oswald as well as his campaign to reverse his undesirable discharge from the Marines, which was issued while he lived in Minsk. In Oswald's petitions and filings, he argued that the unfavorable discharge was based on newspaper accounts (perhaps Priscilla McMillan's) that he had renounced U.S. citizenship. As he wrote to the Marine personnel office with his demand for a complete review: "However, weather [sic] my choice of permanent or temporary residence may be in the USSR, or in the United States, grounds for such arbitrary actions as was instigated against me cannot be judged as being fair or impartial."

In an earlier petition to John Connally, then-secretary of the Navy and future Texas governor, who would be wounded in the JFK motorcade, Oswald noted that Ernest Hemingway resided temporarily in Paris without a loss of citizenship. He should have the same privilege. In his filings of documents for review (some in Minsk, others from Fort Worth), Oswald went so far as to assert his allegiance to the U.S. Constitution and that he wished to reenlist in the Marines to take advantage of his training.

Oswald's crusade to remove an undesirable discharge from his record makes eminent sense given his impending return. His argument hinged on a technicality. Yes, indeed, he did apply for USSR citizenship, but he no longer wanted it when it was offered. Also, the undesirable discharge was based on actions he may or may not have taken after leaving the Marines.

Oswald's letter to Connally served as the foundation for a theory that Oswald really wanted to kill Connally, not JFK. His motive: revenge for the undesirable discharge.

The Oswald file for removal of the undesirable discharge is remarkable for its almost flawless English and rich vocabulary in contrast to the atrocious grammar and spelling in his *Historic Diary* and SS *Rotterdam* ramblings. Could Oswald have enlisted his friends Erik and Pavel or even gotten some assistance from the U.S. Embassy? Back in Fort Worth, he could have used his brother Robert. Or could Oswald actually write effectively if given the time to leaf through his pocket dictionary?

. . .

Lee Harvey Oswald did not have friends. He had pawns, including his nearest relatives. To convince Soviet passport authorities to let him stay, he wrote to Robert that he was breaking all ties to him. As he tired of life in Minsk, he opportunistically resumed correspondence with Robert, informing him matter-of-factly that he had married. He persuaded Robert to lend him money for the return trip. Eventually he extracted an invitation for Lee and family to stay with Robert and his wife, Vada, in Fort Worth, until Lee could get on his feet. Knowing they had a place to stay removed Marina's last reservations about moving to America.

Whereas Lee framed the things he needed from Robert as requests, he posed them as demands to his mother, Marguerite. While negotiating with the Moscow Embassy for return, Lee dispatched a steady stream of correspondence to his mother, who served as his personal assistant. Throughout Lee's time in Minsk, Marguerite continued to write him without receiving signs of life from her son in return. Upon learning of Lee's plans to come back to the States, she volunteered her modest apartment for him, Marina, and her granddaughter, June. They could have the bedroom; she would take the couch. She was used to living without the usual comforts, but don't mind her. She was used to hardship, she complained in classic Marguerite style.

Lee likely understood that he was cut from the same cloth as his mother. His loathing of her perhaps redounded in self-loathing. Like Lee, she had the ability to bluster, harass, and manipulate in order to get her way. The Gregory family would come to understand this as well as anyone.

Although she knew that her youngest son despised her, Marguerite still provided the Moscow Embassy an affidavit of financial support for Marina signed by her employer. To the very end, Marguerite idealized her youngest son. Although Robert was moving up the ladder of a successful business career and had a stable family life, Marguerite placed the erratic and ne'er-do-well Lee on a pedestal. Robert, she would declare, was too soft, too easily influenced by others. Lee was destined for greatness. Robert was humdrum.

• • •

Marguerite Oswald bore three sons from two of her four marriages. Lee and Robert were brothers. John was a half-brother. She did not finish high school although she claimed a high-school diploma to potential employers. Her truculent and demanding manner made it difficult for her to hold a job. She dragged Lee along with her as she moved from New Orleans to Dallas to the Bronx and then to Fort Worth. Her other two sons, Robert and John, she parked in orphanages. Not exposed to the eccentricities of their mother, both had successful careers in the military and business.

In the Bronx (and living with half-brother John), Lee's truancy and antisocial behavior alerted social workers. In their reports, they characterized Marguerite as a "defensive, rigid, self-involved person who had real difficulty in accepting and relating to people." They determined that she did not understand that Lee's withdrawal was a form of "violent but silent protest against his neglect and complete absence of any real family life."

These New York child psychologists got Marguerite right. And while they recorded feelings of sympathy for Lee, there was little they could do for him.

. . .

As Lee, Marina, and June's plane descended onto Dallas's Love Field on June 14, 1962, the prospects for this new phase of life were razor thin. A near-delusional Lee anticipated a tumultuous homecoming with reporters jockeying to shout questions at him. Like in Minsk, he would be a celebrity of sorts. Also, he was no longer a kid; he was a grown man with a family. He had exceptional experiences under his belt. How many fellow Americans had spent three years behind the Iron Curtain? He may not spell well, but publishers would compete to publish his *Historic Diary*. And who else in the Dallas-Fort Worth area could speak Russian as well as he? Surely there would be a job out there. No need to slave as a manual laborer anymore. No more factory floor. The "new" Lee Harvey Oswald would work in an air-conditioned office. Minimum-wage jobs would be a thing of the past. Yes, he could stay with Robert, but it would not be long before he and Marina could enjoy the American dream. This would not mean abandoning his Marxist ideals. He would at last pursue his dream of a college education, during which he would grasp the opportunity to flesh out his ideal socialist society. What better person to do this than Lee Harvey Oswald? He had lived through a failed attempt. He would figure out how to do it right.

PART III

THE GREGORY CONNECTION

My story now switches to Texas and the arrival there of Lee Harvey Oswald, his wife, Marina, and daughter, June; his getting to know Peter Gregory and son Paul; his tempestuous relationship with the "Dallas Russians"; his failed attempt to assassinate General Walker; and finally his killing of the president of the United States. The Gregorys of 3513 Dorothy Lane were unwittingly caught up in the wake of the debris that followed Lee Harvey Oswald, wherever he went.

8

OSWALD RETURNS

The Gregory family's part of the Oswald story began a year and a half before November 22, 1963, in Pete Gregory's office in downtown Fort Worth, as he prepared to greet an unlikely visitor. This appointment was presaged by a brief item in the June 8, 1962, *Fort Worth Star-Telegram*. Headlined "Ex-Resident: U.S. Defector Heads Home," the story informed local residents that an ex-Marine had turned in his passport in Russia and had vowed never to return.

I must have been the only member of the Gregory family who later remembered this news buried on page seven. "Aunt Ruthie," my grandmother's best friend, saw it and sent a clipping to me in Norman with the notation: "Thought you'd be interested in this." She may have mentioned reading it in passing to Pete, but he must have forgotten. He had no inkling of who Lee Harvey Oswald was when the Texas Employment Agency arranged their first meeting.

When Lee, Marina, and daughter June arrived at Dallas's Love Field on June 14, Lee inquired of Robert whether he had received many calls from the press about his homecoming from Russia. Lee was disappointed to learn that he warranted only a brief mention in the Fort Worth newspaper. He had counted on a crowd of reporters waiting with their cameras flashing as he exited the plane with his Russian wife and infant daughter. Lee Harvey's inauspicious arrival offered a taste of things to come. In Moscow, journalists had sought him out in the Metropole to hear his story. In Minsk, he was a celebrity of sorts—the only American in town. In Fort Worth, he was a "defector" to the Cold War enemy. Why waste precious space in the local newspaper on such a misfit?

As Lee and Marina moved into Robert's comfortable ranch-style home on Davenport Street in West Fort Worth, Lee had debts to repay. They could not stay forever with Robert and his wife, Vada, who could scarcely communicate with Marina. Their orderly lives were being interrupted by a stranger who spoke no English. Marguerite had a small apartment on busy West Seventh Street. She would welcome them moving in, but for Lee being around his mother was torture.

Lee had to figure out a way to earn enough money to rent an apartment and pay for food and baby products, and also repay the debts he had built up with the State Department. And then, Lee needed money to hire a typist for his *Historic Diary*, which he reckoned would be a hot property for book publishers.

He hoped the one skill that set him apart—fluency in Russian—might give him a leg up.

He contacted the Texas Employment Office, which was accustomed to filling manual labor jobs. With three years of living in the Soviet Union under his belt, Lee thought that surely someone out there would hire him for his language skills and travel experience.

He was wrong. Soon he would find himself back on the factory floor doing manual labor unsuited to a man of his talents.

9

SEEKING PETE

Pete Gregory's office, located on the fifteenth floor of the Continental Life Building in downtown Fort Worth, resembled Humphrey Bogart's in the 1941 classic *The Maltese Falcon*, except that it was far from run-down. All the individual offices had opaque glass windows, transoms, and black, engraved letters etched in the glass. My father's was labeled "Peter Gregory, Chairman, Yates Engineering Committee." Pete was the chief engineer for the giant Yates oil field located in Texas's Permian Basin.

On June 19, 1962, Lee Harvey Oswald walked into the Continental Life Building to see Pete Gregory. Understanding how Oswald ended up in Pete's office requires some explanation.

* * *

Peter Gregory was born Piotr Petrovich Grigoriev in March 1904 in Khilok, Siberia, a small mining town on the Trans-Siberian Railway. He grew up in Chita, the bustling headquarters of the Trans-Baikal railroad, beyond which lay thousands of miles of taiga forests and then Manchuria.

Like most residents of Chita, the Grigorievs lived in a wooden cottage heated by a single wood-burning stove. Unlike poorer residents, they had electricity and running water (even a "two-seater" toilet). Pete's mother died when he was twelve. With his father away at the World War I front, the three children had to fend for themselves throughout the subsequent civil war between the Whites and the Reds. At sixteen, Pete fled before the advancing Red Army. Although still a teen, he worked as a telegraph operator for the Chinese Eastern Railway in Kharbin, Manchuria.

Many years later, in Texas, Pete entertained my elementary-school friends with his gripping tales of Siberian wolves, his escape from Russia, and his work as a telegraph operator. Some of his tales were so bizarre that we could not tell if they were made up. A grade-school friend of mine, whom I reconnected with fifty years later in Houston, still recalled these stories.

Pete made his way to Tokyo, where he somehow gained admission to the American School in Japan despite his nonexistent English. He studied there alongside young Americans, some the sons of missionaries. One of these, Edwin Reischauer, would go on to become a noted East Asian scholar at Harvard and a U.S. ambassador to Japan. When I later met Reischauer, he could not remember my father, but thought he might be the Russian student they nicknamed "Bubbles." We'll never know.

Thanks to the Russian Student Fund, Pete was able to study engineering at the University of California, Berkeley, starting in 1923. Pete met my mother, Elizabeth Mundhencke, the daughter of a German steel and cotton exporter, in Galveston on his way to West Texas. After Pete's "Shallow Sands Oil Company" denied the Gregorys tycoon status by drilling a number of dry wells near Iraan, Texas, we moved to Forth Worth in 1943, where Pete pursued a successful career as a consulting engineer.

When business was slow, Pete would retire to the city's Rivercrest Country Club for a game of golf or gin rummy. Few could beat him at gin rummy, many at golf. One of his notable coups was trading consulting services for golf lessons from the most famous club member— the legendary Ben Hogan. (The Secret Service used Hogan's luxury Cadillac convertible to transport JFK during his visit to Fort Worth on November 21 and 22, 1963.)

Another of Pete's hobbies was teaching Russian to a small cadre of adult-education students at the Fort Worth public library. Although most of the students had little time and less talent for languages, some of them became family friends—such as the marriage-shy Charlie Ruble, who joined us at family gatherings with his patient fiancée in tow. The marriage proposal never came, the fiancée moved on, and we lost sight of Charlie.

Although the number of students was small, Pete did not memorize their names. It is understandable why he did not remember a middle-aged nurse who introduced herself as Mrs. Oswald.

The free Russian classes at the library became a fixture of the Fort Worth adult-education scene. And in the Fort Worth of the 1950s and early '60s, if anyone was looking for someone who could *speak* Russian, let alone teach it, that someone would have been Pete Gregory.

So . . . on June 19, 1962, Pete received a phone call from the employment agency informing him that they were sending a young man to his office for certification that he was fluent in Russian. He needed a reference for jobs that involved the Russian language (although none existed in Fort Worth).

At 11:00 a.m., a man in his early twenties arrived. He was dressed in a woolen suit in ninety-degree-plus weather. Sweating profusely, he introduced himself as Lee Harvey Oswald. He claimed he knew Russian and hoped to find a job that required him to use his language skills. Pete had him translate passages from two Russian books he chose at random from his bookshelf and was surprised at how well the young man performed.

After they exchanged a few words in Russian, Pete concluded that Oswald was perhaps of Polish origin because he spoke with what Pete thought was a Polish accent. Satisfied on the question of fluency, Pete drafted a "to whom it may concern" letter stating that one Lee Harvey Oswald was qualified to work as a translator of the Russian language.

Conspiracy theorists have latched on to Pete's hunch that Oswald spoke Russian with a Polish accent. Perhaps it was a sign of special language training or of some other conspiratorial plot. Although Pete grew up with Russian as his mother tongue, he would have had no substantive experience in distinguishing one accent from another. Many citizens of the USSR spoke Russian as a second language. A Russian encountering Lee probably would have guessed that he hailed from a Baltic state.

. . .

It was Pete's practice to eat lunch, usually alone, at the Texas Hotel, a couple of blocks from his office. (President Kennedy spent his last night at that hotel.) Curious to learn more about the enigmatic young Oswald, Pete invited Lee to join him. Lee must have been taken aback by the large dining room, with its bustling waiters making sure that each table was amply supplied with melba toast—a signature of the hotel. The dining room was usually full of oilmen, discussing deals and passing the time of day. A number would have worn Texas hats made by our Greek neighbor, J. Peters. Oswald, sweating in his woolen suit, would have stood out in the crowd.

Not being one to pry into other people's personal affairs, Pete tried to engage Oswald in routine conversation about life in the contemporary Soviet Union—such as work and pay—as they ordered and then ate their food. Pete's gentle probes got few answers beyond some basic facts. Oswald volunteered almost nothing about how and why a former Marine and a native of Fort Worth could end up in the city of Minsk, the capital of Belorussia, other than to say enigmatically that he had "gone there on my own."

Upon parting, Lee Oswald gave Pete the address and telephone number of his brother Robert, where he and his Russian wife, Marina, were living at the time. "If anything comes up," Pete said, "I'll be in touch with you there."

When he returned to Robert's home, Lee proudly displayed the certificate of Russian proficiency to his brother and his sister-in-law. He had Robert read it out loud. At least Lee had one accomplishment to his credit that Robert did not.

Our story could have ended at that point. Pete Gregory might not have contacted Oswald, and the recollection of the meeting with this inscrutable young man might have joined other faint or lost memories. But the story did not stop there. In the aftermath of the assassination, Pete and Paul Gregory stood accused in some corners of being part of a conspiracy to deflect attention from the true assassins. Pete became an eyewitness to history. Bubbling below the surface in the Gregory family through all this was a sense of shared guilt. If we had not gotten involved with Lee Harvey Oswald, perhaps President Kennedy would have lived and changed the trajectory of American politics?

Pete Gregory was confronted with this "What if?" question by the Warren Commission counsel:

> MR. LIEBELER: Would it be fair to say, Mr. Gregory, that it was through Oswald's contact with you that he subsequently made the association with and contact with the other members of the Russian community in Dallas and in Fort Worth?
> MR. GREGORY: I think that would be a fair statement, yes.

10

"PAUL, MEET LEE AND MARINA OSWALD"

Until recently, I had not reviewed the transcript of my testimony, but a look at "Paul Gregory, Warren Commission" transported me back to June 1962 as I read my own words describing my first meeting with Lee and Marina Oswald.

Testimony of Paul Roderick Gregory, Office of the U.S. Attorney, 310 Post Office Building, Dallas, Texas. Mr. Wesley J. Liebeler, assistant counsel of the president's Warren Commission presiding:

Mr. LIEBELER: Would you state your full name for the record, please?

Mr. GREGORY: Paul Roderick Gregory.

Mr. LIEBELER: You are presently a student at the University of Oklahoma, isn't that right?

Mr. GREGORY: Yes.

Mr. LIEBELER: You are the son, are you not, of Peter Paul Gregory?

Mr. GREGORY: Yes.

Mr. LIEBELER: Your father is originally from somewhere in Siberia, is that not correct?

Mr. GREGORY: Yes.

Mr. LIEBELER: And he came to the United States approximately when, do you know?

Mr. GREGORY: I would guess about 1920, or '21, or '22. I am not sure of the exact year.

Mr. LIEBELER: Have you had occasion to speak with your father over the telephone or to exchange letters with him since that time he appeared before the Commission in Washington?

Mr. GREGORY: I spoke with him approximately three times since then.

Mr. LIEBELER: Did you discuss with him the testimony that he gave before the Commission?

Mr. GREGORY: No. He only said that he mentioned my name. That is the only thing he said about his testimony.

Mr. LIEBELER: Did there come a time when you met Lee Harvey Oswald and his wife, Marina?

Mr. GREGORY: Yes.

Mr. LIEBELER: Would you tell us when that was and the circumstances of that event?

Mr. GREGORY: I met Lee and Marina Oswald in the summer of 1962—I suppose in the middle of June. I met them both at Lee's brother's house in the western part of Fort Worth. Lee Oswald had become acquainted with my father a week or two weeks earlier. He came to him to get some kind of paper showing his ability in the Russian language; he wanted to get a job as interpreter or some kind of work which would have something to do with his ability to use Russian. I believe he came to my father's office twice—I am not sure, because I wasn't there—and he gave him the address of his brother where he was staying at the time. He may have said, "Come see us." My father and I were both interested in meeting his wife, who was Russian. So, we went there for a visit, a purely social visit, probably in the middle of June 1962, and that was the first time I ever met either Lee Oswald or Marina Oswald.

. . .

Reading these pages of testimony rekindled memories of that first meeting.

Lee left his brother Robert's telephone number with Pete Gregory at the end of their lunch in downtown Fort Worth. Insofar as I was home for the summer, my father and I decided we would like to meet Marina. He telephoned Robert's house and talked to Lee, who in turn talked to his brother, and a meeting was arranged for the same day. Late afternoon, we drove to Robert Oswald's modest, white-frame house at 7313 Davenport Avenue. It was a purely social visit. There was no hidden agenda. We were mostly curious to meet Marina.

Robert and Lee were in the front yard, either waiting for us or just getting some exercise playing ball. Robert, like his brother an ex-Marine, introduced himself, and Pete introduced Lee to me. My first impression of Robert was of a tall, well-spoken man, almost courtly. He seemed to be a solid guy, someone you immediately liked. After serving in the Marines, he had worked his way up the ladder as a division manager at the Acme Brick Company. Over the next two years, Robert and his family would move twice on company assignments, the second one being to Denton, Texas. At the time of the assassination, Robert, like me, had not seen Lee for a year.

You'd have to look twice to determine that Robert and Lee were brothers. Lee was medium height (5'9"), wiry, his hairline noticeably receding. His greeting was restrained. He spoke with a slight southern accent, as did Robert, slightly different from the Texas twang spoken in

Fort Worth—likely a product of their time in New Orleans and of their mother's own way of talking.

My father and I were invited into the house to meet Robert's wife, Vada, and her new sister-in-law, Marina, who was inside with baby June. My first impression of Marina, as she sat alone holding infant daughter June, was of a slender, almost fragile, young woman of natural beauty, unembellished by cosmetics, at least to my unpracticed eye. Like many Russians, she smiled rarely, if at all. (I later learned that she was ashamed of two rotting teeth, a victim of typically horrible Soviet dentistry.) Rarely did her face show any animation.

This was Marina's first opportunity to speak Russian with someone other than Lee, and she seemed to relish the opportunity—all the more so since she knew no English. She had spent her first days in Fort Worth with Vada, who was kind and well meaning but spoke no Russian. She had also met Lee's mother, Marguerite, whom Marina was determined to treat well and with respect, as is expected of Russian wives. Marina was unable to communicate with either woman without her husband's assistance.

Lee had already told her about the Gregorys—that he had found someone with whom she could speak Russian. I later learned that he boasted that he had found Russian speakers as a favor to her. Pete and I sat with Lee and Marina in Robert's living room with him and Vada looking on as bystanders. Pete led the discussion by asking questions about their trip to the United States, life in Minsk, and what it was like to be a young person in Russia. Marina answered most of the questions, speaking quietly, as was her custom. I sat mainly on the sidelines, listening. Lee occasionally jumped into the conversation. Pete apologized to Robert and Vada that the conversation was in Russian, but that was unavoidable given Marina's lack of English.

The conversation itself was not particularly memorable. Lee and Marina brought out photo albums they had brought with them. We examined pictures of their wedding, of her relatives, of Lee's apartment building in Minsk, and snapshots of Lee and Marina with friends in a park.

For Marina, this was her first meeting with a White Russian émigré—my father. In school, she had been taught that the White Russians had been the enemy of the socialist revolution, but experience taught her to ignore most of the nonsense she learned in her compulsory classes on the history of the Communist Party. Pete spoke an old-fashioned Russian from a bygone era. Except for annual visits with his sister in San Francisco, he went for long periods of time speaking no Russian at all. He had the manners of the old guard, not the crudity and bluster of Marina's friends and colleagues in Minsk. In fact, Marina at first regarded Pete as a rather strange specimen with whom she did not feel particularly at ease. I scarcely spoke during this first meeting, but enough for Marina to remark afterward that I did not speak Russian very well. She was correct on this point.

After an hour or so of visiting, we made our way to leave. We all understood that this was an exploratory meeting. It might or might not lead to something, but the door had been opened. Pete Gregory nursed his reservations about this strange fellow, Lee, who had deserted his country. But his wife seemed pleasant enough, and Marina seemed to love her child, as did Lee. As we left Robert's house, it struck me that Marina, unable to communicate with anyone but her husband, was more or less his prisoner in a new and strange land.

11

MY RUSSIAN TUTOR

Shortly after our first meeting with Lee and Marina at Robert Oswald's house, I left town for a visit with my aunt and uncle in San Francisco. Thoughts of the meeting with the Marine defector and his Russian wife faded as I became a small part of that city's fabled Russian émigré scene, of which my uncle's jewelry store at 2050 Filmore Street was a fixture. On Sundays, the émigrés would don their military uniforms, resplendent with medals, and proceed to San Francisco's Russian House for the afternoon *Spektakl* of aging sopranos and overweight former ballerinas.

Upon my return to Fort Worth, my father and I visited Lee and Marina again. They were now living at 2703 Mercedes Street, about a ten-minute drive from our house on the oval-shaped Monticello Park. We decided to ask if Marina would be interested in giving me Russian lessons. True to Lee's form, the couple had no phone, so we just dropped in on them early in the evening.

The Oswalds' cramped one-bedroom duplex lay a short distance from the landmark five-story Montgomery Ward building—the huge edifice of the mail-order empire that once kept rural America supplied with its necessities. "Monkey Wards," as the locals called the Fort Worth store, had already become Marina's "friend." In Lee's absence, she carried June there to marvel at the bulging shelves of clothing, hardware, sporting goods, and other items. Monkey Wards gave Marina, who still knew only a few words of English, the confidence that she had landed in a better place than Minsk.

My father and I found the Oswalds at home—where else would they be? Lee answered. Marina was tending the baby. We stayed a half hour or so, sitting crammed together in their small living room. Pete led the conversation—in Russian—about Marina giving me language lessons. It was agreed that I would come to their house a couple of evenings a week. We would pay her, but no sum of money was decided upon. Marina seemed to look forward to having regular company and something to do. Lee was his usual taciturn self. He gave no sign of being pleased or displeased. He could have easily said no, but he did not. With Lee's low pay and visions of better things to come, perhaps he was tempted by the money. It was to be earned, not one of those "gifts" he so detested.

Pete still had some concerns about my being a regular visitor in the Oswald household. After all, Lee struck him as peculiar, and he was appalled by the family's living conditions: the baby had an improvised bed made of suitcases; the furniture of the furnished apartment was on its last legs. There was no phone or television, probably not even a radio. But Marina again made a good impression on Pete. His son was coming to study with *her*, not Lee. He was merely an inconvenient bystander. Unlike subsequent visitors to Lee and Marina, Pete resisted the urge to help them financially. As someone who had grown up in poverty himself, he could perhaps understand that a husband's pride might be hurt by unsolicited offers of money, bedding, or old furniture. Perhaps Lee tolerated me and Pete because we accepted them for what they were—a couple living at the margin of existence by American standards.

We decided on twice weekly sessions.

Thus began a whirlwind of conversations, shopping trips, and excursions extending until the mid-September semester began. These sessions brought me into the closest proximity of the man who would later shoot President Kennedy. During this period, I became an observer of the Oswalds' lives as Marina made her first acquaintance with a new land, and Lee begrudgingly began his job as a sheet metal worker for the Lou-R-Pack division of the Leslie Welding Company, where he earned $1.25 per hour or $56 dollar a week. The rent on their duplex was $59.50 per month, utilities included. They had no car. There was no air-conditioning; not even a portable fan was visible. Their landlord, who lived nearby, frequently observed Lee walking to the bus stop. On one occasion, he knocked on the Oswalds' front door to offer to install new curtains. Marina was home alone and could not understand enough English to know why he had come. She did not let him in. Later Marina refused entry of an FBI agent on similar grounds.

I observed over the next month and a half their cautious spending of their money on paltry amounts of groceries and household items. Lee was frugal to the extreme. I did not know at the time that he was saving to pay back the travel money loaned him by the State Department and by Robert.

Marina, not having any frame of reference, thought they were living decently and already let her husband know she would not want to return to Russia. What in our eyes was a pitiful existence was well above what she was used to in Minsk, sleeping on her aunt and uncle's sofa. Her wish not to return to the USSR was to make her the subject of spousal blackmail comprised of threats to send her back if she did not toe the line.

. . .

As I prepared to begin my Russian lessons with Marina, neither of us would know that the summer of 1962 would be among the most stable for Lee and her. The almost half year spent in Fort Worth was the longest in duration of the eight places they lived in between their return to America and the assassination. Fort Worth was even a period of some optimism for Lee. Surely someone would recognize his language skills and the value of his memoirs. He could perhaps help Fidel Castro, whose Cuba would appreciate Lee's devotion to Marxism, Leninism, and socialist revolution. Marina had come with him and left her friends and relatives behind. Such an act showed she must love him. They had an infant daughter they both loved. Perhaps a brighter future did lie ahead.

Such hopes would be dashed one by one as the two of them continued their American journey. Each blow and insult would ratchet up Lee's resentment and firm up his resolve to show the world and his wife that he was someone of stature, someone to be reckoned with.

12

LEE LURKS

On the evening of my first lesson, I parked directly in front of the Oswald duplex around seven. The entrance to the Oswald apartment was through the right door of the duplex (I never saw anyone entering the left door into the mirror-image apartment) on a low concrete porch, which required mounting a single step to reach the screen door. Lee's landlord reported that Lee would sit on the small porch without even a lawn chair, usually reading a book on hot evenings.

The Oswalds' clapboard frame house, topped with a cheap composition roof, had a hardscrabble lawn burned yellow by the summer sun, a combination of grass and gravel. I can't imagine either Lee or Marina having an interest in lawn maintenance, much less Lee paying a water bill for the parched lawn. This was a neighborhood where residents came and went, either bettering themselves or moving down to even worse neighborhoods. Duplexes on the street alternated with modest, single-family homes of the same clapboard design.

The homes around Montgomery Ward were among the poorest in the city—a place for families just scratching out a living. On her walks to Wards, Marina would have seen no Blacks or Hispanics until she was inside. As late as the 1950s, Montgomery Ward had separate drinking fountains and restrooms marked "For Coloreds."

I knocked on the door, expecting Lee to answer, but Marina opened it and invited me in. I was surprised that we were there alone. Lee was not in sight.

Marina and I were both twenty-one at the time—my birthday in February, hers in July. She dressed simply in a skirt and blouse that carried with them the drab look of Soviet manufacture. On subsequent visits, she wore clothes she had brought with her or received as hand-me-downs from Robert's wife, Vada. On particularly hot evenings, she wore Bermuda shorts.

We sat opposite one another in the living room and attempted to make small talk. Our first few minutes were awkward. It was not clear how our "lessons" were to proceed. Making things worse, Marina greeted me in rapid-fire, colloquial Russian, spoken in a hushed tone that swallowed the endings of her words. I was accustomed to the precise Russian that my father brought with him forty years earlier or to the classroom Russian I studied at the university. Until I grew familiar with Marina's speech, I had trouble understanding her—not a promising start for language lessons.

As we sat in the bare living room, I still had no idea where Lee was. In our two meetings so far, I had spoken Russian primarily with Lee. The shy Marina had said little unless prompted. Lee's Russian was ungrammatical and clearly that of a non-native speaker, but he was easy to understand. Now my "interpreter" was missing to smooth things out.

I had brought some Russian materials with me, and I showed them to Marina. I told her that I had signed on for an extra-credit Russian class that involved writing a paper on a play by Soviet playwright

Nikolai Pogodin. Entitled *The Man with the Rifle*, or *Chelovek s ruzhyem* in Russian, the play was about a simple soldier who meets Lenin in Petersburg as the revolution unfolds. Their friendship symbolizes the unity of the Bolsheviks and the proletariat. The assignment was for me impossible: to write about Pogodin's use of language—the contrast of an uneducated soldier forming a friendship with the revolutionary genius, V. I. Lenin. It had been suggested to me by Professor Rzhevsky, a Russian teacher who was a newcomer to the University of Oklahoma. He spoke little English and did not understand my limitations. But by the end of the summer, I actually wrote something—very bad, of course—with Marina helping me to identify key passages from the play as we sat at the small table in the Oswalds' dining-room nook.

From Marina's rapid-fire prattling, I fathomed that Lee would be back home shortly. As she and I talked, infant June slept on her improvised bed. With the weather so hot, Marina let June sleep completely naked. As I mentioned earlier, this irritated Lee to no end.

I had not been around many infants at that time, but June was remarkably quiet that evening, as she was on most other occasions. Throughout my time with Lee and Marina, there were only occasional spells of crying to interrupt our conversations.

In looking around the apartment, I could not help noticing that Marina and Lee lacked an essential instrument of Russian parenthood: a baby carriage, or *kolyaska*, as it is called. The typical Russian mother spends an inordinate amount of time parading with her infant in the fresh air. Lacking a baby carriage meant not only missing the Russian promenade but also having to carry June everywhere. Marina must have been annoyed by the lack of a *kolyaska*. Even in Russia, where people have little, mothers at least have a *kolyaska*, but Lee could not provide her with one—another sign of failure and humiliation for him. When local good Samaritan Russians later gave Marina a carriage, Lee flew into a rage, but he accepted it, an indication that Marina prevailed over him in this particular case.

As Marina and I continued our strained small talk, I surveyed my surroundings. The Oswald living room was as bare as one could imagine. The most prominent pieces of furniture were a shabby sofa and chair plus a worn coffee table, on which a copy of *Time* magazine was displayed. A picture of President Kennedy as *Time*'s Man of the Year was on the cover. That magazine was to remain in the same position on that table throughout all my visits. The issue was dated January 5—five months before their return from Russia. How this half-year-old magazine came to occupy a permanent place in their living room was a puzzle to me. I would later learn that Lee had requested Marguerite to send him in Minsk copies of *Time*. For some reason, Lee decided to bring the January 5 copy all the way with him to Texas. I wondered whether the *Time* Kennedy-cover's place of honor was Lee's or Marina's doing. If Lee's, it could have been a sign of fascination, healthy or unhealthy, with the young president.

Off the living room was a small breakfast nook with a table and two chairs. That is where Marina and I worked on my lessons. We brought in a chair if we wanted to sit all three together in the living room. I never used their bathroom or saw their bedroom; the rest of the house remained terra incognita for me.

I saw, too, that Marina kept their modest dwelling in reasonable order. Compared to my own home, managed by a mother from northern Germany, it might have struck me as disheveled, but (as I would later learn from my many visits to Russia) Marina's housekeeping was in the acceptable range of Russian standards.

When Marina and I went over our lessons at the kitchen table, Lee would sometimes putter around, cleaning dishes or doing other small household tasks. In this regard, he was far from the typical Russian husband, who refuses to do any housework or occupy himself with a baby. Lee's willingness to help with the chores may have been one of his few endearing qualities as a husband. Usually, he sat at the sofa reading or pretending to read, as Marina and I conversed over my Russian books just a few feet away. Who knows what he was thinking.

Although Russians are known for hospitality, no matter how meager their circumstances, Marina did not offer me tea or cookies that first night or on subsequent evenings. She was likely under pressure from Lee to economize. Later, only once, after a shopping trip, did Marina offer me a glass of Hawaiian Punch, essentially a glass of water fortified with a microscopic portion of punch concentrate. Although I found Marina's concoction less than appetizing, I drank it down and duly thanked her.

The breastfeeding of June represented another mystery of the Oswald household. Our language sessions often lasted a couple of hours. I have no recollection of Marina withdrawing to the bedroom to feed June. In fact, I have no clear recollection of June crying, except at the Gregorys' the night of the dinner with the Dallas Russians. I guess June was just an exceptionally well-behaved infant. After all, she was a graduate of Russian swaddling.

■ ■ ■

Marina and I were both relieved that first night when Lee bustled rather noisily into the house carrying a stack of books from the Fort Worth public library. Lee was dressed in his customary fashion: simple slacks, a plaid shirt with open collar, rolled up to the elbows. Unlike his fellow welders, he did not go to work in coveralls. I imagine he changed at work to avoid being pigeonholed as a manual laborer during his commute. But his everyday attire might as well have borne a large label: "working class." In the early 1960s, men still wore suits and ties to work.

The books he carried were all thick and weighty, works worthy of an intellectual leftist—H.G. Wells, Marx, Marx and Engels, George Bernard Shaw. I cannot recall exactly. Clearly, Lee wanted it known that he did not waste time on light reading. I suspect he orchestrated his entrance. I dutifully asked to see what he had brought from the library and made some remarks about his selection of reading material. If Lee's strategy had been to focus on his intellectual proclivities and prowess, it worked. Had the books been stacked away in a corner, they would have escaped my attention.

Marina and I returned to the kitchen table to work out a general plan of study, after which we gathered in the living room for conversation—a way to get to know one another. Some of it was small talk; other parts touched on politics. The copy of *Time* gave me the opportunity to talk about the Kennedys. I wanted to know if Marina, fresh from Russia, knew who JFK was. She appeared to know more than I expected. She ventured that he appeared a nice man and that she had seen pictures of his wife, Jackie, whom she thought was quite glamorous. She also ventured that Jackie appeared to be a good mother. Lee, in his curt way, appeared to concur with his wife's positive assessment of JFK.

· · ·

On that first evening together, we avoided sensitive topics, the touchiest one being why Lee had deserted to the Soviet Union. We talked instead about small things. I inquired how the two met, and I asked Lee about his work in the Soviet Union, what his living conditions were, whether he had made friends. Lee did not avoid my questions, but he kept his answers to a minimum. It was clear that he had mastered conversational Russian in his almost three years in Russia. Lee had accomplished the hardest part of learning any language—command of the everyday vocabulary of household items, foods, automobile parts, and curse words.

Marina told me that she was a trained pharmacist who had worked in a hospital dispensary in Minsk. Lee spoke dismissively of his work, suggesting, with a wave of his hand, that the tasks he performed at the Minsk Radio and Television Factory were beneath his capacities. We again went through their collection of photos from their days in Minsk—Lee and Marina pointing out friends, fellow workers, and

Marina's relatives. Prominent among them was a young man, Pavel, who had been among Lee's best friends.

Lee avoided serious discussion of his life in Russia, but he let some of his cynicism be known that first evening. He talked with some scorn about the decision of then-Kremlin-master Nikita Khrushchev to remove Stalin's embalmed body from its place in the Kremlin mausoleum next to Lenin. Throughout Lee's time in the Soviet Union, Nikita Khrushchev reigned supreme. (He would not be removed from office until October 1964.) Stalin's demotion from the mausoleum had been the talk of the Minsk Radio Factory. Lee found the Stalin story ironic: in the Soviet system, one day an eternal hero of the worker state, the next day a surreptitious burial in the Kremlin walls.

The account of life in Minsk that Lee offered to me jibes with his writings in *The Collective* on his experiences at the Minsk Radio Factory. He said that no one really cared about working to build a socialist state, even the party propagandists. Everyone was going through the motions following the saying: "Under socialism property belongs to everyone and to no one." If that is the case, we might as well steal what we can. The most frequent "theft" was theft of time on the job, as they smoked and gossiped.

Although Lee considered the Soviet Union a perversion of Marx's vision, he did not seem to blame its leaders. Some of the things Khrushchev did seemed to make sense, Lee volunteered. At least he wanted to change Soviet communism for the better through his reforms.

As the three of us sat around the small coffee table, the thought that Lee Harvey Oswald a year and two months later would shoot the president, whose visage was staring up at us from the cover of *Time,* would have struck me as the most insane of propositions.

. . .

Lee and Marina needed a lot of help. I could see that. When Lee went off to work in the morning, he left Marina virtually stranded. Her only link with the outside world was the bus, and the nearest bus stop was four blocks away on West Seventh Street. There were no grocery stores in the immediate area. She had to either walk long distances carrying June and the groceries or wait until Lee came home in the evening to ride the bus. Not knowing English, she was wholly ill-equipped to go anywhere except to Monkey Wards, where she could admire the full shelves, without anyone bothering her in English. But Wards had no food department. She and Lee had to rely on the bus.

So she sat alone in a run-down neighborhood. Temperatures in Fort Worth in summer are consistently in the nineties or even hundreds. Lee and Marina didn't own a fan. Marina may have been like other Russians who, having grown up in intolerable cold, welcome hot climates. She never mentioned being uncomfortable in the heat, nor did Lee.

Marina's lack of even an elementary English vocabulary ("Hello, how are you? Where is the bathroom?") is a testament to the isolation that Lee placed her in, and, I believe, his insistence—almost to the point of brainwashing—that she not learn English.

As our first Russian lesson was coming to an end, it occurred to me that I could probably learn much of the everyday Russian language by taking Lee and Marina shopping and sightseeing. We could start with work on my Russian play assignment, after which I would drive them around town so that Marina could get to know Fort Worth, and they could do some grocery shopping and run chores.

At that juncture, it became clear that I was doing Lee and Marina a favor. My taking "lessons" from Marina became an excuse rather than a primary motivation for our getting together. Both Lee and Marina realized this, but he expressed no gratitude. In fact, Lee tended to react angrily to anyone who offered a helping hand. In my case, fortunately, there was nothing to be angry about. After all, this was part of the "lessons" I was taking from Marina.

. . .

As I was preparing to leave their apartment on the evening of that first lesson, Lee raced to the bedroom and returned with a pocket-sized English-Russian dictionary. It was weathered and worn, the pages faded to gray. Clearly, Lee had used it regularly.

"Take this," he told me. "This was the dictionary I always carried with me in Russia. I don't need it anymore."

Although I already had a pocket dictionary, I accepted, telling Lee I was sure I'd find it useful. To me, Lee's giving away what must have been one of his most precious possessions was puzzling. I had little need for it. He did. And this act of generosity was contrary to his personality as I'd observed it—an apparent gesture of friendship and gratitude that was never repeated.

Later I realized that the gift was probably an act of one-upmanship in front of Marina, an intimation by Lee that "I have mastered the difficult Russian language. I do not even need a dictionary anymore. This Gregory kid needs it, and he thinks he is better than me." With Lee, you never knew.

After the assassination, I mentioned to the Warren Commission that I had Lee's English-Russian dictionary. I had already leafed through it to see whether it contained handwritten notes. (There were none.) The commission expressed an interest in having the dictionary, and I agreed to hand it over, but the matter seems to have been forgotten. I gave Lee Harvey Oswald's pocket dictionary to the Hoover Institution Archives, where I knew it would be well taken care of.

. . .

Sixty years later, looking back on that first evening, I puzzle over the fact that Lee left Marina and me alone for, say, thirty minutes before he trundled in with his load of books. In Minsk, Lee was notorious for his jealousy. Unmarried men were not allowed in their apartment. Marina's one extramarital affair (about which he knew nothing) took place when Lee was in Moscow obtaining a visa. He knew that she had

had numerous boyfriends. Why would he let his guard down with this young guy, Gregory?

Throughout our time together, nothing untoward happened between Marina and me. I did find her very attractive, and I remember wondering why she married someone as messed up as Lee. Yes, if she were single, I would have pursued her. For his part, Lee may have figured that Marina would be apprehensive at the thought of receiving a foreigner her age. For her this would be the equivalent of dealing with a man from Mars.

13

HANGING OUT

Marina seemed to look forward to our meetings. To this day, I can still see her sitting in a stifling little clapboard house, husband absent at work in a welding shop, alone with an infant, and no one with whom to talk. At least in Minsk, she had friends and a social life of dances, get-togethers with relatives, and birthday parties. Our evening lessons would have been the only treats Marina could look forward to. It was her one escape from the cocoon Lee had woven around her.

On a typical evening, I would show up around six thirty and leave around ten or eleven. Lee would have been home from work, and he and Marina would have already eaten. On some evenings, Marina and I would work together on my Russian language project. On others, we would climb into the yellow Buick—the Gregory family car. (Pete drove a second vehicle—a big white Chrysler, which we referred to as "the company car.")

Excursion evenings consisted either of shopping or driving around while I pointed out landmarks as we went along. These jaunts certainly gave me my money's worth for the "lessons." By driving, shopping, and talking we could keep up a pretty good stream of conversation. It was Marina's job to correct my mistakes in Russian. Lee did not allow her to correct his; that was strictly taboo, at least in my presence. Even though he maintained that he needed to speak Russian with Marina to keep up his proficiency, Lee did not tolerate Marina teaching him anything, even if it was her native language.

Marina and Lee made sure that nothing got in the way of my lessons. Lee took some pride in informing Robert that I was coming over to learn Russian, perhaps implying that I was learning from him as well as Marina. Although Lee teased Marina that she was teaching me for the money, as a penny-pincher he was probably curious about how much Marina would earn.

. . .

Leonards (the Leonard Brothers department store) was one of our favorite destinations. Fort Worthians knew it had the lowest prices on food and clothing. So that is where I headed with Lee, Marina, and June on grocery-shopping nights. (Because it could be hard to find parking near Leonards, the brothers built the only private subway in the United States to connect their store with a remote parking lot.)

Although Marina loved to browse through Leonards clothing and household sections, there was no money in the Oswald budget for such items, so we usually went first to the grocery area. When it came to food, Lee made the choices, consulting with Marina. They would whisper together, looking intently at the items and then reach an agreement, usually indicated by a nod from Marina. Despite such consultations, Lee controlled every cent they spent. (It had been this way since their first days of marriage. Lee considered Marina a spendthrift.) But Lee's monopoly on food buying gave Marina and me the opportunity to slip away to other departments for Marina to feast her eyes on the unaffordable treasures.

Although it was not normal practice to haggle over prices in a Texas department store, Lee did so as Marina and I stood to the side. His manner was non-confrontational and almost cheerful. He was almost gleeful when he succeeded in getting a special bargain. With Lee's meager earnings, every penny counted. He bargained especially hard for meat, trying to convince the butcher that such an inferior cut should be priced lower. Lee may have honed his practice in Minsk, where meat was always scarce, and he complained he was constantly hungry there.

We usually left the store with only one bag of food—enough to keep the super-thrifty Oswalds going for a week. I was never around Lee and Marina when they ate, but I knew that Marina prepared dinner in anticipation of Lee's return from work. I saw no signs of hunger, such as visible weight loss by either Lee or Marina, even though I knew from their grocery purchases that they bought very little.

Wherever we went, our trio elicited stares. Residents of Forth Worth were accustomed to hearing occasional Spanish but not Russian, which was not only exotic but also the language of our Cold War enemies. On occasion, someone would summon his or her courage to ask what language we were speaking. Lee ignored them. When I answered, "It's Russian," we were met with incredulous stares.

. . .

When the Warren Commission asked me how Lee could buy a sharpshooter rifle and travel to Mexico on his modest earnings, I had no trouble answering: he spent virtually nothing on himself and his family. He saved. And Marina, who had grown up with shortages, would not necessarily have known, at least during her first months in Texas, that other Americans did not necessarily live as poorly as they. As our shopping trips progressed, however, they threatened to destroy any illusions Marina might have harbored about her life in America. She could see that Americans were buying much more than they and were well dressed and owned cars.

Such experiences convinced me that Lee kept Marina in isolation to prevent her from realizing two essentials of their lives: that her husband was an impoverished nonentity and that they had nothing despite living in a land of plenty. He knew that Marina could escape his Svengali-like control if she knew English or had friends, especially female friends, with whom she could compare lives.

Letting me into the house regularly was for Lee a calculated risk. Marina and I could talk, but I did not seem interested in belittling him in her eyes, and he was always around, after that first evening, to keep an eye on things. Also, Lee needed to give Marina small tokens ("See, I have found someone with whom you can speak Russian") to keep her from chafing at her isolation. Lee could, however, think ahead. Eventually Marina would be able to communicate in English and make friends. That this time was coming must have worried him to no end. In fact, it would be the Gregorys who would eventually give Marina her means of escape from Lee's cocoon.

. . .

At my first lesson, Lee and I discovered that we had both attended the same high school, Arlington Heights High. Lee gave me the impression that he had graduated, although he avoided my questions about when he had attended. I would later learn that he had been at Arlington Heights for at most a couple of months before enlisting in the Marines in late October of 1956. We could have crossed paths in the first month of the 1956 school year, most likely on the football field, where we both tried out for the team. Throughout our conversations, however, he let me think that he had graduated from *some* high school (I presumed Arlington Heights) and had every intention of earning a college degree someday. Despite his short stay, Arlington Heights must have made an impression on Lee. He is featured in a photograph in the 1957 yearbook, and he paid a visit to the school in his Marine uniform after basic training.

As was his practice, Lee did not lie outright. He just had a way of creating impressions by speaking vaguely or imprecisely and then not answering inconvenient questions. Already on that first evening, I promised Marina that I would drive them both to Arlington Heights so that she could see where Lee and I went to high school.

Although Arlington Heights boasts many prominent graduates who went on to successful business, medical, and academic careers, four of its most prominent alumni were newsman Bob Schieffer, singer John Denver (John Deutschendorf back then), Cullen Davis (twice-acquitted of murder charges through the skill of lawyer "Racehorse" Haynes, Davis was the son of wildcatter millionaire "Stinky" Davis), and non-graduate Lee Harvey Oswald. I am the only one who knew both Oswald and Cullen Davis, who was a friend of my older brother. John Denver was a couple of years behind me. His school mates would later be shocked to learn that Denver had become a recording star. He showed little sign of musical talent in high school.

After the assassination, reporters converged on Arlington Heights to interview Oswald's teachers. Because of his short tenure, only the gruff assistant football coach, Nick Ruggieri, remembered Lee from football tryouts. He was, the coach said, too small for football and a poor tackler. Trying out for the football team may well have been one of the most conformist things Lee ever did. All the boys knew that the girls liked only football players. If you wanted to "score" with the opposite sex, you had to be on the football team.

Back to the story. We decided one evening near the end of August to show Marina my and Lee's alma mater. The school itself was closed for the summer holidays, but I thought Lee would enjoy seeing his old school again and that Marina would enjoy its picturesque campus backed by a green practice field, track and field facilities, and tennis courts where I, as a member of the tennis team, had practiced.

When we arrived at the campus, Lee behaved in a rather odd way. It was as if he had never been there before. He did not seem familiar with the layout of the school and grounds and appeared to lack interest in what we were seeing. He again evaded my questions as to what years he had attended. As we walked around more, with me pointing out from outside the locations of the cafeteria, auditorium, gym, and classrooms, Lee clammed up, saying absolutely nothing. Had he spoken, I might have picked up on the fact that he had not graduated from the school.

After that nocturnal visit to Arlington Heights High School, it disappeared from our topics of conversation.

. . .

Lee told me he planned to get a university degree with which he could find meaningful work and not toil in a machine shop. Just look how much experience he had! He had lived abroad and could speak a foreign language almost like a native. In fact, his life was so interesting that he was writing his autobiography, and the tightfisted Lee even hired a typist to work on his draft. On a second visit to Pete Gregory's office back in June of 1962, he displayed some pages from his manuscript. He went so far as to brag to Marina that Mr. Gregory had said that publishers would surely want his memoirs. Pete had scarcely looked at the typed pages and said no such thing.

Earlier, Lee had brought home an application for admission to Texas Christian University. It had evening classes, which would mesh with his work schedule, and it was a relatively short drive through Forest Park. He mentioned that Texas Wesleyan University also had a night program, but it was located quite a distance away on the outskirts of the city.

I recall how Lee and I sat one evening in the Mercedes Street house, going over TCU's application forms, which were several pages long. The forms were blank; Lee had not even begun to fill them out. (If he had, I would have learned he could not spell.) Although I doubted that he would have had a good grade point average from high school (remember I thought he had graduated from Arlington Heights), I did not think TCU's evening school had high entrance requirements. Bigger obstacles would have been money (TCU being an expensive private school), the purchase of a car, and the juggling that would be required to add studies to a fulltime job.

I had earlier asked Lee whether he had a driver's license. Again, that drew no direct answer. (Indeed, he *never* got a license.) With a car, even if it was run-down, attending class after work would be more feasible. Lee assured me that he had driven a lot in the Marines; cars, as distinct from licenses, were no problem for him. (But driving was a problem. In Dallas, Lee took driving lessons from a female friend of Marina's.)

Later, on one of our designated evenings with nothing better to do, we decided to drive to TCU so that Lee could inquire about applying for admission. TCU was familiar territory to me. My sister Anita was a graduate. The family frequently went to plays and musical events there, and in those days, parking was not a problem, especially at night. In addition, TCU had a pleasant, green campus with ornate, light-orange brick dorms and a magnificent football stadium built to match its prowess as a regular powerhouse of the Southwest Conference. We could combine a visit to the registrar with a tour of the campus.

Scholar-to-be Lee dressed up in dark slacks and a white shirt. Marina held the baby. When we arrived at the library, Lee motioned us to wait at a distance while he had a whispered consultation with the woman at the desk. There is no way to know whether he actually inquired about admission or just stood there talking for a decent period of time so he could pretend he had. Clearly, the lack of a high school diploma would have been a deal killer, but Lee was not anxious to advertise that fact.

When Lee rejoined us, I asked, "How did it go?" In his usual fashion, he gave no verbal answer, just a shrug that could have meant anything.

After our TCU wild goose chase, discussion of Lee's scholarly ambitions—and desire for a university degree—also disappeared from our topics of conversation.

. . .

Marina and I worked on my assignments at the dining room table. I would show her my latest written draft, and we would read through Pogodin's *The Man with the Rifle* to search for appropriate passages to quote. If Marina found problems with my writing, she would say *eto ne poluchaetsya* (this doesn't work), a common expression new to me at the time.

During our sessions, Lee usually sat reading in the living room. If we had questions, we could call to him. Having lived in complete immersion among Russian speakers for almost three years, he possessed a rich vocabulary for foods, household goods, and other items of everyday life. The fact that he had picked up the difficult Russian language in this period of time speaks to his natural intelligence, which post-assassination pundits and observers have tended to underrate. (When asked by the Warren Commission, Pete Gregory ventured that Lee's Russian proficiency was explained by immersion in daily life rather than attendance at some sinister Russian language school for spies.)

Russian is a very difficult language to learn, even in an ideal classroom setting. It appears that Lee attempted this difficult task on his own. His commanding officer in Japan noted that Lee read all the time and some of his books were Russian. When Lee was cooped up in the Metropole, he wrote in his *Historic Diary* that he used the time to study Russian.

Some conspiracy theorists contend that Oswald's Russian fluency constitutes proof of a conspiracy. They claim that he could not have picked up the language so quickly. Others debate how much Russian Oswald knew. Having spent hours with Lee speaking Russian, I can confirm that his command of the everyday language was excellent. He could express anything he wanted to say, but, even to my unpracticed ear, his grammar was far from perfect. He often spoke in incomplete sentences. He ignored the complex Russian declensions, used ungrammatical endings, and often got the gender wrong. No one would take him for a native speaker, but would, like my father, conclude that he was from a Baltic republic or even Poland with Russian as a second language.

We do have letters Lee wrote in Russian, primarily to Marina, either when he or she were out of Minsk. They vary dramatically in quality of grammar. I suspect he could have gotten Erik or Pavel to help on some of them. The letters that were clearly handwritten by Lee show his lack of understanding of grammar and his use of phonetic spelling. If written for a college course, these letters would be awarded a C-.

· · ·

In our conversations, Marina and I fell back on Lee as our living dictionary. He had already given his own pocket version to me, and there was no other dictionary in the house. So when I stumbled, searching for a Russian word, we would ask Lee if he could supply it.

I recall one evening when Marina and I were talking about foods. I wanted to tell her that I was a finicky eater. I explained in Russian that a finicky person is someone who does not like many types of foods. She could not come up with the Russian word for finicky; so we turned to Lee. I asked him in English: "What is the Russian word for finicky?" Lee himself was stumped, but Marina responded immediately to hearing the sound *fee-nee-kee*. That, she explained, is the Russian word for figs, and *finiki* was her favorite fruit.

Somehow this small exchange has stuck in my mind over the years. I've never been at a loss for the Russian word for figs.

· · ·

On another one of our late-summer excursions, I drove Lee and Marina to what I considered the most beautiful spot in Fort Worth. Turning off University Avenue to the serpentine Old Garden Road, on to the oval Rock Springs Road, we reached a small parking lot overlooking the city's botanical garden. We got out of the car to admire the panorama of lush plants and flowers below us. It was almost dark, but there was enough light to walk down a pathway through different gardens. Lee carried June, pointing out to her the sights and sounds. We were all in a good mood. The air was cool and delightful for a Fort Worth summer evening.

As we walked past the flowers and fountains, we dwelled on pleasant things. Marina explained how they had met at a dance, and that she, at first, was puzzled by Lee's nationality. Marina said that her friends and relatives resisted her engagement to an American, about whom they knew little, but Marina's girlfriends had been impressed that her American boyfriend had his own apartment. Marina related that she had visited Lee in the hospital when he became ill. (I suspected incorrectly that it was the hospital where she worked.) Marina related that she encountered vocal opposition to her marrying an American both at work and from her friends. Surprisingly, Marina's aunt and uncle gave their blessing. Marina suspected they welcomed the freeing up of the scarce apartment space that Marina occupied.

Marina and Lee married on April 30, 1961. Marina waivered when Lee proposed she come with him to America. But June was born in February of 1962 as Lee was negotiating their return to America, and the birth sealed the deal that she would go with June's father to America. Marina was ostracized and ridiculed at her work and party cell meetings when it came out that she wanted to leave Russia. It was so hard on her that her health suffered.

As I watched the two of them, I wondered why a normal young Russian woman, particularly one as attractive as Marina, got involved with and married an American of such questionable background and prospects, and not particularly handsome at that. Marina and Lee were no "beauty and beast" combination, but to my eye they appeared mismatched.

In my own experience, I subsequently saw a number of marriages of beautiful Russian women to plain or even ugly Western men. Many of these marriages failed; some succeeded, but in Marina's day such liaisons simply did not occur.

Marina may have been attracted to Lee as a rare and exotic specimen almost from another planet. At that time, the Iron Curtain limited the flow of information about the sky-high living standards of the United States. I doubt that Marina saw Lee as a ticket to a materially better life. She didn't seem to know much about life in America. But perhaps she, like Lee, yearned for something better, for a new start; and a new life in America filled that bill. If she had been happy in Minsk, she would not have given Lee a second look as a foreigner, I believe. She would have selected from among her many Russian suitors.

• • •

We chatted casually as we strolled by the Japanese garden, the Oval Rose Garden, the Lower Rose Garden and its fountains, and the Fragrance Garden as Lee shifted June from one hip to the other. I remember that balmy evening in the beauty of the Fort Worth botanical garden vividly, as if it were yesterday. I recall even my own thoughts with great clarity: *Life is remarkable. Here I am walking around with two misfits from the USSR in the city of Fort Worth, Texas. They are living at the margin of subsistence, but they seem, at least at this moment, content with the hand that fate dealt them.*

For a brief, rare moment, even Lee Harvey Oswald appeared almost happy—in his way.

Although still in his early twenties, Lee's disappointments were not limited to his life in the Soviet Union. The Marines had failed him by not recognizing his talents. When I asked him about the Marines, his look of disdain told me he did not want to speak of his experience as one of them. Perhaps it was the mood of the evening. Or Lee still held out hope for the better life for which he had returned to America. The translating job that Pete Gregory told him did not exist could material-ize someday. Publishers would decide to print his *Historic Diary*. Their rocky start in America would prove to be just a small bump in the road. Fellow leftists would come to understand the remarkable contributions he, as a Marxist scholar and revolutionary, could make to the cause. Marina would come to understand he was a man of consequence.

14

THE "DALLAS RUSSIANS"

Word was out in the small Dallas-Fort Worth Russian émigré community. A pretty young Russian woman from Minsk with family ties to Leningrad (St. Petersburg) was living in their midst. Her marriage to an oddball—a former U.S. Marine who had defected to the Soviet Union—suggested something fishy about the whole thing. After all, the émigrés believed, we cannot trust any communist, and the husband claims to be a Marxist. Cautious by nature, the area Russians weighed carefully whether they should meet this odd couple; it was not an easy decision to break bread with a defector, much less a Marine who'd elected to embrace the land they had fled.

This Russian émigré community of some fifty persons, spread across the greater Dallas-Fort Worth area, was divided between the few who fled Russia in the aftermath of the Bolshevik revolution and civil war and the greater number, from the geographic areas of Soviet conquest, who found their way to America from displaced persons (DP) camps in Germany. The civil war émigrés, like my father, had arrived in the

1920s. They now spoke English well and had had time to establish themselves professionally and financially and integrate themselves into the broader community. The later emigrants tended to be Poles, Lithuanians, or Ukrainians who knew Russian as a second language. In several cases, Russian women had come to the area as wives of GIs. Both generations and various ethnicities were united in their hatred of Soviet communism.

Two mainstays of the Fort Worth Russians were Pete Gregory and Gali Clark, the wife of a respected Fort Worth attorney. Gali occupied the ceremonial top rung of this small society. Her husband, Max, had met the beautiful and elegant Gali in Paris while he was serving as an officer in the U.S. Army legal corps. She was from a noble family, which Leo Tolstoy presumably used as a model in his novels. The Clarks attended Russian émigré functions regularly. They did their best to blend in, but everyone understood that Gali Clark was something special.

The leader of the Dallas community was a fifty-eight-year-old life-long bachelor, George Bouhe (pronounced Boo-he). (See the photo of Bouhe with my parents in the photo section.) He had managed a successful accounting business and, now semi-retired, he continued to keep the books for a few wealthy clients. His father had occupied a high administrative post in the Czarist administration before the revolution.

George Bouhe possessed a strong sense for pedigree. A highlight of his life was being received by Gali Clark's "princess" mother in her expansive Parisian apartment. He returned to Dallas swooning about her gentility and culture. In a word, George was a snob, but a well-meaning one at that.

Bouhe had a sensitive nature. He worried about his stomach. When invited to dinners, he either refrained from eating or brought along his own food. (After the assassination, he fretted about being called to Washington to testify because his delicate constitution would not allow him to fly.)

A native of St. Petersburg, Bouhe was the most anxious to meet Marina, who had grown up in that same city with her grandmother. Bouhe missed his hometown, which he knew he would never see again. A bundle of energy, he turned his efforts to helping others. Bouhe had the time and the means to assist former fellow countrymen, particularly a young woman from the Soviet Union with ties to his beloved St. Petersburg. While not wealthy, he was financially comfortable, especially compared to the more recent émigrés, who had trickled into Dallas from the DP camps of Europe.

Bouhe dressed in understated elegance. Tall and thin with a prominent nose, his manners were "old school." He kissed the hands of women to whom he was presented, and he arrived at dinner parties with the appropriate gifts and compliments for the hostess. He was not averse to letting it be known that his father had been a prominent official in the Czar's government and that he descended from Germans invited to Russia by Catherine the Great, herself a minor German princess in her youth. Growing up in a sheltered home of the minor elite of Czarist Russia, Bouhe had a series of governesses who spoke successively French, German, and then English with him until he reached his twelfth year. He attended Petersburg's elite *Gymnasium* for young men. That education was the equal to an undergraduate degree from a good American university. Graduation from a top *Gymnasium* was considered more than enough "learning" to prepare one for a top-flight career. Only a few wishing to pursue an academic or professional career (doctor, engineer, or lawyer) continued their studies in universities or scientific institutes. (Few of Russia's leaders, either before or after the revolution, attended universities.)

Bouhe's knowledge of languages, particularly English, probably saved his life. Had he remained in the Soviet Union, Stalin would have imprisoned or executed him as a "former person," the term reserved for those faithful or suspected thereof to the *ancien regime*. While still in his teens, Bouhe had the good fortune to be taken on as an employee of Herbert Hoover's American Relief Association in what had been renamed Petrograd. American mentors, noting his precise English and meticulous attention to detail, arranged a visa for him to immigrate to the United States.

. . .

The displaced person émigrés from World War II were the foot soldiers in Bouhe's Dallas-Fort Worth army. When asked by the Warren Commission whether he was the "leader" of the Russian community, Bouhe put on an air of humility and did not say no. Representative of the DPs were Teo and Anna Meller, who had met as displaced persons in Germany. They ended up in Dallas under Bouhe's watchful mentorship. Anna got a job as a draftsman with Dallas Power and Light, while Teo worked as a packer and floor walker in a downtown department store. Although he had been a university professor in Poland, he did not complain about being reduced to a department-store packer.

Anna Meller was a tall, striking women in her mid-forties, with blond hair fading into gray, a graceful figure, and a face that hinted strongly at great beauty in her youth. Like husband Teo, Anna did not dwell on the atrocities she had seen and experienced as she fled Russia with retreating German troops. She had to decide whether it was better to leave with the Germans or stay in a Soviet Union she detested. As a Ukrainian, she had lived through Stalin's 1932–33 famine, which killed more than five million of her fellow citizens. So, she went over to the German side and subsisted on the scraps of food they gave her. In the Soviet Union before the war, Anna had completed her training as a dentist, and she, like Marina, bore the scars of Soviet dentistry—a smile marred by a sparkling array of silver fillings.

. . .

After my lessons with Marina began, Pete had to field the curious calls coming in from Dallas, especially from George Bouhe. Would it be a good idea for the émigrés to meet Marina? Who was this no-good husband who had deserted to the Soviet side?

You could imagine the trepidation of the Dallas Russians. Marina was married to a traitor to their beloved United States of America. They were avid anti-communists and considered their new home the land of milk and honey. How could they agree to sit at the same table with Lee Harvey Oswald? He had made his home in the despised Soviet Union. Gali Clark, for one, had made up her mind early. She would not come to any gathering at which Lee was present. She and husband Max limited their contact to a few telephone calls.

. . .

The fact that Max Clark served as a lawyer for General Dynamics made him a ready target for JFK assassination theorists. Somehow, as a pawn for the military-industrial complex, the by-the-book Max Clark was supposed to have masterminded through Oswald the assassination of the president. What General Dynamics was supposed to gain from the murder of JFK is never spelled out, and Clark's minimal contacts with Oswald were secondhand through his wife.

Max Clark also served as the private attorney for Pete Gregory. *Aha!,* chortled the assassination lobby. *In Gregory and Clark we have a grand merger of oil and military-industrial interests!* Poor JFK did not stand a chance against such powerful interests, especially when they settled on the master assassin Lee Harvey Oswald as their instrument of death.

. . .

Among themselves, the Dallas Russians agreed that they would wait and see. After all, the Gregorys were already in contact with the Oswalds through Paul. If the Gregorys give the go-ahead, the thinking went, we'll meet them. A dinner at the Gregory house, whenever it came, would be an appropriate way to break the ice.

15

ABUSE

The Dallas Russians would have lost their appetite to meet the newcomers had they witnessed Lee's dismissive attitude toward his wife. They would not have been put off by Lee and Marina's poverty. Many were poor themselves. But one particular incident would have left the Russians so appalled that social contact between them and the Oswalds would have been impossible. It involved an accident that threatened serious injury to Marina and daughter June.

By way of background, both Marina and Lee worried constantly about June's health. Marina would regularly check June's temperature by touching her forehead. Lee worried alongside her. They had no money for a doctor. Instead, they consulted a thick book on children's health written by some Dr. Spock of the Russian language. What I witnessed one day in front of their house told me that Lee's concern did not extend to his wife.

As we prepared to leave for shopping on that evening, there was the usual bustling around. Did they have June's bottle or rattle? Did they have the right baby blanket? These things had to be considered before leaving the house via the front door onto the small concrete porch, which rose one or two feet above the ground.

I went out first and proceeded toward the car. Marina and Lee came out together. Marina held June, facing the door, as Lee locked up. By mistake, Marina took a step backward and fell with a hard thump on the ground. Her back and the back of her head absorbed the bulk of the impact. June fell separately to the ground, screaming. I looked on, frozen in place. June seemed all right, just scared, but Marina had taken a severe blow to the back of her skull.

To my shock, Lee began to scream at Marina, who was lying faceup. I feared she was unconscious and needed to be hospitalized. Lee rushed to pick up June and continued to rant at Marina for her clumsy mistake. As Marina slowly regained her senses, Lee raced inside for the baby book. Marina made it to her feet, and they began frantically leafing through the pages to find the right information. All the while Lee continued to curse and rage at Marina.

Ignoring Lee's tirade, the dazed Marina took the book and read about the kinds of injuries to look for. June had quieted down, and she seemed fine. She had been frightened by the fall and by her father's screaming at her mother. Lee, satisfied that June was not seriously injured, quieted down too. But he scarcely cast a glance at Marina, unconcerned about her condition.

Ashamed, they looked at me, a stunned witness to the inner workings of their marriage. For Marina, her mistreatment by Lee had become routine. Beatings had begun when they lived in Robert's house. Although Robert knew, he did not intervene. In the privacy of their own home, Lee could beat Marina without repercussion.

That evening, we drove silently on our usual rounds, trying to ignore what had occurred. I felt pangs of guilt that I had not rushed to aid Marina, who could have sustained a serious injury. It all happened too fast.

As I drove, I wondered what my father and the Dallas Russians, especially the fastidious George Bouhe, would have thought if they'd witnessed Lee's behavior that evening. I chose not to tell my father about the incident. Had he known, he would have had no further dealings with Lee Harvey Oswald. Some sixty years later, I ask whether I made a mistake by keeping quiet.

16

DISAGREEMENTS ON CUBA

Lee Harvey Oswald considered himself a Marxist intellectual. He continued to pile up weighty tomes from the public library, strewn around the apartment. He used his meager earnings to order the *Daily Worker*, *The Militant*, and books by Leon Trotsky.

Contemporary readers probably do not realize how rare someone professing Lee's radical beliefs was in Texas in 1962. The 1950s and early '60s were far from the later days of "leftist chic" of Che posters on dorm walls, reverence for the left-wing politics of Daniel Ortega and Fidel Castro, and the teaching of post-modernism in universities. We young people had grown up watching the TV series *I Was a Communist for the FBI* (apparently one of Lee's favorites as a youth). *The Manchurian Candidate* was one of the most popular films of 1962. Professors thought to be leftists at the nearby University of Texas in Austin had trouble holding their jobs.

We Texas children knew who the enemy was when we climbed under our elementary-school desks in mock preparation for a nuclear attack. Although Senator Joseph McCarthy had been disgraced in his anti-communist Army hearings, the general public definitely shared his fear of communism and worried that the USSR might blow us all to kingdom come. JFK himself had based part of his 1959 campaign against Richard Nixon on a presumed missile gap that had opened between the USSR and the United States under President Eisenhower.

In my home state of Texas, the Democratic Party was bitterly split between the "leftist" Ralph Yarborough (who happened to be in the fateful motorcade on November 22) and his longtime political rival and vehement anti-communist Price Daniels. The "America First" movement kept a vigilant eye open for "communists." In high school, our one history teacher with a Ph.D. (Dr. Kathryn Garrett) delighted in repeating the slogan: "The United Nations out of the United States, the United States out of the United Nations." We began each day with the Pledge of Allegiance and a daily Bible reading led by the theology teacher over the school intercom.

· · ·

Lee Harvey Oswald rebelled against this us-versus-them view of the Cold War. At the time, it was my impression that he did so not out of conviction but to stand out in a world where uniformity reigned and where he was being overlooked and ignored.

Two documents burrowed in the dense appendices of the Warren Report were instrumental, however, in changing my impression of Lee Harvey Oswald. As we were meeting in 1962, I considered him a poseur Marxist, who had taken on a radical leftist persona to divert attention from his many failings. However, his essay on the Soviet socialism he experienced in Minsk (aptly dubbed *The Collective*) reveals him as a keen observer, a fact obscured by misspellings and grammatical errors. His extensive scribbled musings on ideal forms of socialism, composed on the SS *Maasdam* underway to America, are confusing and rambling, but they show at least someone groping for answers to big issues.

Yes, through the Warren Commission files I became convinced that Lee Harvey Oswald was the dedicated Marxist he declared himself to be. Lee taught himself a working understanding of radical Marxist thought. He was indeed, as he identified himself, a Marxist, albeit disappointed with its real-world manifestations. As a "Marxist," Lee dreamed of a pure form of a worker state in which equality and peace prevailed.

Lee dreamed of a worker state—but for others. Despite lacking formal education and working as a manual laborer, he was convinced he deserved the privileges of the vanguard of the revolution. That the Soviet state assigned him to manual labor in the Minsk Radio Factory was an insult he would never forgive.

Not that I was an expert on Marx then, as I looked forward to my senior year as an economics major at the University of Oklahoma. I had taken the usual courses in the history of thought, micro and macro, but my understanding of Marxism-Leninism was at best superficial. In fact, no courses were offered on what would now be called "political economy." Nevertheless, I could perhaps have provided Lee with a sounding board for the weighty philosophical tomes that he spent his time studying. This happened only to a limited degree. I clearly got a mouthful of Lee's disenchantment with the communist system he experienced firsthand in Minsk. Perhaps Lee thought that I was there to learn Russian, not to talk politics. Or he considered me wet behind the ears, not capable of an intelligent conversation on exploitation and surplus value.

Let me be clear. Lee Harvey Oswald could be a dedicated Marxist even without delving that deeply into its intellectual foundations. All that was required was a conviction that capitalism was unfair and doomed and a belief that it must be replaced by something better. And that something was socialism.

· · ·

Prompted by my curiosity, Lee was willing to talk about his personal world of Soviet socialism, namely the Minsk Radio and Television

Factory. As in his *The Collective* (of which I knew nothing at the time), he recounted his disillusion with the Minsk version of the worker's paradise. Lee recalled a party "agitator" visiting his factory and finding that the machines were not lined up so that the operators had a proper view of the portrait of Lenin looking down on them. The factory management had the layout changed in time for the agitator's next visit.

Lee did not hide his feeling that his first brush with Soviet socialism had been a devastating disappointment. He was denied a university education and given a menial job, just like any ordinary Russian. Marina grew up with the system and knew its foibles. But Lee had expected more.

Lee had not abandoned *all* hope. Castro's Cuba might become a truly just society run according to Marxist principles. After all, Cuba had defended itself against the mighty and imperialist USA when Fidel Castro's forces repulsed the Americans at the Bay of Pigs at the start of the Kennedy presidency. That fiasco, Lee contended, revealed that America was basically an imperialistic bully, except when challenged by brave foes such as Castro.

. . .

As we sat together, Marina listened with a bemused look on her face to Lee's roster of complaints. She had no interest in such things. In fact, they bored her. They reminded her perhaps of the tiresome lectures she had to endure in school or during party meetings in her workplace. She and her classmates learned to ignore these "political agitation" lectures. Moreover, she could see that the "agitator" was just going through the motions himself. He did not believe what he was saying, and Marina and her classmates were not paying attention anyway. The whole thing was a farce to her.

On one occasion, Marina could not resist chiming in when the subject of Cuba arose. She knew that the Soviet Union was spending its precious resources to prop up Castro's regime. From her perspective, people in Minsk had so little that it was ridiculous to waste Soviet treasure on a faraway country. Cuba had done her and her fellow citizens no good, other than to stock their shelves with expensive sugar.

This difference in views on Cuba exposed a rift in a fragile marriage. Far from being a supportive wife, Marina viewed her husband's "deeply held" views with scorn. Further, she must have been aware that such views—which she regarded as crackpot—could get her and her family in trouble in the United States.

. . .

Marina's mocking of Lee's politics was only one irritant to their marriage. My suggestions that she learn English was another. As my evenings with Lee and Marina settled into a routine, Marina had still not acquired the most rudimentary elements of English vocabulary. This despite my repeated inquiries: "What English words have you learned? Are you doing anything to learn the language?" I imagine that each and every such question grated on Lee's nerves, but he held his tongue.

Both ignored my offers to bring materials that would help Marina learn English. I had English-Russian flash cards. Marina could have used them by herself to build up a small English vocabulary. When I made such suggestions, however, Lee remained silent, and Marina promised this was something she would do "soon." Marina knew that defying Lee was not something to be done lightly. She would have feared the consequences of crossing him. She knew her husband did not want her to learn English, and it would have required enormous effort, persistence, and daring for her to proceed on her own.

17

UNDER SURVEILLANCE

As a former Marine undesirably discharged and a defector to the Cold War enemy, Lee Oswald, I assumed, would be under surveillance by the FBI. The circumstances of his return, along with a Russian wife, were, at the least, suspicious. It took assurances from lawyer Max Clark to convince the Dallas Russians that Lee *was* under the careful watch of the FBI, and it was therefore safe for them to meet him. Clark's assessment carried weight. He was personally acquainted with a local FBI agent, John Fain. Surely the FBI would not let a foreign enemy roam the streets unobserved.

Indeed, Special Agent Fain called Lee to the local FBI office on June 26, 1962. In an interview that lasted more than two hours, Fain and his assistant, Tom Cutter, went over Lee's defection to the Soviet Union, his contacts with the KGB, and his possible affiliations with the American Communist Party. The agents described Lee throughout the interview as insolent and growing increasingly recalcitrant. He answered most of their questions but stubbornly refused to explain his motivation for going to the USSR. In the cover letter to their June 26 report, Fain reported that Oswald refused to take a polygraph test on whether he had supplied information to the Soviets or been recruited by Soviet intelligence.

Fain and another agent, Arnold J. Brown, re-interviewed Oswald in their car parked on Mercedes Street on August 16. They had Lee's approximate address from Robert. From a neighbor, they learned that a young couple had moved into 2703 Mercedes. Fain and Brown surmised from her description that the couple was Lee and Marina. By the agents' account, they intercepted Lee on his way back from work on that Thursday evening. They invited him into the back seat of the car, with Fain in the front seat and Brown in the back. The two agents questioned Lee for nearly two hours. This time, they reported, he was more cooperative, but he still stubbornly refused to answer why he had deserted to the Soviet Union. In his report Fain wrote that "he said it was a personal matter to him. He said, 'I went, and I came back.'" Anyone asking Lee why he had gone to the USSR was definitely striking a nerve.

Marina recounted this FBI incident differently. She said that two men came to the front door and asked Lee to accompany them to their car. (The FBI account says they intercepted him on his way home.) Both the FBI's and Marina's accounts agree, however, that the agents questioned Lee for almost two hours. Marina grew more irritated as time passed and Lee did not return. She had to take dinner off the stove. When Lee finally came through the front door, he explained that the two men were from the FBI, saying they were the equivalent of the KGB, the feared security organ of the Soviet state. He told Marina that the agents instructed him to contact them if any Russians attempted to recruit him.

Although Lee expected that the FBI would continue to keep an eye on him, FBI records show no further contacts with Oswald until after his return from the Cuban and Soviet Embassies in Mexico City on August 2, 1963. Lee had already warned Marina that "it has begun," namely, that his harassment by the American version of the KGB was just getting started.

The surveillance of Lee Oswald did not escape my own notice. One evening, it must have been late August, as we were leaving the Mercedes Street duplex, Lee's experienced eye spotted a dark sedan sitting idle in the dying heat of the day. The window was down, and its visible occupant was dressed in shirtsleeves, his jacket resting over the passenger's seat. There may have been another man in the car. I could not tell from that distance.

Lee told us to wait. "I'll be back in a minute," he said. "I have to go talk to that guy." Lee walked over to the car and got in. They talked for about five or ten minutes, out of our hearing range. Lee returned to us nonchalantly, as if nothing had happened. And from my perspective at that juncture, nothing had. Why should I be interested in the fact that he had spent five to ten minutes talking to a stranger staked outside his house? Marina raised no questions either, but for a different reason: she had seen the same thing before.

As I pulled out of the driveway, what had happened became clear to me. The appearance of the car and its occupant reeked of police or FBI. They were, I could see, still keeping an eye on one Lee Harvey Oswald.

■ ■ ■

The Fort Worth FBI reports say that the last time they interviewed Lee Harvey Oswald was August 16. This "last" FBI interview lasted for nearly two hours, not the brief back-seat interview I witnessed. Perhaps the meeting I witnessed was of such short duration that the FBI felt it not worth mentioning, but it did occur before my eyes.

FBI agent James Hosty Jr. later visited Marina at the home of her friend Ruth Paine to question her about Lee's trip in late September through early October of 1963 to Mexico City, where U.S. intelligence recorded him entering the Cuban and Soviet Embassies. Marina claimed to know nothing of Lee's Mexico adventure. She grew frightened when the FBI agent threatened her: if she didn't cooperate, they would send her back to Russia. For Marina, who wished to remain in America, the FBI was a potent threat. Her own visa status was still up in the air.

Upon his return to Dallas from Mexico, the irate Lee subsequently told Marina to write down the agent's license plate number if this happened again, and he made a cheeky call to the FBI's Dallas office to tell its people to leave his wife alone, even accusing Agent Hosty of coming on to his wife.

When the FBI, led by Hosty, first questioned Marina (under Secret Service protection) three days after the assassination, she clammed up. She would talk only to the Secret Service. She remembered her earlier, unpleasant encounters with America's KGB, the FBI. Fear of the FBI was one of the few lessons she had learned from Lee. The FBI's threat to deport her back to Russia had her unsettled.

18

FROM FRIENDS IN MINSK

On a number of occasions, Lee and Marina showed me photographs of their life in Minsk. Unlike Fort Worth, where Lee had no friends, the photographs suggested that Minsk afforded him an active social life. As perhaps the sole American in that provincial city, he cut an exotic figure. In Dallas-Fort Worth, Marina was similarly a rare species as the area's only direct arrival from the contemporary Soviet Union. Lee had been a celebrity in Minsk. Outside of a handful of people, no one knew of Marina's existence. That would change shortly when Marina got to know the Dallas Russians. Marina would become the star and Lee the wallflower.

The photos taken in Minsk showed birthday parties, fishing outings, days at the beach, and family gatherings that included a smiling Lee cavorting for the camera. Marina's pictures showed her surrounded by her relatives and friends from work. The sharp contrast between her bright pictures from Minsk and her dull existence in Fort Worth made even more puzzling her preference for life in America. In Minsk, she had friends and family. In Texas, she had neither, just a sweltering, run-down apartment, a baby to care for alone, and an abusive husband.

The answer to the puzzle seems to be the contrast between dreary Minsk and what she had seen of the better sides of American life outside her house—Robert's home and family, my parents' house, Montgomery Ward, her own modest cottage, riding around in a big Buick, and shopping in grocery stores laden with foods of all kinds. As we looked at the photographs, Lee and Marina would identify the people in them with a dizzying array of names and places. The names Lee mentioned most frequently were "Pavel" and "Erik." I remember Pavel especially because it is the Russian equivalent of my name. Lee regarded Pavel as his best friend, someone on whom he could rely, someone to have fun with. Pavel, Lee told me, worked in the same factory, although he was the son of a general who'd been promoted to that rank for his heroic feats during the Great Patriotic War, as Russians call World War II.

Pavel's picture revealed a young Adonis with wavy blond hair, a handsome face, a pleasant smile, and fashionable attire. He and Lee appeared to be about the same age. Lee explained that, actually, Pavel had sought *him* out. Pavel claimed he wanted to practice his English. In return, Pavel helped Lee, as a new arrival, learn enough Russian to carry out his work in the factory. Unlike other "English speakers" in provincial Minsk, Pavel had a good command of English and could carry on intelligent conversations with Lee. Lee seemed proud of the fact that his friend was the son of a general and war hero. He hastened to introduce Marina to Pavel as they shared in his luxurious lifestyle. Indeed, Pavel lived the life of the Soviet elite—a beautiful, roomy, and well-furnished apartment, the latest electronics, and American recordings.

■ ■ ■

One evening I arrived to find both Lee and Marina in good spirits. As I entered, Lee waved a blue airmail envelope and a letter of several pages written on thin airmail paper. A letter from Pavel had arrived. Lee thrust it into my hand, as if he wanted me to read it (I declined, thinking it was none of my business). I did not know that Pavel's letter contained a message for me.

Much later in reading through the appendices of the Warren Commission report, I discovered that Lee and Marina had conscientiously saved their correspondence with friends in Minsk. Among them was the lengthy letter from Pavel that Lee had offered me to read. This letter (undated), like two others, related gossip, addresses, weather, and requests for magazines. To my surprise, Pavel's letter offered advice to Marina in her tutoring of me: "By the way, Marina, try to explain to Paul that the basic idea of Pogodin's play is contained in the words 'now we don't have to fear the man with the rifle.'" I guess that Marina's "work" with me constituted a big enough event in their lives to share with their Minsk friends.

Pavel's letters (three in all) read as if they were prepared with a Soviet censor in mind. He sticks to routine matters and suggests that Lee and Marina subscribe to "correct" reading material. He even seems to be pushing for minor intelligence information, such as items they might read in the press about Mariner 2, NASA's first successful interplanetary spacecraft.

Pavel had been encouraged to make Lee his friend and to introduce him to female students at the foreign language academy, a training ground for spies and diplomats. The KGB had leverage with Pavel, a known ne'er-do-well who was skating on thin ice despite his father's influence and reputation. They made clear that he could rehabilitate himself by cooperating with them on the Oswald case. We can imagine that when the Minsk factory bosses suggested to Pavel that he befriend Lee Harvey Oswald, he accepted without hesitation.

In the twisted world of Soviet spying and counterespionage, Pavel's assignment to keep an eye on Lee Harvey Oswald does not mean that real friendship did not develop between them. At least as far as Lee was concerned, Pavel was his true friend, perhaps the first one in his short lifetime.

Pavel was just a minor player in the KGB's monitoring of Lee Harvey Oswald, of course. KGB officers followed Lee's activities, including bugging his apartment and taping his phone conversations. Lee's most intimate moments with Marina (and some of their worst arguments) likely remain preserved on tape in Minsk's KGB vaults, still inaccessible to the outside world.

. . .

Lee and Marina received other letters from friends and relatives left behind in Minsk. Marina received more than Lee, from relatives, friends, and colleagues. There was a jocular letter from Ernst (Erik) addressed to both of them, with Lee's portion in English. Marina's letters expressed curiosity about her life in America. Her friends wanted to know if Marina had learned English and was turning into a real American. Another urged Marina to come to her senses and return to where she belonged.

Letters from back home were limited by the fact that unauthorized correspondence with foreigners could still lead to trouble. Soviet citizens could not dispatch letters to enemy states without permission. Soviet people still remembered that, during the Stalin years, unauthorized contact with the West was grounds for a prison sentence or worse. In the 1960s, having friends in the West was grounds for a visit from the KGB and a black mark on the work record.

Marina would have understood this hard fact of Soviet life better than Lee. She would have immediately understood that Pavel's letter was not an act of friendship but that he had been ordered to check up on Lee.

Lee would likely never understand that the KGB had created something of a virtual life for him in Minsk. Lee Harvey Oswald was open to friendships in his three years behind the Iron Curtain. He noted in his *Historic Diary* that he was beset by loneliness. To ensure that he did not make trouble, they gave him a "best friend" and even girlfriends from the language academy.

19

A WOULD-BE PHARMACIST

Marina seldom spoke about her life in Minsk. There seemed to be little there that interested her or gave her joy. Despite the letters she received from them, she did not seem to miss her friends and relatives. She had not particularly enjoyed her work. If anyone was ready for a new life, it was Marina.

I had to draw her out about her work in Minsk. She explained that she was employed in a hospital pharmacy preparing prescriptions for doctors. This sounded to me like a responsible position and interesting work. (It also may explain why she visited Lee regularly when he was hospitalized for an ear infection. Lee may have interpreted her visits as a sign of special affection.)

I was impressed that Marina had worked in a profession that—in the United States—required considerable training. I did not then understand that "pharmacists" like Marina received cursory vocational training in the USSR, nothing like the four or five years of concentrated study required in our country. In any case, in my mind, Marina's work in a pharmacy was on a much higher level than Lee's in the factory. At least I had the good sense not to let Lee know that this was how I saw things.

In Fort Worth, as in most other U.S. cities, pharmacies—or drugstores, as they were then known—were usually located next to grocery stores. When one evening in early September we stopped by Kleinschmidt's grocery to pick up a few items, I decided to show Marina an American pharmacy, or *Apteka*, as they are called in Russian. Marina and I, with Lee tailing along carrying June, wandered into the Cunningham Drugs next to Kleinschmidt's.

In the early 1960s, stores like Cunningham Drugs not only dispensed drugs but also sold a sundry variety of everyday items and still had a soda counter with stools, where a "soda jerk" prepared sandwiches and ice-cream sodas. (As a twelve-year-old, I had delighted in walking the fifteen minutes to the same Cunningham store for a milkshake that cost the grand total of a quarter.) Marina and I wandered through the store. Lee held June and looked at some item that caught his attention. I decided to show Marina the pharmacist preparing prescription drugs for pickup.

We walked to the back of the store where the pharmacy was located. Bottles of medications were stacked on white shelves behind the counter. Seeing that the pharmacist was not busy, I introduced Marina to him as a fellow pharmacist from another country. The middle-aged man in his white coat was intrigued by the attractive, non-English-speaking pharmacist standing in front of him. He wanted to know what country Marina was from. To his great surprise, I responded "Russia." His interest piqued, he asked if Marina was currently working as a pharmacist. When I answered no, he came back with an unexpected proposal: if Marina could learn English, he might have a job for her as his assistant. He could, he said, always use people with experience.

I translated for Marina. She could not believe that he was serious. Such a nice place to work, and in her mind, the pharmacist clearly was earning a lot of money. All she needed to do was to learn English.

A suspicious Lee joined us. Marina proudly informed him that, if she knew English, she could get a job in this nice *Apteka*. Unsaid was the fact that she would probably earn much more than he. Lee dismissed Marina's excitement with a shrug.

I could see that Lee was not happy with what had just transpired. In a rare show of emotion, he threw a look of irritation across his face as if to say to me: *What trouble have you caused me now?* What thoughts had this privileged kid, who knows nothing of the real world, put into his wife's head?

The incident showed that Marina might be better equipped to navigate her new world of the United States than he—an American, but one with no marketable skills. I cannot say whether this topic of conversation continued after I dropped them off, but Lee's pride must have taken a jolt. I do not know if Marina decided to rub in her triumph. If she did, she would have paid a price.

20

DINNER WITH RUSSIANS

Pete Gregory reported to the Dallas Russians what I told him about my lessons with Lee and Marina. From this information, George Bouhe concluded that, although Marina might be a respectable young Russian woman and a good mother, she had obviously made a rather poor choice of husband. The fact that Marina had grown up with her grandmother in Leningrad, Bouhe's beloved hometown, was, however, enough to warrant a meeting. The Gregorys volunteered to host a dinner at their house. Bouhe began his own preparations to meet his fellow St. Petersburg native.

This meeting would have untold consequences. It resulted in Lee and Marina moving to Dallas, for one. After Lee lost his job in Fort Worth, Bouhe activated his extensive network to find Lee a job (but again at $1.25 per hour). He welcomed the opportunity to have Marina nearby, where he could help her as he had helped other Russian émigrés. The others, however, did not come with the baggage of a Lee Harvey Oswald as a husband.

The place: the Gregory residence at 3513 Dorothy Lane. The date: Saturday, August 25, 1962. My mother prepared the meal. She did not cook Russian dishes; only my father did for special occasions. This meal featured standard American fare. I recall something simple like pot roast. In attendance: two envoys from Dallas, the Oswalds, and the three Gregorys. Although she had been invited, the cautious Gali Clark steered clear of the whole affair. Who knew what kind of rapscallion this foolish Russian girl had dredged up in Russia?

George Bouhe decided to bring Teo and Anna Meller with him, but Teo had to work that night. George arranged to drive Anna, only, of course, after the gallant Bouhe received formal approval from her husband. These were men of the old school. After all, Teo had been a professor in his native Poland. Standards had to be observed even if Teo had been reduced to a department-store clerk.

George planned the evening carefully. He wanted the first meeting to be non-confrontational. He brought along albums of maps of St. Petersburg at various stages of its history, with an eye toward probing Marina's knowledge of the city. He wanted to know whether she was familiar with the areas of the city where he had lived and gone to school.

It fell to me to pick up Lee, Marina, and June. I was taken aback to see Lee dressed in a brown suit, cleanly shaven, clearly intent on presenting himself in the best possible light. He could not have been happy about being dragged into a room full of strangers. They would likely ask embarrassing questions in Russian that he could not filter before they reached Marina. Maybe he could avoid the worst by dressing well and acting with decorum.

Marina had brought a good dress with her from Minsk for such occasions. My memory suggests a red dress, perhaps the very dress she had worn when she met Lee. So far, I had only seen her in her everyday drab attire. Made up, with jewelry, she cut a fine figure, one with whom the solicitous George Bouhe would surely sympathize. Lacking a baby carriage, Marina packed blankets for June in a bag.

We arrived before George and Anna Meller. Marina settled June on the blankets in the bed in the downstairs master bedroom. At first, June fussed and cried. We feared she might turn the evening into a fiasco, but she settled down, fell asleep, and did not disrupt the conversation around the dinner table.

The doorbell rang. George entered, dressed immaculately as an English gentleman for an evening at the manor house. He entered toting his maps and heavy albums. Anna Meller bore small gifts for Lee and Marina and for the hostess. As was her custom, Anna remained in the background, saying little.

After an awkward moment or two, the Oswalds were introduced to George and Anna. True to plan, George's maps did serve to break the ice. He and Marina repaired to the living room, where they spread out the maps on the carpet and huddled together, pointing at various landmarks. No one paid attention to Lee, who went off to the den, where he sat alone, waiting to be called to the dinner table. Tonight Marina, not he, was the center of attention. Having little to do myself, I went in to keep him company.

Back in the living room, George and Marina were hitting it off. He asked Marina where she had lived with her grandmother, the schools she had attended, and what kind of person her grandmother was. Left unspoken was the fact that Marina had no grandfather—a likely victim of starvation during the siege of Leningrad. George was particularly impressed that Marina spoke educated Russian, not the lingo of factory workers. Most surprising was that Marina's grandmother had attended an exclusive women's *Gymnasium*, well known to the class-conscious George Bouhe. Marina disclosed as well that her grandmother was a "believer," a particularly pleasing fact to George, who had single-handedly organized Russian Orthodox services in Dallas. It was the grandmother who insisted that the infant Marina be baptized, as was often the case in Soviet Russia.

After a short while, Bouhe concluded that this young lady needed his assistance and that he would do whatever he could for her, even if that meant helping her ne'er-do-well husband.

My mother called her odd group of guests to dinner, and we took our places at the large dining room table. Lee and Marina sat at one side of the table, alongside me to my left. The Dallas Russians sat opposite them. Pete sat at the head of the table, with my mother at the other end, near the swinging door that led to the kitchen.

Trying to keep the conversation on an even keel, George began to probe Lee and Marina about life in Minsk. He turned his attention to the silent Lee and attempted to elicit information about contemporary Russia and his life when he lived there. George asked trivial things like: Where did you work? How much did you earn? How much did a pair of shoes cost?

When he learned what Lee's salary was, the accountant in George started doing mental arithmetic as to what that amount would buy by asking how much specific items cost in rubles. Anna Meller realized that although these figures sounded meager, Lee had been given a rent-free apartment. Anyone familiar with the USSR, a group that did not include Bouhe, would understand the incredible privilege of having one's own apartment—and for virtually nothing. Most workers lived with relatives or in communal apartment flats. Marina had shared a cramped apartment with her aunt and uncle.

Anna, who had experienced life in the USSR, had always wanted a room of her own. And this upstart newcomer, an ordinary worker in an ordinary factory, had a whole *apartment* to himself. Anna thought to herself: *Maybe Marina took this unpleasant guy simply to get her own apartment.* And Anna was not entirely wrong: Lee's having an apartment placed him above Marina's other suitors.

Lee Harvey Oswald certainly did not sit well with Anna Meller.

Although the assembled group had collectively decided to avoid delicate questions, it was the unassuming Anna who burst out with the one everyone wanted answered: "Lee, why did you leave the United States for the USSR? How could anyone do that?"

Anna had picked the very question that Lee detested above all others. His lips had turned white and his face pale when asked the same question twice by the FBI. Here, at a supposedly social dinner party, people were taking advantage of him to ask this hated question!

Unlike at his FBI interviews, where he could give flippant and insolent answers, Lee found himself with his back to the wall. He could not answer truculently, as he had to the FBI, that he "went to see the country." He could not say, "I went for my own reasons" (which was his answer to Pete Gregory at their first meeting). Marina was present, the company awaited his answer, and the conversation was in Russian.

Lee, who had been on his best behavior, grew agitated and defensive. His voice rose as he mouthed slogans familiar to me: "I left because capitalism is a terrible system. It exploits the workers. Life is unfair under capitalism. The rich get everything, and the poor get nothing."

Anna could not let Lee's response go unrebutted: "But, Lee. I know the Soviet Union. It is a terrible place. There is nothing good about it. And you left the United States, which I consider a welcoming land of opportunity and freedom, for that place. I cannot understand."

Lee responded defensively that, yes, he saw many things in Russia that were not right. He did not think that the party faithful believed in communism anymore. It was far from a worker's paradise. It did not appreciate his talents, but that did not make America a great place. Just look at the Marine Corps. He had served in it, and although the corps was held in high esteem, he had seen many bad things there.

As Lee became more and more agitated, Bouhe decided that it was time to bring the evening to an end, but not before—unwittingly—striking another of Lee's most sensitive nerves. Bouhe and Anna both began to insist that Marina learn English. Bouhe had arranged English lessons for so many Russian émigrés, he could do the same for Marina.

They should stay in touch. Bouhe would get to work on the arrangements. He himself might be willing to tutor Marina.

Again, Lee's voice rose in agitation: if he allowed Marina to learn English, his Russian would suffer. It was very important that he retain his fluency in Russian.

Anna could scarcely keep her anger under control. What a selfish man! Marina desperately needs to learn English and her no-good husband is keeping her in suffocating isolation for his convenience. She had had enough of this guy, and she felt pity toward Marina, stuck with this ungrateful oaf.

The evening ended. George and Anna drove Lee and Marina home. Lee must have thought to himself: *Now these people know exactly where we live. They are going to be trouble.*

The two Russians had their own thoughts: *We need to help Marina, but that jerk of a husband is going to get in the way.* How could they help Marina without his cooperation? Basically, he had her as his hostage.

It wouldn't be long before George Bouhe began showing up at Mercedes Street loaded with largesse for Marina.

As Lee and Marina climbed out of George Bouhe's car on Mercedes Street, they did not realize that their lives would change dramatically in the embrace of George Bouhe and his fellow Dallas Russians, no matter how hard Lee resisted.

The dinner at 3513 Dorothy Lane would prove a turning point in Lee and Marina's complex and troubled marriage. Lee had succeeded in building for Marina a shabby isolation cage at Mercedes Street. Robert's kindly wife, Vada, could not penetrate it even if she wished because of the language barrier. Pete Gregory did not have any interest in meddling in their lives. Gali Clark kept her distance. I was the biggest potential threat, but Lee understood that I was not there to judge him.

As a recent arrival from Minsk, Marina concluded that her living conditions had not worsened, and she had only a little insight into how those around her lived. I had no desire to clue her in, and, by the way,

I'd be out of their hair once school resumed in mid-September. Bouhe, Anna Meller, and the other Dallas Russians they would soon meet were a different matter. They would want to meddle, to help out, to tell Marina the facts of life about America and her husband. Marina's Dallas Russian friends would become a constant source of friction and conflict. They also gave Marina an escape. If life with Lee became intolerable, they would offer her shelter and protection.

On that evening, Lee must have had an inkling of what was to come. It would spell the end of his complete domination of his dependent wife. That did not sit well with him.

21

"CAPITALISM— ALL FOR THE RICH!"

The consequences of the August 25, 1962, meeting between Lee and Marina and the Dallas Russians would begin to make themselves felt over the next weeks. In the meantime, I still had some time before the start of the semester at the University of Oklahoma. I continued my twice-weekly evenings with Lee and Marina. Less time was spent on excursions and more on completing my summer assignment. Marina and I worked together at the kitchen table with books spread out in front of us as Lee read in the living room.

I still drove Lee and Marina for grocery shopping and for other outings. On one such evening in early September, I decided to show Marina the estates and mansions around Rivercrest Country Club that the oil wealth of Texas had built.

In 1962, Fort Worth was a study in contrast between rich and poor. In the 1950s and 1960s, much of the city's middle class worked for Convair, a large defense contractor that built military aircraft. Fort Worth's fortunes rose and fell with those contracts. The most notable

Convair event of my day was the building of the B-36 bomber, a six-engine plane (with the engines mounted backward) that could fly nonstop to Russia with A-bombs on board. As children, we were kept awake at night by the sound of the test B-36 (piloted by the test-pilot father of a school friend) circling the city for hours on end. Then Convair began to build jet aircraft; so children and adults alike had to live with the thunder of jets breaking the sound barrier.

The city's wealthy set made their money in the rough oil fields of Texas as wildcatters. After striking it rich, many moved to Fort Worth, where they built mansions, raised spoiled kids, and played golf and gin rummy at the Rivercrest or Colonial country clubs. Their mansions were located around those two spreads. The wealthiest people lived in the plush Westover Hills subdivision. At the apex of Fort Worth society was Amon Carter, the industrialist, philanthropist, and publisher of the *Fort Worth Star-Telegram*. It was Amon Carter's goal to turn Forth Worth into a city comparable in affluence and amenities to rival Dallas. When Fort Worth's city fathers built an international airport in Grand Prairie halfway between the two cities, Dallas refused to relocate flights from Love Field and the early version of DFW airport died a slow death.

The poor of Forth Worth were less visible. Some lived in Black communities to the south of Camp Bowie Boulevard, remarkably close to the wealthiest parts of town. Poor white families lived in the areas around Montgomery Ward and in White Settlement, so named in frontier days to distinguish it from a nearby settlement of Native Americans.

On that evening in early September of 1962, I drove the Oswalds past Rivercrest Country Club, after which I took a right turn down the winding road into the Westover Hills subdivision. As we crisscrossed Westover Hills, Marina's eyes were riveted to the magnificent mansions and estates, surrounded by acres of gated land. They may have reminded her of pictures of the grand homes of the St. Petersburg nobility before the revolution. Lee looked on, saying nothing.

On a whim, I decided to drive next down the red-brick-paved Camp Bowie Boulevard and take a left into the poor neighborhoods to the south. We drove first by a motel with a neon sign announcing coloreds welcome. Just as we had done with the mansions of Westover Hills, we traversed neighborhoods of small single-family homes and some shacks. They were built largely of white wooden siding and composition roofs.

Lee did not pass up the opportunity to engage in a little preaching. "See!" he said. "The capitalist system is all for the rich. They live like kings, and the poor live like this." Marina assumed a bored air, having no interest in her husband's commentary.

Although the contrast between this poor Black neighborhood and Westover Hills could not have been more striking, I realized that these homes did not look much different from Lee and Marina's Mercedes Street residence. Marina and Lee could not have missed this fact either. Again, I had inflicted another blow to Lee's carefully constructed image of himself. My excursion unintentionally drove home the point that Lee and Marina themselves were among the poorest of the poor. They lived little better than those in the poorest neighborhoods I had singled out for pity.

I imagine Marina was dreaming that evening about living in one of the Westover Hills mansions, as opposed to her modest Mercedes Street dwelling.

22

A $35 PAYCHECK

My last language lesson with Marina took place on Friday, September 14. I was scheduled to leave for Norman, Oklahoma, on the following Sunday. I had told Lee and Marina that I would drive the short distance home for Thanksgiving and Christmas holidays, and I expected to see them again within a couple of months.

My work with Marina had not been unproductive. With her help, I completed my assignment on Pogodin's *The Man with a Rifle*. Performed frequently in Soviet times, the play now rests in deserved obscurity.

The assignment proved to be the equivalent of pulling teeth for Marina and me. I somehow had to compare the idiomatic speech of Lenin (the play's key figure) with an almost illiterate soldier when the two met during the days of the revolution. Marina and I sat many hours over the text trying to pick out appropriate passages. But in the end, the paper was done. I handed it in to get the credit for a Russian minor at the June 1963 graduation.

When we'd begun the lessons, we had not settled on Marina's compensation. My father and I had discussed paying Marina a dollar an hour, but much of the time together was spent driving around town on errands. After some thought, we decided on a check for $35. In retrospect, I realize that neither of us knew whether Lee had a checking account. But if not, he could endorse it to his brother Robert. At that time, I had no checking account either, so my father wrote out the check. I thought the sum might be too small, but there was no precedent to follow.

It turns out that the $35 sum was somewhat less than one week of Lee's pay.

When I arrived for the final lesson, we three sat and talked. Much had happened since our last meeting. Lee and Marina had fallen under the umbrella of the benevolent Dallas Russians. They were taking my place even before I departed the scene. George Bouhe had begun showing up at Mercedes Street, always in Lee's absence, with his car full of presents—a crib, a baby carriage, used clothes, and household goods. He continued to discuss English lessons with Marina. When Lee returned home to find Bouhe's largesse, he ordered Marina not to accept any more presents and not to open the door to him. Notably, his orders did not require Marina to actually return Bouhe's bounty of things they really needed.

Knowing Bouhe's interest in arranging English lessons, I asked Marina whether she had begun to learn the language. She shrugged. That, she said, was something she would get around to one of these days. Lee said nothing.

Neither Marina nor I regarded this farewell as a real parting. We figured that she and Lee would continue to live at Mercedes Street and that I would drop by on my periodic visits to Fort Worth. We did not count on the intervention of Bouhe, who would arrange for the Oswalds to move to Dallas, where he could better take care of Marina.

Before we parted, Marina gave me a pin, a memento from her days in the Communist Youth League. The pin bore Lenin's image, chin jutted out in a defiant but thoughtful pose. Marina pressed it into my hand saying, "I think you'll appreciate this pin. I do not need it anymore." In retrospect, I suspect she assumed, from my paper on the Pogodin play, that I might share some of Lee's leftist sentiments. She did not understand that I was looking at the play as an abstract example of the genre of socialist realism—the rather hackneyed and often trivial form of literature that evolved under Stalin.

More likely, Marina just wanted to give me some kind of memento, a token of our friendship, and that was all she had to offer. It is better not to read too much into her gesture. I must confess that I lost the pin and never wore it.

When I ceremoniously handed Marina the envelope with the check, she did not want to accept it. She burst out with a rare show of emotion, "Paul, I did not do it for the money!" This was her sole confession that she and I had become friends. Friends do not do things for other friends for money. I, too, had come to consider Marina a friend, but no more than that. She and I were the same age. She was attractive. I guess I would have been regarded as handsome. I was leading a life that Lee could only dream of. But there was no romantic spark. If there had been, Lee would have been on hand to extinguish it.

Marina and I were alone together only on that first lesson when Lee arrived late. Subsequently he was never more than a few steps away from the two of us. Later, Lee did harbor jealousies, even under curious circumstances. There were stories that he thought that a Dallas FBI agent had come on to Marina.

I insisted on making the payment and handed the check over to her. When she opened it, she was amazed to see the small fortune of $35. She had never seen such a sum of money in her life. She went to Montgomery Ward the next day and spent it on herself, June, and Lee. Her urge to splurge was understandable. Lee gave her two dollars a week from his meager earnings. But the $35 was money she had earned, and it was hers to spend. That must have been an exhilarating moment for Marina.

Lee watched with studied indifference as I prepared to leave. We parted with a few banalities about seeing each other soon and a brief handshake. In retrospect, I imagine that he watched me go with some relief, but the damage to his domination of his wife had already been done. I had given Marina a lifeline to the Dallas Russians.

Lee Harvey Oswald and wife Marina (holding baby June) on a park bench in Minsk shortly before their departure to the United States in June of 1962. EVERETT COLLECTION HISTORICAL / ALAMY

Picture of Lee, Marina, and June, taken on Thanksgiving Day 1962 at the Fort Worth bus station where they were dropped off by the author. CORBIS HISTORICAL / GETTY

(Above) The author in front of the Gregorys' home on Dorothy Lane, with Monticello Park in the background. Fort Worth, Texas, 1962. (Below) Pete and Paul Gregory standing in front of the family yellow Buick—Marina's introduction to American cars. 1962.

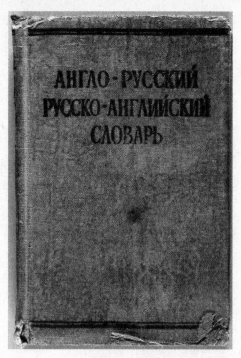

Lee Harvey Oswald's pocket Russian-English dictionary he gifted the author on the occasion of their first Russian lesson in June 1962.

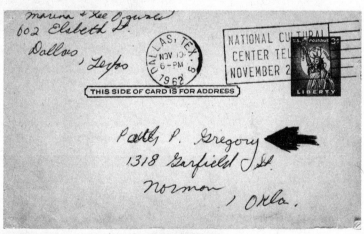

Postcard from Lee to the author announcing their new address in Dallas and an invitation to visit. Author thought it was written by Marina because of errors and lack of punctuation. November 29, 1962.

(Above) Pete and Elizabeth Gregory with George Bouhe, leader of the Dallas Russian community, who brought his picture albums to show Marina his family's time in Russia and connect about their shared homeland. This was the first meeting of Lee and Marina with the Dallas Russian community. August 25, 1962. (Below) Lee Oswald with his "best friend" (by order of the KGB), Pavel, and his first love, Ella German, who turned down his marriage proposal (upper right). SVINTAGE ARCHIVE / ALAMY

Lee posing with the assassination rifle in the backyard. In her interrogation translated by Pete, Marina reluctantly admitted she took the picture. Dallas, Texas, March 1963. THE WARREN COMMISSION, A US GOVERNMENT REPORT. FROM WH VOL.16 PAGE 510.

Students at the OU student union watch Walter Cronkite declare JFK is dead. The author is wearing glasses in the right corner. November 22, 1963.

Assassin suspect Lee Harvey Oswald in the Dallas Police Department surrounded by Dallas detectives in cowboy hats. November 22, 1963. ZUMA PRESS, INC. / ALAMY

Picture of an unidentified man entering the Soviet Embassy in Mexico City during Oswald's stay identified as Jack Ruby by Marguerite, or as an Oswald decoy by various conspiracy theories.

Pete translating for Marina as Agents Mike Howard and Charles Kunkel interrogate her at the Six Flags Inn. November 25, 1963.

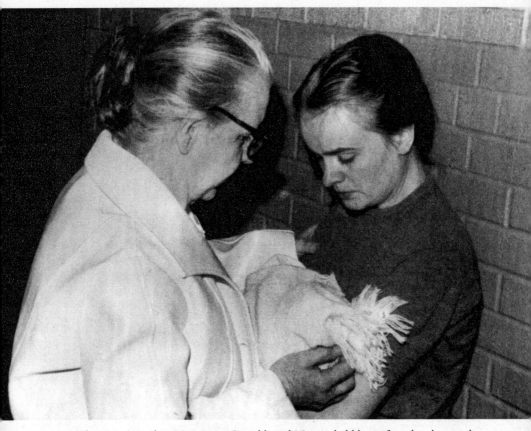

(Above) Lee's mother, Marguerite Oswald, and Marina hold her infant daughter at the Dallas police headquarters. November 24, 1963. EVERETT COLLECTION INC / ALAMY

(Below) Marina and Marguerite insist on seeing Lee's body at Parkland Hospital. They are accompanied by Agents Howard and Kunkel. Pete Gregory is in the rear out of sight.

PART IV

LEE WREAKS HAVOC

My summer of 1962 with Lee and Marina had ended. I said
my goodbyes and returned to the University of Oklahoma
for my senior year. I left knowing that they were now
in the benevolent arms of the Dallas Russian community,
which I imagined would fill any void left by my departure. Lee himself may have breathed a sigh of relief that
I, the Russian-speaking intruder, was out of the picture,
at least for the time being. But he had bigger problems
in George Bouhe and any number of good Samaritans ready
to take care of Marina.

23

AS THE GOOD SAMARITANS LOOK ON

As I expected, George Bouhe and company sprang into action. Bouhe found Lee a job in Dallas after Lee lost (or said he lost) his job at the Fort Worth welding company. Bouhe arranged for Marina to stay with a Russian couple while Lee lived at the YMCA as he settled into his new low-paying position and searched for an apartment. Although the Dallas Russians sought to find Lee and Marina a place in their neighborhoods, Lee, perhaps in spite, selected one on Elsbeth Street in the Oak Cliff district, on the other side of Dallas from where most of the Russian benefactors lived.

Bouhe's mercy missions did not sit well with Lee, who resented outsiders—especially Russian speakers—butting into his and Marina's lives. With every new gift or gesture, Lee's resentment grew, though not quite enough to turn down the largesse the Russians brought to his door. Shocked by Marina's decaying teeth, Anna Meller arranged for dental work and drove her to the office for the procedure. Lee never seemed to have money in his pocket. Marina had even less. Their Russian-speaking friends were expected to pick up the tab when they were together with the Oswalds. Yet Lee treated such "gifts" as insults. When friends volunteered to take the sick June to the doctor, Lee shouted that he would take care of his own child. When asked if he had thanked one of their Russian friends for getting him a job, Lee's response was, "Why be grateful for a $1.25 per hour job?"

In his Warren Commission testimony, Bouhe declared that the surly Lee would not speak with him while all of this was going on. Lee and Bouhe clashed on occasion. Once, Lee pointed to his copy of Marx's *Das Kapital* and declared it "*the* book." Bouhe could not contain himself and stated that Lee should go back to Russia.

All the while, Lee attempted to maintain his hold over Marina. He discouraged meetings with her growing list of Russian friends. He himself did the grocery shopping, leaving Marina at home alone with June. At least with me around, she could go along for the shopping trips. Now Lee was depriving her of even that simple pleasure.

Lee's working again at a menial job and the tensions caused by gifts, assistance, and offers of English lessons wore on the troubled couple. Lee's physical violence against his wife intensified. She admitted freely to the Dallas Russians that her black eyes were not due to accidents but a result of Lee hitting her in the face. Lee's resentment of Bouhe rose to the point that the would-be benefactor feared Lee would attack him.

Marina did not move from her more comfortable life as a guest of Russian benefactors to 604 Elsbeth Street in Dallas until November 4, 1962. The place was filthy, and Marina worked until five in the morning to clean it up. Almost immediately, the fighting began as Lee kept Marina a virtual prisoner in their new apartment. To her rare visitors she gave the appearance of a malnourished hostage.

On November 6, Lee accused Marina of "whoring" after the money and possessions that Bouhe and the other Russians were offering her. Disgusted, she left the apartment and somehow managed to phone the Mellers from a gas station. Anna Meller instructed her to come by cab, and a trembling Marina arrived at their front door carrying June. She had had enough.

As news of Lee's latest outrage spread, the worried Russian community organized shelter for Marina. She and June could not continue to sleep on a makeshift bed in the living room of the Mellers' tiny apartment. Bouhe found more suitable accommodations with Katya Ford, a Russian married to an ex-GI. The Fords had a home that could comfortably harbor guests.

Lee became frantic. His wife had deserted him. She and his daughter were living with people who detested him. He pleaded with Bouhe to arrange a meeting where he and Marina could talk things through. Bouhe reluctantly did so—for Sunday morning, November 11, at the apartment of one of the more robust male members of the Russian community. Bouhe recruited him to protect him—and Marina—from Lee.

The meeting began on a confrontational note, with Marina throwing Lee's brutality in his face and Lee countering with complaints of Marina's nagging. Marina refused his plea to reconcile with him. They decided to part ways under the watchful eyes of Bouhe. Returning to Elsbeth Street with Bouhe and his "bodyguard," a subdued Lee helped to load Marina's things into a car. As they pulled away, Marina called to Lee that she did not want to see him one more second.

Notably, Marina did not shield from Lee her current address and phone number. Knowing Marina was living with the Fords, Lee began a barrage of phone calls; Marina rebuffed him, saying in no uncertain terms that she was not coming back. On the third night of telephone calls, Lee told her that Robert had invited them for Thanksgiving, and he would be humiliated if he had to go alone. The Thanksgiving invitation weighed on Marina's conscience. She worried that Robert would think badly of her for leaving Lee. Lee chose his line of attack well, for Marina thought highly of Robert and Vada.

The Dallas Russians hoped that Marina would not yield to Lee's increasingly desperate entreaties. They upped the pressure. If she returned to Lee, they would wash their hands of her. It was her choice to make.

Bouhe, hopeful that Marina would yield to his group's ultimatum, was busy organizing a life for her that would be free of Lee. He introduced Marina to Anna Ray, another Russian woman married to an American. Anna had three small children and invited Marina and June to live with them. She herself would teach Marina English—a seemingly perfect arrangement.

Marina moved in with the Rays on November 18, but not before telling Lee where she was going. He telephoned within minutes of their arrival, and Marina caved in, telling him to come over.

When Lee appeared at the door, the two retreated to Marina's room. He pleaded with Marina on his knees, crying, telling her he loved her. He declared that he could not live without her and pledged that he would be a good husband. He repeated that Robert expected them for Thanksgiving, and he could not bear to go alone. Thanksgiving was only four days away.

Marina relented and agreed to a reconciliation. Her host's husband drove them to Elsbeth Street as word spread through the irate Russian community. That very evening, Lee wrote to Robert: he and his family would be happy to accept their invitation for Thanksgiving dinner—a narrow escape from the humiliation Lee so feared.

I look back and see that Lee Harvey Oswald was proving more than Bouhe and his troops could handle—perhaps a first for them.

24

MY MISTAKE

I n Norman, Oklahoma, I was unaware of Lee and Marina's marital turmoil. I was anticipating seeing them at Thanksgiving in Fort Worth on November 22. It would be my first trip back after parting with the couple two months earlier. I had left my Norman address with Lee but had little expectation I would hear from either of them.

It was a postcard that thrust me back into the havoc of Lee and Marina's marriage.

Our Norman mailbox rarely contained any mail, but on November 12 it contained a simple penny postcard, as they were called in those days (although it cost three cents). (See photo of the postcard in the photo section.) Handwritten, it had been posted two days earlier (November 10) in Dallas in the midst of the Oswalds' marital dogfight. The return senders were listed as Lee and Marina Oswald of 602 Elsbeth Street, Dallas. I kept the card for their address. Perhaps I would be in Dallas in the near future and drop by for a visit. I assumed that Lee and Marina had no telephone. Any meeting would have to be arranged by mail.

The postcard (reproduced below with original spelling and punctuation—or lack thereof):

"Dear Paul! We have moved to Dallas Where we have found a nice apartment and I have found work in a very nice place, we would like you too [sic] come and see us as soon as you get a chance we live in the Oak Cliff section of Dallas at 602 Elsbeth St. *Do svidanya* [goodbye] M).

The scribbled signature was something of a mystery. To me, it looked like a poorly written Russian "M," despite the fact that it appeared to have an extra line attached to the "M." (In looking at the card more than a half century later, I realized that I should not have missed the fact that the ending to the Russian *Do svidiania* (goodbye) was botched—an unlikely error for Marina, but it was my mistake that I did not see it.)

From the primitive handwriting, lack of punctuation, and misspelling ("too" instead of "to"), I assumed the postcard was from Marina. After all, it appeared signed by her ("*Do svidania* [goodbye] M"). I was surprised, to say the least, that the message reported that the writer of the postcard—I thought Marina—had found work at a "nice place."

It was a rather stupid mistake, but I concluded that Marina, not Lee, wrote the postcard reporting that she had somehow found a job. I read it over quickly and put it in a drawer. Had I taken more time, I would not have made such an egregious error.

My mistake concerning who wrote the postcard constitutes a story in itself. The content and timing of the postcard from "Lee and Marina Oswald," I came to realize, also offers a rare, documented example of Lee's wily and deliberate maneuvering after Marina left him in early November 1962.

Lee took it upon himself to write one of the few people he knew outside the Dallas Russian community, who might not know that Marina had left him. In his few and simple words, he reported to me that he and Marina were leading an almost happy life. They had a nice apartment. Lee had a good job. They looked forward to welcoming me to their new abode in Dallas. Everything was fine.

Of course, everything was not fine. Lee wrote this message sitting alone in his Elsbeth Street apartment, deserted by his wife. She had resisted all his pleas and entreaties, swearing never to return. He had been labeled as a beast and a boor by the good Samaritans who sought to save his wife from his abuse. In two weeks, he was scheduled to attend Thanksgiving dinner at his brother's house with his wife and daughter at his side, but she was refusing even to talk with him.

Lee surely wrote the postcard in a high state of agitation.

. . .

Robert had arranged for their half-brother, John Pic, to drive down from San Antonio with his family for Thanksgiving so that Lee could see him for the first time since his teen years. A refusal of this invitation would tell Lee's two brothers—each successful in their own way—that his family life was in shambles. What a humiliation for Lee to either refuse this invitation or make a lame excuse for not attending. In either case, his marriage would be revealed as a failure, just like almost everything else in his life.

Why, then, did Lee Harvey Oswald choose to send *me* an upbeat message that his work, his marriage, and his life were finally taking shape—at the very time they appeared to be crumbling around him? I had never felt a particularly strong tie to this cipher of a man; but I, unlike others, had never belittled him or diminished him in the eyes of his wife. Perhaps I was the only remaining person with whom he felt some sort of closeness, a kind of friendship. Even those Dallas Russians who'd been willing to give him the benefit of the doubt were now ready to wash their hands of him. I suppose I was the last one left.

Why did Lee Harvey Oswald describe to me a Potemkin-village life in which good things were happening for him? The most likely explanation for the "all is well" postcard is that Lee was preparing a second line of attack to get Marina back. If the pressure of Robert's Thanksgiving invitation did not work, he could tell Marina, "Paul is coming to visit.

Just imagine what he will think if he finds you have taken June and deserted me."

The reconciliation with Marina took place eight days after Lee mailed his postcard to me. He indeed had his second chance to make his marriage work. When Marina returned to their house, she and Lee danced in the kitchen. He brought her coffee and doughnuts, and even took her to a bowling alley as they prepared for the family reunion on Thanksgiving Day.

I did not know it, but their Thanksgiving plans included a last meeting with me, instigated by Marina herself.

25

"OUTING" LEE

Marina herself would have picked up the letter I sent to her in response to Lee's postcard, which I had mistaken to be from her. Lee was surely at work when it arrived. The letter would have reached Elsbeth Street only a day or two after her reluctant return to her husband. I remember its contents as if I'd written it yesterday.

Remember, I thought that Marina—not Lee—had written the "all is fine, come and visit" note, completely lacking in punctuation and with "too" instead of "to." So, I wrote back in Russian how pleased I was that Marina had found a job and was studying English, and that I was impressed by her attempt to write in her new language. Taking on the uninvited role of tutor, I instructed her about punctuation and the difference between "too" and "to."

In those few lines written in Russian, I unwittingly demolished Lee's claim to Marina that he was an underappreciated author of an autobiography that was sought after by publishers. How could anybody write an autobiography if they could not spell and punctuate? (Lee and Marina saved virtually every letter they received. My letter is not among them, for obvious reasons.)

The parsimonious postcard and my untoward reply played a role in my final meeting with Lee and Marina on that Thanksgiving Day, November 22, 1962, exactly one year before the Kennedy assassination. I had last seen them two months earlier at their Mercedes Street address.

. . .

The day before the holiday and the Gregory family's Thanksgiving dinner, I drove down from Norman in my newly acquired 1959 Volkswagen. I did not expect to see Lee or Marina. There had been no mention in the postcard that they would be in Fort Worth. (In fact, Lee would not have known when he wrote the postcard that Marina would return and that he could accept Robert's invitation.)

In the late afternoon of Thanksgiving Thursday, I answered our phone. It was Marina, calling from Robert Oswald's house in Fort Worth. She wanted to see me. She had apparently escaped the crowd of in-laws, nieces, and nephews in the dining room to call in private.

Her first words came tumbling out as if blurting a state secret: "I did not write that letter. Lee did."

Marina spoke softly but in an agitated manner, so rapidly that I did not understand every word. But I did understand that she was upset. Lee had been doing bad things to her. He had alienated her Russian friends. He kept her almost prisoner in the apartment with June. She had threatened to leave him.

Marina asked that I come over to Robert's house, pick up the three of them, and drop them off for the late bus to Dallas. I agreed.

I arrived to collect Lee, Marina, and June around four in the afternoon. The party was breaking up. A small crowd of Oswalds was assembled in the front yard, saying their goodbyes. Robert greeted me, saying he had volunteered to drive Lee and Marina to the bus station, but Marina insisted on calling me. Lee was wearing a light brown sports

coat and white shirt open at the collar. Marina wore a woolen knit suit
with a high collar underneath a light overcoat. (See the picture taken at
the Fort Worth bus station, that day, November 22, 1962.) Together in
Robert's front yard, they gave the impression of a happy young couple.
June was warmly dressed in a jaunty white cap askew on her curly hair.
As usual, Lee had little to say, other than a casual hello. Likely he would
have preferred to have Robert drive them to the bus station, but Marina
had taken matters into her own hands with the phone call to me.

Lee introduced me to a man in his late thirties, whom he identified as
his half-brother. This was John Pic, with whom Lee and Marguerite had
lived in New York when Lee was twelve years old. John and his family
were living in San Antonio, having recently returned from a military
assignment in Japan. The well-intentioned Robert had followed through
on his promise to use the occasion of Thanksgiving to bring together the
three brothers. By not inviting the volatile Marguerite, he hoped that
the get-together would go well.

Lee and Marina's bus did not leave for Dallas until 9:00 p.m. We
drove back to our house on Dorothy Lane. The three of us said our
short hellos to my father and mother. We went to the kitchen and made
turkey sandwiches from leftovers and proceeded to the den, where we
lingered over conversation. They would not arrive back to Elsbeth Street
until 1:00 a.m., so they needed food in their stomachs.

Marina had already had her say about Lee on the phone. I now
knew about my faux pas with respect to authorship of the postcard. I
suspected that Lee must be seething at me for my inadvertent betrayal.
This conversation in the den was tense but notable for its lack of content. Marina came across as more forceful than on Mercedes Street. She
temporarily had the upper hand. Lee had to be on his best behavior after
luring her back. She did not know then that he would quickly revert
to form.

Much had happened since we had last seen each other—the move
to Dallas, the interventions of George Bouhe, Lee's new job, but we

sat together making strained conversation. Lee remained largely silent, withdrawn into his shell. There was also a notable lack of discussion of the Dallas Russians. We definitely avoided Lee's postcard, my response, and what it revealed about Lee's clumsy use of the English language.

Under other circumstances among friends, my mistaking Lee's writing for Marina's could have evoked a hearty laugh, but not in this case. The damage to our relationship had already been done, and we all knew it. The only unknown was whether Lee knew that Marina had informed me of my mistake concerning the authorship of the postcard. Yes, she had done so in our hurried phone conversation a couple of hours earlier.

A little after 8:00 p.m., I drove them downtown to the bus station. We were all in a subdued mood. When I'd had no alternative transportation, I had ridden the Dallas-Fort Worth bus, and it was not a pleasant experience. The bus was filled with drunks and down-and-out souls. I remember one occasion where a drunk vomited all over the aisle. Someone tossed a newspaper over the result as if this were an everyday occurrence. Riding the bus and walking constituted Marina's routine in her life with Lee.

As we drove up, the last bus to Dallas was preparing to depart. The Oswalds hurried so as not to miss it. Marina turned and waved, and they climbed aboard. Lee did not look back. That was the last time I saw either of them.

My next view of Lee was exactly one year later as the police hauled him into the Dallas police station as the prime suspect in the assassination of the president of the United States. The next time Robert Oswald would see his brother would be behind bars in the Dallas city jail.

What a contrast: from an impoverished figure with his wife and child climbing aboard a dilapidated bus on November 22, 1962, to a man at the center of world attention in the Dallas police station on November 22, 1963. In his perverted way, Lee Harvey Oswald had achieved his goal.

. . .

After that day, I had no time to drive to Dallas to see Lee and Marina. There were no postcards awaiting me with new addresses or invitations to visit. I was in Fort Worth only for Christmas and Easter. On the latter occasion, I attended a gathering of the Fort Worth and Dallas Russians. George Bouhe took me aside and spoke disdainfully about "our mutual friends," who were causing him and the other good Samaritan Russians no end of aggravation. In Bouhe's words were hints of dark deeds and transgressions, even physical abuse. He was too refined, too much a gentleman of the old school, to go into details. But he had clearly given up on the Oswalds. Lee was more than he wished to handle, and Marina did not have the sense to break with him permanently and accept Bouhe's benevolent offerings.

At that Easter gathering, Bouhe would scarcely have known that Marina had become pregnant in the aftermath of her reconciliation with Lee. As word spread among the Russian community, plans for freeing Marina from the grasp of her abusive husband were set aside as she gave birth to a second daughter, Rachel, just thirty-three days before the infant's father shot and killed the president of the United States. Marina's pregnancy did not affect Lee's frenetic activities as he plotted to move to Cuba, narrowly missed killing a leading Dallas right-wing figure, fled to New Orleans, and visited the Cuban and Soviet Embassies in Mexico City.

26

SHOOTING
GENERAL WALKER

George Bouhe and company fretted over the marital pyrotechnics of Lee and Marina and the hostility of Lee toward them. They did not know that they had a much more serious problem on their hands to which only Marina was privy.

On the night of April 10, 1963, Lee Harvey Oswald took his sharpshooter rifle to the backyard of Major General Edwin Walker's house, aimed toward the window where he was working, and narrowly missed a shot to his head. Lee fled the scene on foot and ran to a distant bus stop and returned home to Marina late at night. Walker was a stark anti-communist voice, a leader of Dallas's right-wing community.

When the Warren Commission met on February 3, 1964, to hear testimony from Marina Oswald, among the topics covered was Lee Harvey Oswald's attempt to kill General Edwin Walker in his Dallas home. Marina was questioned by commission counsel Lee Rankin and she answered through a translator:

MR. RANKIN: How did you first learn that your husband had shot at General Walker?

MRS. OSWALD: That evening he went out, I thought that he had gone to his classes [typing] or perhaps that he just walked out or went out on his own business. It got to be about 10 or 10:30, he wasn't home yet, and I began to be worried. Perhaps even later. Then I went into his room. Somehow, I was drawn into it—you know—I was pacing around. Then I saw a note there.

MR. RANKIN: Did you look for the gun at that time?

MRS. OSWALD: No, I didn't understand anything. On the note it said, "If I am arrested" and there are certain other questions, such as, for example, the key to the mailbox is in such and such a place, and that he left me some money to last me for some time, and I couldn't understand at all what can he be arrested for. When he came back I asked him what had happened. He was very pale. I don't remember the exact time, but it was very late. And he told me not to ask him any questions. He only told me that he had shot at General Walker. Of course I didn't sleep all night. I thought that any minute now, the police will come. Of course I wanted to ask him a great deal. But in his state I decided I had best leave him alone—it would be purposeless to question him.

MR. RANKIN: Did he say any more than that about the shooting?

MRS. OSWALD: Of course in the morning I told him that I was worried, and that we can have a lot of trouble, and I asked him, "Where is the rifle? What did you do with it?" He said, that he had left it somewhere, that he had buried it, it seems to me, somewhere far from that place, because he said dogs could find it by smell. I don't know—I am not a criminologist.

MR. RANKIN: Did he tell you why he had shot at General Walker?

MRS. OSWALD: I told him that he had no right to kill people in peacetime, he had no right to take their life because not everybody has the same ideas as he has. People cannot be all alike. He said that this was a very bad man, that he was a fascist, that he was the leader of a fascist organization, and when I said that even though all of that might be true, just the same he had no right to take his life, he said if someone had killed Hitler in time it would have saved many lives. I told him that this is no method to prove your ideas, by means of a rifle.

MR. RANKIN: Did you ask him how long he had been planning to do this?

MRS. OSWALD: Yes. He said he had been planning for two months. Yes—perhaps he had planned to do so even earlier, but according to his conduct I could tell he was planning—he had been planning this for two months.

MR. RANKIN: Did he show you a picture of the Walker house then?

MRS. OSWALD: Yes, Mr. Rankin.

MR. RANKIN: That was after the shooting?

MRS. OSWALD: Yes. He had a book—he had a notebook in which he noted down quite a few details. It was all in English, I didn't read it. But I noticed the photograph. Sometimes he would lock himself in his room and write in the book. I thought that he was writing some other kind of memoirs, as he had written about his life in the Soviet Union.

MR. RANKIN: Did you ever read that book?

MRS. OSWALD: No.

MR. RANKIN: Do you know of anything else he had in it besides this Walker house picture?

MRS. OSWALD: No. Photographs and notes, and I think there was a map in there.

MR. RANKIN: There was a map of the area where the Walker house was?

MRS. OSWALD: It was a map of Dallas, but I don't know where Walker lived. Sometimes evenings he would be busy with this. Perhaps he was calculating something, but I don't know. He had a bus schedule and computed something. After this had happened, people thought that he had a car, but he had been using a bus.

MR. RANKIN: Did he explain to you about his being able to use a bus just as well as other people could use a car—something of that kind?

MRS. OSWALD: No. Simply as a passenger. He told me that even before that time he had gone also to shoot, but he had returned. I don't know why. Because on the day that he did fire, there was a church across the street and there were many people there, and it was easier to merge in the crowd and not be noticed.

MR. RANKIN: Did you ask him about this note that he had left, what he meant by it?

MRS. OSWALD: Yes—he said he had in mind that if in case he were arrested, I would know what to do.

MR. RANKIN: The note doesn't say anything about Walker, does it?

MRS. OSWALD: No.

MR. RANKIN: Did you ask him if that is what he meant by the note?

MRS. OSWALD: Yes, because as soon as he came home I showed him the note and asked him, "What is the meaning of this?"

MR. RANKIN: And that is when he gave you the explanation about the Walker shooting?

MRS. OSWALD: Yes. I know that on a Sunday he took the rifle, but I don't think he fired on a Sunday. Perhaps this was on Friday. So Sunday he left and took the rifle.

MR. RANKIN: If the Walker shooting was on Wednesday, does that refresh your memory as to the day of the week at all?

MRS. OSWALD: Refresh my memory as to what?

MR. RANKIN: As to the day of the shooting?

Mrs. Oswald: It was in the middle of the week.

MR. RANKIN: Did he give any further explanation of what had happened that evening?

MRS. OSWALD: When he fired, he did not know whether he had hit Walker or not. He didn't take the bus from there. He ran several kilometers and then took the bus. And he turned on the radio and listened, but there were no reports. The next day he bought a paper and there he read it was only chance that saved Walker's life. If he had not moved, he might have been killed.

MR. RANKIN: Did he comment on that at all?

MRS. OSWALD: He said only that he had taken very good aim, that it was just chance that caused him to miss. He was very sorry that he had not hit him. I asked him to give me his word that he would not repeat anything like that. I said that this chance shows that he must live and that he should not be shot at again. I told him that I would save the note and that if something like that should be repeated again, I would go to the police and I would have the proof in the form of that note. He said he would not repeat anything like that again.

. . .

Fast-forward and note the difference between Oswald's two assassination attempts, other than the fact that the first one failed. As Marina's testimony makes clear: Lee did have a reason for wanting to eliminate General Walker. Walker was, in Lee's opinion, a dangerous person, a fascist. He believed in the opposite of Lee's professed beliefs. Kennedy, on the other hand, was a centrist in American politics. Lee would scarcely pick him out for ideological reasons. Besides that, his wife admired the Kennedys. He would have known she would be devastated if he inflicted harm on the young president.

Ernst Titovets, Lee's friend in Minsk, could not believe Oswald killed President Kennedy because such a murder did not fit into Oswald's mindset. Titovets would have no problem accepting the fact that Lee had tried to take out General Walker. Walker was abhorrent to Oswald's Marxist beliefs; Kennedy was not. My response to Titovets is that the Kennedy assassination was about several factors, and Kennedy's political philosophy would not have been one of them.

The note Lee left behind for Marina gave her instructions as to what to do in case he was caught and was being held in jail. It also provides valuable information on his command of Russian. The note is composed in the phonetic spelling of Lee's ungrammatical Russian. The endings are wrong; he mixes Cyrillic and Roman letters, and there is no punctuation; yet the message is understandable. But this Russian bears no resemblance to what one might expect from an agent instructed at an exclusive Soviet spy training camp.

27

THE PERSECUTED RADICAL

The Dallas newspapers of Thursday, April 11, 1963, ran front-page stories about the attempt on Walker's life. Lee left the apartment to buy the papers, and he listened to radio bulletins. A Walker neighbor's report of suspicious cars at the scene prompted Lee to chortle to Marina that no American would think of using his legs. A quick arrest of a disgruntled Walker associate proved to be a false lead. The trail had gone cold, but Lee Harvey Oswald concluded that he would be safer if he left Dallas. He chose his place of birth, New Orleans. He would go ahead, and Marina would follow. In the meantime, she could stay, as usual, with friends, leaving him free for his schemes.

· · ·

Already during his stay in the Dallas-Fort Worth area, Oswald had sought to establish relationships with communist and pro-Cuba organizations. He sent a "fraternal" letter to the chairman of the American Communist Party, Gus Hall, praising him as a "fighter for peace." The

Socialist Workers Party threw cold water on his offer to form a Dallas branch but offered him "a close sympathetic relationship" and encouraged him to promote subscriptions to their journal, *The Militant*. (Lee held a copy of *The Militant* in his photo dressed in black and holding the assassination rifle.) On the eve of his departure, he wrote the Fair Play for Cuba Committee (FPCC) volunteering to found a branch in New Orleans. On May 29 he received from the FPCC national office a membership card, the FPCC's constitution, and instructions for forming a new chapter.

Lee regarded New Orleans as a fresh opportunity to burnish his radical credentials. Once there, his plans became grandiose. He leased at his own expense(!) an office, and he organized demonstrations, a recruitment campaign, and a media debate. FPCC's response was less than enthusiastic on his chances in Louisiana: unlike the Northeast, there were few potential pro-Castro recruits in New Orleans, they wrote. Undeterred, Oswald printed application forms, which he handed out on New Orleans street corners. Oswald reported "considerable attendance" at his demonstrations, but his net brought in zero applicants other than his own alias, A. J. Hidell. Other New Orleans activities included a fistfight with a Cuban exile, overnight jail time, a fine, and then a radio appearance.

After his unsuccessful attempt on Walker's life, the restless Lee started assuming a new persona as a Marxist organizer one step ahead of the ruthless FBI. Cuba beckoned. According to Marina, Lee had even considered skyjacking a plane to Havana, but had abandoned that idea in favor of pursuing a Cuban visa. As a part of his Cuban designs, Oswald requested a Soviet visa from the Soviet Embassy in Washington.

According to his self-description in his visa applications, Oswald was a dedicated Marxist, an activist, committed to the cause. The visas were urgent. The FBI was closing in on him.

Lee convinced a very reluctant Marina to join his quest for a visa back to her homeland. She began filling out the paperwork, but the process required months and her eventual presence at the DC Embassy itself. Oswald's last letter to the Embassy on the visa business was dated November 9, 1963 (postmarked November 12), just a couple of weeks before he killed the president.

· · ·

In Oswald's mind, he was developing a plan to convince the Castro regime that he had been a valuable cog of American support. As such, he should merit special consideration when it came to a visa request. After all, he was the secretary of the New Orleans FPCC chapter. On a curious note, Lee listed his alias, Hidell, as chapter president. The New Orleans FPCC was a shell, but Lee had garnered endorsements from some influential American supporters to show Cuban authorities.

It fell to Lee to figure out a way to obtain a Soviet visa, with which he could extract a transit visa for Cuba. Once in Cuba, he figured he'd be difficult to dislodge. That was a lesson he'd learned from his three years in the USSR.

The closest city that had both Cuban and Soviet Embassies was Mexico City—a tolerable bus ride from New Orleans.

· · ·

On September 27, Oswald arrived in Mexico City via a bus from Nuevo Laredo. He registered at a nearby fleabag hotel. His first step was to visit the Soviet Embassy, where he met on September 28 with a consular official later identified as V.V. Kostikov. By Oswald's account, Kostikov (he thought the name was Kostin) assured him that he would indeed get an entry visa. (Kostikov was a KGB agent disguised as a consular official, as was common practice in Soviet embassies and consulates.)

It should be noted that Lee's one-on-one meeting in the Mexico City Soviet Embassy with Kostikov provides the foundation for the Cubans-killed-JFK-through-Oswald theory.

Oswald didn't come to the notice of U.S. intel (the CIA) until they intercepted a telephone call on October 1 to the Soviet Embassy by a man "speaking broken Russian" and identifying himself as Lee Oswald.

The call originated from the Cuban Embassy through the intermediation of a Mexican communist, Silvia Duran, who worked at the Cuban Embassy. Oswald showed her his New Orleans FPCC credentials. He assured her that the Soviet Embassy had confirmed his visa was on the way, but a telephone call to the Soviet Embassy said otherwise. The frustrated Oswald was then told that the Cuban Embassy would not issue a transit visa without the Soviet visa, regardless of his service to the Cuban cause.

As tension rose, the irate Oswald accused the Cubans of not standing behind those who were helping them. They must issue the transit visa even without the USSR visa. The consul himself came out and began a heated conversation with Oswald. The consul confirmed that he would not authorize the visa and told Oswald "a person of his type was harming the Cuban Revolution rather than helping it."

In his five days in Mexico City, the frustrated Oswald had toured the capital. He purportedly attended a party with Silvia Duran. Attendees described him as standing in a corner by himself. This truly sounds like Oswald. The more sensational accounts claim an unlikely sexual relationship between Oswald and Duran.

. . .

The goings-on in Mexico City were "Oswald theater." His real goal was to obtain a transit visa to Cuba, which he understood required a Soviet visa. He already knew that, at best, the Soviet visa would require four months to process. He decided therefore to travel to Mexico City where he could play one embassy against the other. He planned to bluff the Cubans into thinking that he was assured a Soviet visa. He would then obtain a Cuban transit visa and leave Mexico City with a green light to travel to Cuba. In his gambit, the Soviet visa was only a means to an end. He apparently had no intention to start a new life in the USSR, where it had all begun. Oswald knew that once in communist Cuba, he could stave off expulsion as he had in Moscow four years earlier.

The disappointed Oswald returned from Mexico City to Dallas on a Greyhound bus on October 2—his plan for a new life in Cuba temporarily set back. Back in Dallas, Lee and Marina lived separately; she with a friend, Ruth Paine, and he in a rented room.

When Marina first saw Lee after his return to the United States, he was disappointed by his failure to reach Cuba, but he was still intent on acquiring a Soviet visa through the DC Embassy. With a Soviet visa, he could then reactivate his quest for his Cuban visa.

Meanwhile, news of the interception of Oswald's telephone call to the Soviet Embassy in Mexico City was passed on to the FBI. Even before his return to Dallas, FBI Agent James Hosty had visited Marina at Ruth Paine's home. He demanded to know from the frightened Marina what her husband was up to in Mexico. He purportedly threatened her with deportation if she did not cooperate.

When Lee learned of Hosty's visit, he ordered Marina to take down the agent's license plate number if he appeared again. He visited the Dallas FBI office to confront Hosty, who was not in the office at the time. He left behind a letter, which Hosty flushed down the toilet. For this act, Hosty was later reprimanded for obstructing the Warren Commission's work.

· · ·

Back in Dallas, around October 15, Lee began work at the Texas School Book Depository on Dealey Plaza—a job opening brought to his attention by a Ruth Paine neighbor. That Oswald would begin a new job at a facility on the president's motorcade route could not have been a part of a concerted plot. At that time, plans for JFK's Texas trip were still in embryonic form. The Secret Service and Dallas police did not settle on the motorcade route until November 18—about a month after Oswald began work at the book depository.

On Saturday, November 9, Lee Oswald spent hours in the Paine home typing a letter for the Soviet Embassy in Washington. Typing was a new tool in Oswald's arsenal—the product of typing lessons at a nearby community college. He worked his way through numerous revisions, intent on making a good impression. He retyped the envelope address ten times because of repeated mistakes. Despite Oswald's extreme care, the final draft contains the typical Oswald misspellings (visted, interrest, visa's, etc.) as well as nonexistent punctuation.

Through his missive to the Soviet Embassy, Oswald wanted Soviet consular officials to know he had been treated shabbily by the Cubans in Mexico City, but he had no complaints concerning his treatment by the Soviets. Oswald wrote that Mr. Kostin (Kostikov) of the Soviet Embassy simply had no time to prepare for his visit. Oswald probably assumed that the Cubans would have reported his heated visit, and he needed to preemptively repair any damage.

Oswald's most important message followed: his and Marina's Soviet visas remained an urgent matter. Because of his activities on behalf of communist causes, including service for the USSR, the FBI was coming down hard on him and was attempting to get his wife to "defect." Oswald ended the letter on a personal note, announcing the birth of his second daughter, Rachel, on October 20, as if Soviet diplomats in Washington cared.

· · ·

Oswald's letter to the Soviet Embassy was not posted until November 12. For the Soviets, the Oswald letter would be a nightmare to say the least, coming less than ten days before the assassination. To make matters worse, Comrade Kostikov turned out to be a high-ranking KGB officer from the 13th directorate specializing in sabotage and assassinations. Would a KGB officer of his rank deal with a walk-in American seeking a visa?

The fact of a conversation in Mexico City's Soviet Embassy between Oswald and a KGB assassin has served as proof that somehow the Soviets were involved in the Kennedy assassination with Oswald as their Manchurian candidate. That Oswald met with a 13th directorate KGB agent performing routine consular duties, however, was not exceptional. KGB officials commonly used official duties as their cover in embassies and consulates worldwide.

The Soviet Embassy feared dire consequences from Oswald's November 12 letter and of his September 28 visit to their Mexico City Embassy. Their course of action: declare Oswald's letter a fake and issue instructions to Mexico City to lie low.

The Soviets enlisted American Communist Gus Hall to spread the story that the assassination was organized by ultra-right plotters. The Soviets were concerned that if the finger pointed toward them, right-wing American generals might launch a coup and then unleash a nuclear attack on the Soviet Union.

Back in Moscow, the Politburo was convinced that a single gunman operating alone could not conceivably have brought down the world's most powerful man. They considered their view confirmed when Jack Ruby gunned down Oswald. Yes, it was a conspiracy, and that conspiracy surely came from the right.

. . .

Oswald's visit to Mexico City raises a number of "what if" questions. We suspect that his main reason was to get a visa to Havana. The Soviet visa was simply a means to an end. Oswald's mind had already turned to Cuba. He had even begun to compile a list of common Spanish phrases. If he could learn Russian, Spanish would be a breeze.

If Oswald had gotten his Cuban visa, he could not have flown to Havana immediately from Mexico City. He had less than $15. He would have had to return to Dallas where he had a larger amount hidden with Marina. So, even if he had gotten his Cuban visa, he would have had to return to Dallas and would have been there during Kennedy's visit.

His serendipitous job in the Texas School Book Depository was to give Oswald a unique chance to fire on the president from a relatively short distance. Without his job at the depository, had he persisted in attempting to kill the president, normal Secret Service precautions would likely have foiled his chances.

28

A VISIT TO DEALEY PLAZA FOR MYSELF

Jumping ahead to March 31, 1964, almost four months after the assassination, I was scheduled to testify. I had driven the evening before from Norman to Fort Worth for a deposition in Dallas. The Warren Commission had set up an operation within the U.S. Attorney's office in the post office building. I was supposed to report there early afternoon to explain my relationship with Lee and Marina Oswald to the commission's assistant counsel, Wesley Liebeler.

I had passed the Texas School Book Depository literally dozens of times. From downtown Dallas to the Dallas-Fort Worth toll road, you had to drive the semicircle of Dealey Plaza to go through the correct underpass leading to the Dallas-Fort Worth Turnpike.

Having seen hundreds of images of Dealey Plaza and read the debates as to whether someone with Oswald's shooting experience could have killed the president from his sixth-floor window, I wanted to judge for myself.

This was my first visit to Dallas since the assassination. I felt an eerie sense as I found a spot on a side street to park my '59 Volkswagen and wandered onto the plaza's infamous "grassy knoll." I was not the only one there. A group of German tourists were pointing their cameras at "the window." I resisted an irrational urge to tell them what I knew. Had I done so, they would have taken home a strange tale to tell their friends.

As I, too, looked up at the window, I conjured an image of the wiry Lee Oswald, dressed in his usual dark slacks and plaid, open-collar shirt, crouching there as the motorcade passed. I could not picture Lee in the role of patsy or as someone incapable of carrying out such a horrendous act.

From the grassy knoll, I walked alongside Houston Street to its intersection with Elm. I measured with my eye the distance between Lee's window and the street. It seemed short enough for him—or anyone else who was a decent shot with a rifle—to have killed a passenger sitting in an open limousine. Moreover, the motorcade needed to make a sharp left down Elm as it reached its closest point to the depository. At that junction, the president's car would have had to brake to a slow speed. The shot seemed easy to me, but who was I to say? The only rifle I had ever fired was a .22 caliber in ROTC class in college.

· · ·

My personal due diligence complete—yes, Oswald could have killed the president from his sixth-floor perch—I proceeded back into the heart of downtown Dallas. I rode the elevator to the city attorney's office and was invited into a good-sized office with large glass windows that allowed me to see the Dallas city attorneys bustling about their business. I caught sight of Bob Travis, who worked as a deputy city attorney and was a good friend of my elder brother, Don. I felt somehow like tainted goods sitting before officers of the Warren Commission testifying about my knowledge of Lee Harvey Oswald. I had spent considerable time together with Bob Travis, but after my testimony, I left without making any effort to say hello to him. Such was the odd feeling of shame we shared—but I think I felt it much more than most.

A copy of my deposition was subsequently sent to me in Norman for proofreading and signature, and I remember taking it to the Norman post office. The postal clerk made some joke about accepting an envelope covered with "Top Secret" seals. I kept quiet about the contents.

PART V

EYEWITNESS TO HISTORY

The story now moves to Pete Gregory, my father.

Little did Pete know on the morning of November 22, 1963, that he would be a close-up witness to history over the next five days as he accompanied Marina, Marguerite, and the Secret Service from a hideout hotel room, to Parkland Hospital, to the Six Flags Inn, and then to Lee Harvey Oswald's burial and back. The story he told us on Thanksgiving Day (November 28, 1963) as the Gregory family assembled for the first time since the tragedy made each of us secondhand eyewitnesses to history.

Our father, a natural raconteur, told us what he saw and heard during the days between November 24 and our family gathering, except he disclosed nothing of Marina's answers to the Secret Service interrogators. He was also sworn to secrecy with respect to Marina's hiding places at the Six Flags Inn and the James Martin home. Even Marguerite did not know Marina's refuge, although she suspected it was our house.

29

PETE GETS THE NEWS

November 22, 1963, Fort Worth, Texas. The president of the United States had flown into Carswell Air Force Base outside of town the night before from Houston. He and Jackie had spent the night at the Texas Hotel, near my father Pete Gregory's office in the Continental Life Building.

Pete arrived early to join the crowd swelling twenty deep in front of the ornate portico entrance of the Texas Hotel. A speaking platform had been erected in front of the building's massive, red-brick frame. Despite a light rain, a jovial JFK appeared without a raincoat, accompanied by his beaming Texas-born-and-bred vice president, Lyndon B. Johnson. Special Secret Service Agent Mike Howard stood immediately behind the president, indistinguishable from the assembled political dignitaries. After Johnson's rousing introduction, the president made brief remarks, apologizing that Jackie was busy preparing herself for the day's events. He assured the audience that she looks very good at any time of day.

JFK's remarks concluded, while Pete watched from the back of the crowd as the president shook hands with the well-wishers pressing forward. Few security operatives were evident, just some scattered policemen. The crowd appeared to be in the same upbeat mood as the president. Women, wearing plastic head covers for the light rain, vied with one another to touch his hand or shoulder. Pete watched the president vanish back into the hotel to address a waiting assembly of the Fort Worth Chamber of Commerce. Kennedy ordered the Secret Service to bring Jackie downstairs as the attendees had begun to call out "Jackie! Jackie!" She appeared in a stunning pink outfit trimmed with a fur collar and matched by a pink pillbox hat. Within a matter of four hours, this outfit would be covered in her husband's blood and brain matter.

Having seen and heard the president outdoors, Pete proceeded to his office for his day's work. He did not witness the president's motorcade (with the president in golfer Ben Hogan's Cadillac convertible) departing for the short flight from Carswell Air Force Base to Dallas's Love Field.

· · ·

When Pete emerged from the Continental Life Building in the early afternoon, he noticed something awry. People were agitated, talking frantically. Some were wandering aimlessly. He heard above the hubbub: "The president has been shot!" Pete ducked into the Texas Hotel, where he could see the television coverage. He watched the same story unfold that I, in the University of Oklahoma's student union, was glued to: the shocking image of a bruised Lee Harvey Oswald, surrounded by a police escort, arriving at the Dallas police station.

Pete telephoned home. His wife, Elizabeth, answered. She had also seen the whole TV sequence and telephoned daughter Edith in Arlington. I called around 5:00 p.m. When Pete arrived home, both of my parents knew they were in for a troubled night. Indeed, they were awakened by Special Agent Mike Howard's persistent ringing of the doorbell at 3:00 a.m.

30

THE OSWALD WOMEN

At the time of the Secret Service's early-morning November 23 visit to Pete, Marina and her two daughters, along with Marguerite, were sleeping at the Arlington, Texas, home of Ruth Paine. A Quaker and an activist, Ruth had become Marina's hostess and confidante. After his return from Mexico City, Lee lived in a rooming house, separate from Marina. Lee, a frequent weekend visitor to the Paine home, had stored his sharpshooter rifle, covered by a blanket, in Ruth's garage. He picked it up on his final visit with Marina on the evening before the assassination. After Marina heard of the shooting, she discovered to her horror that the rifle was missing.

Upon hearing the news of Lee's arrest around 2:00 p.m. on Friday, November 22, Marina and Ruth hurried to the Dallas police headquarters in the hopes of seeing Lee.

The resourceful Marguerite, meanwhile, called the *Fort Worth Star-Telegram* to get one of their reporters to drive her to Dallas. The driver was newsman Bob Schieffer, coincidentally also a graduate of

Arlington Heights High School. Robert Oswald rushed to Dallas from nearby Denton.

The three Oswalds reunited in the police headquarters. Lee was being interrogated and was not allowed to visit with family. Robert met Ruth Paine for the first time. He did not like what he saw. For a straitlaced ex-Marine, Ruth was too much of a hippie activist for his taste. He would later forbid Marina from moving back in with Ruth.

Robert had last seen Marina on Thanksgiving Day 1962 when I picked them up at his house for the ride to the bus station. Marguerite had not seen Marina for well over a year. She learned for the first time that she had a new granddaughter, Rachel, at the Dallas police station. The Dallas district attorney's office was working full speed to prepare indictments against Lee, first for killing Officer J. D. Tippit, second for wounding Governor John Connally, and third, for killing the president of the United States.

FBI agents approached the small group to question Marina and Robert. But Robert would not allow it, stating that until he and Marina had legal representation, they would answer no questions.

Marina and Ruth, after waiting in vain to be granted a visit with Lee, were driven back to Irving by a reporter and photographer from *Life* magazine. They arrived around 6:30 p.m. at the Paine house. After consulting among themselves in the car, the *Life* staffers knocked on the door and began to take photos of Marina and Ruth.

One journalist followed Marguerite into her bedroom, and when she objected to the rude invasion of her privacy, he soothed her irritation by floating the idea of a $17,000 honorarium for her life story. She was not surprised when management at *Life* turned down the idea. Marguerite worried out loud that Ruth was trying to sell her own story to *Life* and, worse, was horning in on her own limelight. After all, as she would regularly complain, she was the mother of the accused assassin. It was she who deserved the limelight, not Ruth Paine or even Marina.

The *Life* reporters' interviews in the Paine home that evening dissolved into farce because of Marina's poor English and Ruth's poor Russian. At times, Marguerite would chime in with what she claimed were statements from Marina. The *Life* reporters departed with their photos, leaving the women alone.

. . .

In a telephone call from jail later that evening, Lee instructed Ruth to contact John J. Abt, a prominent civil liberties lawyer in New York. He figured Ruth was capable of making the connection because she was a member of the ACLU. As to Abt, he was spending the weekend in a cabin in rural New York and began receiving telephone calls from friends that Oswald had requested his legal representation. Abt, however, never received a formal request for representation from Oswald or any member of the Oswald family—and he had no idea who Oswald was, anyway.

Later, before the Warren Commission, Abt said he could only assume that Oswald knew of him through his ACLU work on behalf of American communists.

. . .

The next morning at 9:00 a.m., Marina and Marguerite were met at the Paine home by the same *Life* crew, now accompanied by a Russian-speaking translator. The *Life* operatives spirited them to the exclusive Adolphus Hotel in downtown Dallas, offering them free accommodations and food. *Life* arranged through a Dallas detective for Marina, Marguerite, and Robert to meet with Lee at the Dallas jail that same day.

In their brief meeting separated by glass, Lee warned Marina what not to tell the police. He professed his innocence, and assured Marina that everything would be okay. His shaking voice told her otherwise. During their four-to-five-minute conversation, Lee apparently caught sight of

June wearing hand-me-down tennis shoes from Ruth. Lee instructed Marina to make sure to get June a new pair of shoes. Apparently, Marguerite was close enough to hear Lee's comment on the shoes. She would later use this small incident as proof of what a good father her Lee was.

From his frightened voice, Marina understood that Lee was in real trouble. She left thinking he was guilty and worried what the consequences would be for her.

. . .

After the jailhouse meeting, the *Life* reporters returned with Marina and Marguerite to the Adolphus, where they were confronted by Dallas police officers and an FBI agent, demanding to see their press credentials. The *Life* reporters knew that the place would soon be swarming with police and FBI. They bundled Marina, Marguerite, and the two infants into a car and drove evasively until they'd lost any trailing cars. The *Life* reporters deposited the foursome in a luxury suite at the Executive Inn near Love Field, and then they handed Marguerite a fifty-dollar bill to pay for the suite and left, saying they would be in touch. With room service, the bill came to $48, according to Marguerite. The hotel room soon became a mess with diapers, hand-washed clothes, and uneaten food strewn about.

The location of the Oswald women at the Executive Inn turned out to be an unkept secret. Marina was in touch with Ruth Paine, who knew their location. The Paines, in turn, were acquainted with Bardwell Odum, a Dallas FBI agent. They told him where the women were, and Odum knocked on their hotel room door around 6:30 p.m., asking to see Marina. He was turned away by Marguerite, but not before Odum showed her a photo of a man he hoped Marina could identify. The photo had been passed along by the CIA. Presumably, it was a photograph of someone, possibly Oswald, entering the Soviet Embassy in Mexico City. (See the picture of the unidentified man in the photo insert.) Marguerite glanced at the photograph and declared she had never seen the man pictured. (She would later claim it was Jack Ruby.)

The Secret Service had their own clue as to the location of the Oswald women. An agent, in checking the vacated Adolphus room, found a piece of paper with "Executive Inn" written on it. Agent Howard, whose detail had been ordered by the new president, LBJ, to protect Oswald's family, spent the entire night monitoring comings and goings from their vantage point in the Executive Inn parking lot, ready to make their move in the morning.

31

"MARINA, GET A HOLD ON YOURSELF"

Pete and Elizabeth Gregory had gotten little sleep before Secret Service agents woke them in the early hours of Saturday, November 23, to conduct a first interrogation. When the agents left, they told Pete to stand by in case they needed his help. Pete's sleep from Saturday night to Sunday morning was fitful at best.

The phone rang at 7:00 a.m. on Sunday. Pete heard a woman's voice on the verge of tears: "Mr. Gregory, I need your help. The reporters, the news media, are badgering me." She sobbed before continuing: "I wonder if some of your friends, or you, could provide a place for me to hide from them?"

Pete asked, "Who are you?"

The caller answered, "I'd rather not tell you who I am, but I will identify myself by saying that I am one of the students in your Russian class in the library."

Pete responded, "I do not talk to people who do not identify themselves."

Caller: "You know my son and daughter-in-law well."

Pete then linked the voice with a short, stout woman—a practical nurse—who had sat largely unnoticed in the back of his Russian class some ten days earlier. She had at one point introduced herself as "Mrs. Oswald," but until this phone call, the name had failed to register. He remembered her because one evening her car broke down, and he volunteered to drive her to her West Seventh apartment, not far from Pete's house on Dorothy Lane.

He now realized that he was talking with Marguerite Oswald, the mother of Lee. Now it became clear why this woman with little interest in the language came to his class. Her son knew Russian, and her daughter-in-law spoke little or no English. This was Marguerite's way of bridging the language divide between her and her daughter-in-law.

Pete said, "Oh, you are Mrs. Oswald."

Marguerite replied, "We are at the Executive Inn in Dallas."

Pete wrote down the room number and instructed Marguerite to stay where she was. He would organize help for Marina and Marguerite and would come to them himself.

Marguerite may have been angling for the Gregorys to put them up in their house, but the thought never crossed Pete's mind. The possibility remained firmly embedded in Marguerite's, however.

After hanging up, Pete called Agent Mike Howard to inform him where the Oswald women were and of their call for help. Howard agreed to come pick Pete up right away. He would organize a hiding place for the Oswald women. Howard then called Robert Oswald, who broached the idea of taking the women to his in-laws' ranch, some forty-five minutes from Dallas.

Back in the Executive Inn in Dallas, Marguerite had told Marina she was going to call "Mr. Gregory" for help. She was surprised to learn that Marina knew who Mr. Gregory was and brightened up. Marguerite regarded this as a favorable sign that she was doing the right thing in calling "Mr. Gregory."

Around 10:00 a.m. at the Howard Johnson Inn on the Dallas-Fort Worth Turnpike, Pete and Agents Howard and Kunkel met up with Robert Oswald driving in from Denton. As the four men drove toward Love Field, they worked out a preliminary plan to take Pete to the Dallas jail to see if he could, as a familiar face, persuade Lee to talk.

Once at the Executive Inn in Dallas, the four men went straight to the room whose number Marguerite had given Pete. They instructed Marina and Marguerite to pack their things. Pete and Robert, who had not seen Marina for a year, were shocked at her appearance. She had lost considerable weight. She was having difficulty producing milk for Rachel, the daughter she had borne only thirty-three days earlier. Both children were sick, and they had no spare diapers or clothing. Obviously, Marina was not in shape for intensive interrogation. But time was passing—and what if she was part of a larger conspiracy? What if she had information about an imminent plot against the government? The Secret Service could not wait for more favorable circumstances to interrogate Marina.

After consulting Robert, they came up with a plan. South of Fort Worth, at Robert's in-laws' farm, they would be free from hordes of reporters, and Marina could perhaps recuperate while being questioned. Agents Howard and Kunkel agreed they should head for the ranch.

In the hotel room, Marina did as she was told and started packing, but Marguerite refused to budge. She wanted to tell "her story" to the two agents before she would go anywhere, but they "just wanted to get us out of there." She insisted she would not be put "out in the sticks." She had to be in Dallas to help her son. The exasperated Robert lost patience as he tried to break down his mother's resistance. Pete warned her that if she made further trouble, he would wash his hands of her. He lectured her that she had asked him to find a place to hide, and here they were with a solution.

Chastened, Marguerite agreed and began to pack her things for the journey to the farm. She gave Robert the $50 from *Life* magazine to settle the bill.

As the men loaded up one of the two cars, one of the Secret Service agents whispered to Robert and Pete that Lee had been shot. A fringe member of the Dallas gangster community, soon identified as Jack Ruby, the owner of a strip club, had just shot him in the Dallas police station's parking garage. The entourage spoke quietly and agreed not to tell Marina or Marguerite for the time being.

Robert left immediately in his car for Parkland Hospital, where Lee had been taken. There was no word on his condition. Mike Howard, together with Pete and the Oswald women and children, proceeded in the general direction of the farm. Marina insisted that they stop at Ruth Paine's house in Arlington to pick up some clothes plus diapers and additional baby things. Both children had diarrhea, which created conditions in the car that Pete later described as nearly intolerable. Nonetheless, fresh diapers or not, the Paine stop was ruled out: Ruth's house was surrounded by a mob of reporters. Instead of Arlington, the car was diverted to the home of C. J. Wirasnik, the Irving chief of police. From there, Marina could telephone Ruth to prepare the things she needed. The Secret Service could arrange for the baby supplies to be couriered over to the Wirasnik place, a half hour drive.

Because Agent Howard appeared to be driving aimlessly, Marina and Marguerite gained the impression that they were being taken to the jail to see Lee. In fact, Howard did not really know where to drive until he knew Lee's condition. If his wound was slight, they could proceed to the farm. If Lee did not survive, Marina would become the most important witness in the investigation. She could not be isolated on a remote farm under that circumstance. Marina's testimony, as translated by Pete, had to be airlifted to Washington following each session.

As he drove, Howard decided he had no choice but to tell the two Oswald women that Lee had been shot. He softened the blow by maintaining that the injury appeared not to be serious—a shoulder wound. Even Marguerite grew silent.

At the Irving police chief's house, Marina telephoned Ruth to give her a list of things she needed. As Marina admired the Wirasniks' home and sipped the glass of water Mrs. Wirasnik brought her, Pete approached her with a somber look on his face. The time was close to one in the afternoon. She knew what he was going to say: "Marina, get a hold on yourself. Lee is dead." Agent Howard told the agitated Marguerite the same news: "Your son has expired."

. . .

Marina's first thought was that her daughters, June and Rachel, were now without a father. June was just learning to walk. Marina had herself grown up without a father and had lost her mother at age fifteen. She said she wanted to see Lee's body. Pete warned that doing so would be a risk to her and even the children. It would be better, he said, to view the body at a funeral home after it had been "prepared."

Mrs. Wirasnik brought the two weeping women coffee as the men tried to convince them not to go to Parkland. Marguerite insisted that she "as an American citizen even if I am poor" had the same rights as Jackie Kennedy. No one kept Jackie from seeing her dead husband, and Marguerite should be allowed to see her dead son. In a rare case of agreement between mother and daughter-in-law, Marina said she wanted to go to the hospital too.

Pete's warning proved prescient: at Parkland, the small group, led by Agent Howard, made their way through a growing and at times belligerent crowd. Marina carried June, followed by Marguerite. As Howard later remarked to Pete: "If anyone had a 'Why the hell am I here?' look on his face, it was you at that moment."

The doctors were kind. They advised Marina against viewing Lee's body, which Pete described as being in awful shape. But Marina insisted. Indeed, Lee looked terrible—yellow and unshaven, his face bruised. Marina opened his eyelids and saw moisture accumulating. According to Marguerite's account, Marina said in broken English: "He cry. He eye wet." Marina wanted to look at the wound that killed him. But as she began to pull the sheet from over the wound, the doctor stopped her. Instead, she stooped to kiss Lee's forehead—by then ice cold—as is the Russian custom.

From Parkland, the Secret Service took Marina, Marguerite, Pete, and Robert to a new hideaway: The Inn at Six Flags, halfway between Dallas and Fort Worth. Orders had come directly from President Johnson himself for the Secret Service to protect Marina and Marguerite. The last thing its agents needed on their record was another murder.

Who knew what kind of nuts were out there? And rumors were floating that Marina herself was a Soviet agent—a co-plotter with her husband. The Secret Service needed any clues that Marina could supply of possible collaborators in the killing of the president. Even if uninvolved, Marina would be among the most likely to finger the plotters. The Six Flags Inn was not ideal, but it was the best they could do on short notice. On the back side were woods, and the inn complex fronted on a major highway. Howard's partner, Charles Kunkel, had served on the Arlington police force and could recruit volunteer detectives—one to guard the wooded rear, the other the front side. Both would be heavily armed, instructed to be inconspicuous, and not let anyone through without proper identification. (Mike Howard said that one volunteer came armed with a machine gun.) The Inn itself consisted of bungalows around an oversized swimming pool. This decentralized design made it possible to place the Oswald women in quarters separated from the other guests.

One key piece of evidence troubled Agents Howard and Kunkel. Searches of Lee's belongings at the Paine house and Lee's rooming house yielded a photo of Lee posing in his backyard in black apparel, holding what appeared to be the assassination rifle. If that picture had been taken by someone other than Marina, an organized plot would have become a likely explanation.

Indeed, Marina Oswald was the most important witness to the assassination, but she was going to be a reluctant witness unless there was someone who commanded her confidence, and that person was Pete Gregory, the reluctant translator.

32

A WARY MARINA

The Oswalds and their protectors arrived late afternoon at the Six Fags Inn on Sunday, November 24, after viewing Lee's body at the hospital. Marina, the two children, and Marguerite were assigned a suite with adjoining rooms (423 and 424). The room reservation came directly from the Secret Service to the general manager, James Martin. Robert Oswald and Secret Service agents Mike Howard and Charles Kunkel occupied the two rooms on either side of the Oswald women.

At the end of each day of the ensuing five-day residence at Six Flags, Pete Gregory would drive the forty-five minutes to his home in Fort Worth, exhausted.

The suites of rooms at the Six Flags Inn played host to a confusing blur of activity. Marina and Marguerite took turns taking care of the children. Marina and Robert were questioned in the Secret Service rooms, with Marguerite doing her best to eavesdrop to make sure nothing bad was said about Lee. There were constant comings and goings, with no one person able to take in all that was happening. Pete stuck close to Marina as her translator. As Marguerite later complained: "Mr. Gregory did all the Russian talking."

There were also practical matters to take care of. Marina had two young daughters. Rachel was breastfeeding. As she needed supplies, Marina wrote out shopping lists. Pete translated them into English for Mike Howard, who went to a nearby grocery store. On one such occasion, Mike Howard looked to Pete and asked about one particular request from Marina: beer. Pete queried Marina, whose answer was that it was Russian custom for breastfeeding mothers to drink beer.

Meanwhile, all interrogative attention focused on Marina. The Secret Service agents, Howard and Kunkel, posed questions to Marina, as Pete translated. The agents were particularly interested in Marina's knowledge of her husband's guns and the photo of Lee dressed in black holding what appears to be the rifle recovered from the Texas School Book Depository building.

Marina was understandably frightened. If she had found herself in such circumstances back in Russia, her life or at least her freedom would have been at stake. She would likely lose her children. She feared that the American authorities would send her back to Russia. She remembered that Dallas FBI agents (specifically James Hosty) had threatened her with deportation when they had earlier questioned her about Lee's trip to Mexico. Obviously, if Marina had been part of a conspiracy, she would have faced a long prison sentence or worse. Although Marina did not have legal representation at the time, she would have understood the danger she was in even without legal advice.

Six adults were cooped up in cramped hotel rooms, shuttling back and forth, sick infants crying and needing medical attention. Yet, to Marina, Robert, and the Secret Service, the irascible, unhinged Marguerite proved the greatest source of irritation. She fumed as the agents taped their interviews with Marina (with Pete translating). They questioned Robert but did not bother to interrogate her and "put her on tape," even though she was the mother of Lee Harvey Oswald.

At Six Flags, Marguerite formulated a twisted form of the truth as she saw it. According to her version, Lee had been a secret agent for the government all along. He was innocent and actually a hero. She asserted that someone (FBI Agent Odum) had shown her a picture of Jack Ruby the day before he shot Lee. She also had a photograph that she claimed put Lee and Marina outside the book depository shortly after the president was shot. She had teamed up with activist lawyer Mark Lane. Marguerite claimed that they had received 1,500 tips from outsiders. She claimed to know more about her son than anyone, although she had not seen him for more than a year. She had all the "records," but no one wanted to hear her story.

Howard and Kunkel attempted to limit the watching of TV. Guests looked on with curiosity at the goings-on in rooms 423 and 424, unable to imagine that the family of the presumed killer of the president was staying at the same hotel.

Marina endured the questioning, answering as best she could, heeding Pete's advice that it was best to tell the truth. Although she answered most queries, she did not want to admit that she took the picture of Lee dressed in black. Nor did she want to concede she knew about Lee's attempted shooting of General Edwin Walker on April 10, 1963.

As Marina talked, Marguerite's behavior became more erratic. Robert attempted to calm her down. Pete, trying to render a correct translation of Marina's answers, felt like he was confined in a mad house.

Marguerite's antics drove the sleep-deprived Secret Service agents to the breaking point. Marguerite kept insisting that Lee was innocent and really an agent of the FBI. As television coverage showed Lee's rifle, Marguerite said: "How can they say Lee shot the president? Even though they might prove it is his gun, that doesn't mean he used it. Nobody *saw* him use it." Agent Kunkel had had enough. He said flatly, "Mrs. Oswald, we know that he shot the president."

Marguerite appealed to Mike Howard: "What's wrong with that agent? That agent is about to crack. All he has done is taunt me ever since I have been here." Howard replied: "Mrs. Oswald, he was personal bodyguard to Mrs. Kennedy for thirty months and maybe he has a little opinion against you." Marguerite snapped back: "He should keep his personal opinions to himself."

Marguerite grew increasingly irritated that her daughter-in-law was getting the "red carpet" from the Secret Service. She complained: "My son [Robert], in my presence, was questioned and taped, and Marina was continuously questioned and taped. But I have never been questioned. They were not interested in any papers I have. They were not interested."

Even worse from Marguerite's standpoint, the Secret Service had visited Robert's company to inform his boss that he was helping the government investigation. No one had bothered to do the same for her. The Secret Service favored Marina because she was young and beautiful, she claimed.

On Monday, November 25, the day of Lee's funeral, Mike Howard was fed up with Marguerite's whining. He decided to put her "on tape" and let her have her say, no matter how irrational. As Robert came into the room, frustrated by his inability to find a minister to perform the funeral service scheduled for that day, Marguerite insisted, with reference to her ongoing taped testimony: "I would like Robert to hear this. Maybe he will learn something."

Robert and Agent Howard exchanged meaningful glances as Marguerite babbled on. Robert urged in a whisper that this nonsense be terminated. Howard responded that it would be best to let her "get it out of her system." Howard's thirty-minute-plus taping of Marguerite, supposedly to let her demonstrate Lee's innocence, would later drive a hole in her claim that no one let her talk on record. She would continue to deny that the Six Flags Inn recording of her existed even after it was played in her presence with Chief Justice Earl Warren listening in during her Washington testimony.

For her part, the terrified Marina answered questions, smoked, drank coffee, and tended to her two sick children. Robert was essentially in shock from Lee's death.

Then, Marguerite became even more erratic. She would stand in the middle of the room, announcing that she was making "a statement," as if anyone was in a position to take down what she said. Her first "announcement": "I feel that my son cannot be buried anywhere but Arlington National Cemetery." Shortly thereafter, Marguerite issued another nonsensical statement: "Just remember how, on our last visit in the jail, Lee wanted to buy June a new pair of shoes."

Eavesdropping on Marina's interrogations, Marguerite grew increasingly irritated by her answers that incriminated her "hero" son. She began to berate Marina: she didn't know anything about Lee; his mother knew much more. She claimed that Marina was being compelled to say that Lee was guilty of everything, and Mr. Gregory was in on it. According to Marguerite, Marina had maintained for three days this was not Lee's rifle and that she planned to live with "her Mama" (Marguerite). Marina then "turned against her Mama . . . Marina has been changed to a different personality." Kunkel, Howard, and Mr. Gregory—according to Marguerite—were manipulating Marina to implicate her son.

Although Marina had always tried to have a good relationship with her mother-in-law, as was the Russian custom, she now saw that any life that included Marguerite, with Lee gone, would be impossible. Marguerite kept insisting that Lee was innocent, and she knew that Marina's testimony was incriminating her son. Marina felt that if she told her mother-in-law that she was simply testifying truthfully, Marguerite "would scratch my eyes out."

It was chaos inside the rooms at the Six Flags. Watching Marguerite's antics, Pete better understood why Lee had turned out as he did.

. . .

As Marguerite was sounding off with her "announcements," Robert was frantically trying to finalize arrangements for Lee's funeral, scheduled for that afternoon (Monday, November 25). After a number of rejections, Robert found a helpful funeral director who confirmed that Rose Hill Cemetery on the outskirts of Fort Worth would accept Lee's body. But that still left the problem of finding a minister to officiate. A Reverend French, invited to meet with the family in the Six Flags redoubt the evening before, refused to officiate, despite Robert's and Marguerite's pleas. Robert was a devout Lutheran, who placed great importance on a proper religious burial for his brother. Marguerite berated Reverend French, insisting that the church should be willing to bury a "lost sheep like Lee. . . . The good people don't need to go to church. Instead, it is the murderers that we should be concerned about." After the failure with Pastor French, a Lutheran minister associated with the National Council of Churches promised to be at the cemetery at 4:00 p.m. Monday, the next day.

As Pete drove that Sunday evening to the sanity of his own home, he could not imagine that the days to follow could be any crazier. He was wrong.

33

WHERE IS THE MONEY FOR LITTLE ME?

Monday morning, three days after the assassination, Pete Gregory arrived at the Six Flags Inn to find Marina and Marguerite glued to the television. Agents Howard and Kunkel had requested that they keep the TV off, but when Marina learned that the Kennedy funeral was being broadcast live from Arlington National Cemetery, she demanded that the agents switch on the set. She watched with tears in her eyes as another new widow and her children bade farewell to their husband and father. Marina continued watching until it was nearly time to leave for Lee's own funeral.

The guests in room 423 and 424 watched, with the rest of the nation, the images that became part of our historical memory: the horse-drawn caisson with the casket; John-John Kennedy, at age two, solemnly saluting his father's casket; the disciplined Jacqueline Kennedy, with her stiff upper lip, immaculately dressed in black; the twenty-one-gun salute; the lighting of the "eternal flame" at Arlington National Cemetery.

Marguerite became increasingly frustrated as she waited for her daughter-in-law to prepare herself for the services, but Marina was unhappy with the two dresses the Secret Service had brought over from the Paine house in Arlington. She complained that one was too long, and that the other did not fit well. Marguerite, a self-proclaimed arbiter of fashion, assured Marina she'd look fine. After all, between the church and grave site, she'd be wearing a long coat that would cover the dress. Marguerite's efforts to hurry Marina along paid off: the Oswald women, Robert, Pete, and the Secret Service agents left for the funeral on time. They drove to the Rose Hill Cemetery on the outskirts of Fort Worth. The cemetery grass was barren, a brownish gray in November, interspersed with scattered trees of modest height. Rose Hill seemed a cemetery that cried out "working class," the very label Lee Harvey Oswald had detested all his life. Rose Hill's only other notable inhabitants are a major league baseball player and a former U.S. congressman.

The small group arrived to see a cordon of police stationed along the chain-link fence and surrounded by reporters. It was clear that the Oswalds were not to be admitted to the chapel for a service. Instead, they were told to proceed directly to the graveside. A group of reporters volunteered as pallbearers to carry the casket from the hearse to the grave site, but the Lutheran minister failed to show up as promised. Fortunately, a minister from the Council of Churches in Fort Worth had driven down on his own initiative, and he agreed to officiate.

Lee Harvey Oswald was laid to rest under a simple, flat gravestone labeled "OSWALD," no first name, middle initial, or dates. It was as if his final resting place should fade into obscurity, although his name and deeds most certainly would not. The management of the cemetery was worried that relatives of those buried there would protest having the notorious Oswald next to their departed loved ones.

A photo of the casket being lowered into the ground shows Marina holding June and dressed in a long overcoat that covered her dress, as Marguerite had promised. Robert stands to her left, with Marguerite to *his* left holding Rachel. An unidentified man in glasses (perhaps the minister) is slightly behind Marina. In the background are reporters and Secret Service personnel. Pete does not appear in the photo although he was present. The sober looks on the faces of the family members emphasize the solemnity of the event.

Robert, being the only solvent Oswald, was left holding the bill for the funeral.

• • •

Marina felt humiliated by the furtive and rushed service, although it is unclear what she should have expected. She returned to their Six Flags hideout in a deep depression. Her mood lifted as Pete Gregory translated for her a telegram from a group of college students: "We send you our heartfelt sympathy. We understand your sorrow and share it. We are ashamed that such a thing could happen in our country. We beg you not to think ill of us. You have friends and we are with you."

Letters, packages, and telegrams continued to flood in unsolicited. When Pete arrived at the Six Flags Inn the next day (Tuesday morning), he found Marguerite and Robert going through the deluge of condolences flooding in from all over the world. Some were hateful, but, for the most part, they were sincere expressions of sympathy for the ordeal of the new widow. Many letters contained money—a sign of things to come.

Marguerite complained that few letters were for her, the grieving mother: "All this for Marina and not a single one for me. Doesn't anyone pity poor me?" Particularly disturbing to Marguerite was the fact that checks were made out to Marina. Did people not understand that she herself was a poor widow?

The largesse spontaneously directed toward widow Oswald did not go unnoticed by opportunists, who saw Marina as a possible golden goose. It was left up to the harried Robert to protect Marina's interests from those scenting an easy payout from a naïve widow, and there were many. Robert would fire Marina's "business manager," James Martin, for misusing the considerable contributions that Marina received from sympathizers. Legal battles broke out among the Dallas Russians as to who should represent Marina's business interests. Even George Bouhe got involved in this internecine struggle. Various "representatives" negotiated with publishers for Marina's life story. Despite all this, Marina was able to retain enough money to buy her own house and to live the American life that Lee had promised her back in Minsk.

34

THE FBI AND SECRET SERVICE CLASH

When they parted Monday night, November 25, Agent Howard warned Pete Gregory that he would, in all probability, be approached the next day by the Federal Bureau of Investigation for an interview. It was a worrying proposition. The Secret Service had sworn Pete to silence about the events he had witnessed in the past two days. He was particularly concerned about being asked where the Oswald women were being isolated—a fact that he had pledged not to disclose to anyone. Howard advised Pete that, if the question came up, he should refer the FBI to the Dallas regional office of the Secret Service.

Pete had translated for Marina virtually nonstop as Howard and Kunkel walked her through the weeks leading up to Lee's last visit the night before the assassination, and his departure for work on November 22 carrying a bulky package. Marina's testimony clearly led to the conclusion that Lee had fired the shots at Kennedy. Marina supplied no evidence pointing to a conspiracy—because she had none. Like everyone who knew him, she described her husband as a loner with no one with whom to conspire. That he was also stubborn, hotheaded, and sometimes violent (like his mother) made him even a less appealing participant in a conspiracy.

Pete was not a professional translator. Understanding that questions could be raised about the accuracy of his translations, the Secret Service flew the tapes daily to Washington to be checked by professionals. Their verdict: Pete's translations were "faultless without deviation."

Despite the enthusiastic endorsement from Washington, some conspiracy theorists claimed that Pete deliberately mistranslated Marina's description of Lee's rifle as "dark" (*tyomny* in Russian). They claimed that the metallic stock of the rifle was not "dark." Hence the rifle in Oswald's hand in his picture could not have been the assassination weapon. On this point, they had the backing of Marguerite who claimed that Marina had been browbeaten into saying it was Lee's rifle. Personally, I would not build a theory on one spoken word, especially as Marina testified that she had not examined the rifle, only its butt. Moreover, it did not help to have Marguerite on your side.

■ ■ ■

Indeed, as warned by Howard, two FBI agents arrived at Pete's office on Tuesday morning (November 26) to interview him about the events of the past few days. Pete told them what he could, including the fact that he was present when Marina Oswald was questioned. When asked where the Secret Service was holding Marina, Pete gave them the number of the Dallas Secret Service office and offered the use of his phone.

From what Pete garnered, the call was not completely friendly. The FBI agents thanked Pete for his cooperation and left. The Secret Service appeared to be way ahead of its rival and seemed to relish the FBI's discomfort.

As Pete understood, the two agencies would agree that the FBI interview Marina Oswald later that day. They would do so without Pete's participation. A Russian-speaking Secret Service agent, Leo Gopadze, had flown in the night before and was supposed to take over from Pete. Gopadze himself was not enthusiastic about his assignment. It had been a while since he had used his Russian.

The friction between the Secret Service and the FBI was fed by the Secret Service's conviction that the FBI had overlooked a potential assassin in their lack of surveillance of Lee Harvey Oswald. The FBI had concluded that any danger to JFK would come from the right-wing fringe for which Dallas was noted. Indeed, in the first minutes after the assassination, the FBI was already scouring its files for local right-wing extremists. J. Edgar Hoover's operatives were as shocked as anyone when an avowed communist, Lee Harvey Oswald, was led into the Dallas police headquarters.

Incredible as it may seem in such a crisis, one agency of the federal government (the Secret Service) was stiff-arming the nation's number-one law enforcement agency (the FBI). The Kennedy assassination shows that even in the worst of tragedies, agencies do not forget their rivalries. In the case of the Kennedy assassination, the bitterness between the FBI and the Secret Service was readily evident, even to bystanders like Pete Gregory.

• • •

The November 26 meeting between Marina and James Hosty of the Dallas FBI (Leo Gopadze translator) did not portend well for future questioning.

From earlier experiences, Marina mistrusted the FBI, identified by Lee as America's "KGB organization" that had threatened her and her children. She, of course, immediately recognized Hosty for his threats made at Ruth Paine's house. The Secret Service, on the other hand, had rescued her from the Executive Inn, treated her kindly, seemed to want to help her, and recruited the familiar face of Pete Gregory to translate for her. Marina harkened all the way back to the FBI's rude disruption of the dinner she had prepared for Lee back on Mercedes Street in Fort

Worth in August of 1962. Even with her limited language skills, Marina distinguished between friend—the Secret Service—and foe, the FBI.

In fact, when two FBI agents, one being James Hosty (the other a T. Brown), arrived Tuesday afternoon at the Six Flags Inn to interrogate Marina, they were accosted by the private detective Kunkel had arranged to patrol the wooded side of the grounds. Armed with a rapid-fire rifle, the detective prepared to shoot as they advanced yelling out "FBI, FBI." Mike Howard interceded before the hostilities escalated and admitted Hosty and his fellow FBI agent to the makeshift compound.

Once inside, they found Marina to be an uncooperative witness.

■ ■ ■

It was agreed that Secret Service Agent Gopadze would accompany the FBI agents to their first interview with Marina. As prearranged, Gopadze was not to identify his affiliation. Marina assumed that Gopadze's silence on this issue meant he was FBI. She took an immediate dislike to him and clammed up. She complained that she was worn out from the interminable interrogations. She recognized Hosty as her tormentor at Ruth Paine's house. Marina accused the FBI of causing employers to fire Lee.

Gopadze could see that Marina, who had confidence in Pete, was upset that a new unknown translator was to occupy Pete's place. To make matters worse, Marina worried that Gopadze's rusty Russian could mean trouble for her if he mistranslated. Whereas Pete translated for Marina in a low-key fatherly way, Gopadze was a by-the-book interrogator whose approach frightened Marina.

Shortly after Pete persuaded Marina to proceed with Gopadze, he departed, thinking Marina would cooperate. He was wrong. The FBI interrogation of Marina ended abruptly. She declared she would answer no more questions and declared the interview over.

The following morning, November 28—Thanksgiving—Pete was surprised to find a frustrated Gopadze waiting for him in his Fort Worth office. Gopadze explained that Marina did not want to talk to him: "She is frightened of me. She thinks I am a Jew." Pete asked about Gopadze's ethnicity, which he learned was Georgian. His swarthy appearance, typical of Georgians, somehow convinced Marina that he was Jewish. Further, Gopadze said, he had not spoken Russian for a long time, and his translating skills were rusty, to say the least.

What probably lay behind Marina's concerns was that she thought Gopadze was from the FBI, not the Secret Service. His translating for two men who were indeed from the FBI the day before was doubtless enough to cement Marina's suspicions.

Pressed again into service, Pete agreed with Gopadze to leave immediately in separate cars to meet up with Marina at the Six Flags Inn. Their plan was to smooth the transition from Pete to Gopadze. When Marina saw them both together, she made clear to Pete her antipathy to this stranger. She pointed to his poor Russian; she feared again that he might mistranslate and get her into trouble with something she did not say.

I suspect that Marina used Gopadze's presumed Jewishness as one of many excuses not to talk with the FBI. In fact, one of her first suitors in Minsk was Jewish. Marina was looking for any and all reasons to avoid interrogation by FBI Agent James Hosty, whom she feared and detested.

Pete tried to put Marina at ease. He told her that Gopadze was Georgian, not Jewish, and asked him in to confirm this fact. Pete asked how the Secret Service was treating her now. Did she have any other complaints or problems? He then encouraged Gopadze to talk a little about himself—especially about his growing up in Soviet Georgia. Through this gentle approach, Pete acquainted the two. Gopadze, Pete emphasized, certainly meant her no harm. And if he mistranslated, that would be picked up by experts checking the tapes in Washington. In addition, Pete pointedly reminded Marina that he himself had been working with her on a volunteer basis, and he had to get back to making a living. He could not be at her side forever. Moreover, the whole Gregory family was assembling later that day for Thanksgiving dinner. Marina and the girls had their own plans.

Satisfied that he had smoothed things over, Pete prepared to leave, only to be called back into the fray. Marina, who had so far cooperated, was refusing to answer the FBI's most urgent question: Did Marina Oswald take the photograph of Lee holding a "Fair Play for Cuba" poster in one hand and the assassination rifle in the other, the pistol used to gun down Officer Tippit hanging at his waist. The FBI agents wanted to hear for themselves who took the picture and when.

Marina refused to answer the question. Pete called Marina aside. Trying to apply logic and looking at the matter from Marina's point of view, he explained that simply taking a picture of Lee in his bizarre getup did not make her an accomplice. If all she did was to take the picture at his insistence, she should not worry about answering the question. Marina decided to answer: yes, she had taken the photograph, but it was made under duress from Lee. In fact, she ridiculed him at the time for wanting to have such a strange picture taken.

Marina confessed that she had taken two photographs in the back-yard of their Dallas Neely Street address. Lee had to instruct Marina how to take the picture with a camera he had purchased. At last, Marina had made the key confession: the photograph was not taken by a co-conspirator. Marina had done so to humor her erratic husband. She made this confession only after Pete and Gopadze assured her she could not be prosecuted for such an action.

. . .

As Gopadze's Russian came back to him and Marina's comfort level rose, Pete no longer had to serve as Marina's translator (though the Warren Commission did use Pete as a translator for Marina in some of its formal hearings). This did not mean that Pete was free of the craziness in the Oswald Six Flags suite. Marguerite was not going to allow the Secret Service and her own family to move her from the spotlight where she was convinced she belonged.

. . .

Some conspiracy theorists see in Pete's role as translator a White Russian plot to insure that "communist" Lee Oswald was identified as the lone gunman. The plot had Pete Gregory, assisted by other rabid local White Russians, worming his way into the critical position so he could alter what Marina actually said. Pete stands accused of deliberately mistranslating Marina and purportedly threatening Marina and her children with deportation.

Indeed, under normal circumstances, the Secret Service or FBI would have used an agency translator, but these were not normal circumstances. The Secret Service had to determine urgently whether there was an organized conspiracy that could threaten the U.S. government as a whole. The Secret Service needed a readily available translator for Marina, and better if it were someone she could trust.

The November 23, 7:00 a.m. phone call from Marguerite already placed Pete Gregory on the Secret Service investigation team. Agent Howard could see that Pete had the confidence of Marina, and, if anyone knew something about an organized plot, it would be she. The difficult switch of Gopadze for Pete showed that precious time was required for Marina to gain faith in a translator. As the sleep-deprived Howard and Kunkel would attest, time was one commodity they lacked.

The Warren Commission made sure that tapes of Pete's translations were checked in Washington and certified as accurate. The accuracy of Pete's translations would have come as no surprise. He was a recognized translator of Soviet scientific literature on geology. He had been tapped to accompany President Eisenhower to Moscow for the summit that was canceled after Francis Gary Powers, piloting a CIA U-2 spy plane, was shot down over Russia and captured on May 1, 1960, causing a rift in USSR–U.S. relations. If the government was looking for one of the nation's best Russian interpreters, it would have been Pete Gregory, and he happened to know the widow of the assassin and lived less than an hour away from Marina's hiding place.

Somehow the presumed White Russian cabal had been activated well before November 22, 1963. I apparently was an integral part of this conspiracy as a supposed native speaker using language lessons as a pretext for my so-called forty-eight visits to the Oswald household. What conspiratorial work I did within the Oswald household is not elaborated. The conspiracy theorists also cite the leader of the Dallas Russians (George Bouhe) who testified (incorrectly) that I was giving Marina English lessons. Also, I stand accused of amnesia for inconsistencies between my first and second FBI interrogation. (There was no second FBI interrogation.)

35

MARGUERITE'S BAYONET

Thrust back into the Six Flags circus on Thanksgiving Day, Pete could see that the situation was approaching the boiling point. Marguerite was getting on the Secret Service agents' nerves with her adamant insistence that her son was innocent. She continued to whine that she was being neglected, overlooked, and abused by agents who did not like her. (She got that one right.) She particularly worried that the monetary contributions flowing in were for Marina, not for the deserving mother of the assassin.

Marina, who had tried to maintain a good relationship with her mother-in-law despite Lee's hostility, was also nearing a breaking point. Eavesdropping shamelessly, Marguerite accused Marina of implicating her innocent son in the assassination.

Robert and the Secret Service understood that, for everyone's sanity, they had to separate Marina and the children from Marguerite. They also knew that Marguerite would come down with a vengeance on anyone who attempted to exclude her from the picture.

On the morning of November 27, Agent Mike Howard had approached Robert with a proposal. The manager of the Six Flags Inn, James Martin, a Gregory Peck look-alike, was volunteering to take Marina and her daughters into his Dallas home to live with his wife and three children. On an odd note, Martin made the offer without consulting his wife. Martin vowed that there were no strings attached. He was doing this out of Christian charity. Marina could stay as long as she liked. They would keep her location secret, and she could begin a new life.

The Martins lived in a modest, single-story structure on a shady lot at the corner of Farrar and Sinclair, an area of modest homes nestled amid tree-lined streets. Lochwood Park was only a one-block stroll away for Marina and the children. Cramped quarters aside, Marina was impressed, but she worried whether the Martins would like her (Mrs. Martin, it seems, was understandably unhappy with the guest arrangements). Marina asked Mike Howard whether she was expected to work for the Martins. Martin sent back assurances that Marina could stay as long as she liked and that she and her children would be treated as members of the family.

Although false rumors later floated that a rich woman had provided Marina shelter, the Martins were far from rich. Their house had three bedrooms and two baths to hold the five Martins, the three Oswalds, and accommodate the constant presence of Secret Service security. Such living arrangements would have strained any normal American family, although they would seem quite normal to Marina, who had grown up in cramped Soviet housing.

Robert considered it his responsibility to take Marina and the children into his home in Denton, but its location was already known and would not serve as a suitable refuge. Although Ruth Paine expressed a willingness to have Marina and the children live with her again, Robert ruled this out. Ruth had made a bad impression on him when they had met at the police headquarters in Dallas the afternoon of the assassination. Marguerite began lobbying for Marina to move in with her. She was prepared to take the $833 cash value of her life insurance policy to arrange suitable housing for her, Marina, and her grandchildren. After all, a "foreign girl" like Marina with no mother and father needed to live with a loving mama like herself.

Marina had not met hotel manager James Martin, but Robert pointed out the tall and handsome Martin so that she would know who he was. Robert discussed the matter with Martin himself and again over lunch with Howard and Kunkel. By early afternoon, he had decided that Martin's house was Marina's best option. To break the ice and give Marina a sense of his home, Martin invited Robert, Marina, June, and Rachel, along with two Secret Service agents, to Thanksgiving dinner at his house on 11125 Farrar Street in Dallas. It was understood by all that Marguerite was not to be invited.

When Pete arrived back at the Six Flags Inn, Robert approached him and explained the Martin offer. Robert and Pete took Marina aside and explained it to her. She herself expressed a preference to return to Ruth's place in Irving. Robert could not put his feelings into clear words, but he "didn't think they [the Paines] were the proper or correct people for her to be associated with."

For its part, the Secret Service understood that it could not continue to shuttle Marina and the children from one hiding place to another, a step ahead of the press. Marina needed some stability and Martin seemed the best bet. After some consideration, Marina acceded to Robert's urging and agreed to the Martin plan. For one thing, she realized that it would free her from Marguerite.

Marina was scheduled to move to the Martin home on Friday, November 29. She delayed the move until the next day. During that one-day period, she had an odd reason to keep her distance from Marguerite.

. . .

Pete learned from Marina, well out of Marguerite's hearing, that she considered Marguerite a danger to her and her children. She had gone through Marguerite's suitcase as she was sleeping and discovered, of all things, a bayonet. In the middle of the night, Marina knocked on Mike Howard's door and whispered, "Mama, knife." Together, they slipped into the bedroom and Howard removed the bayonet. Marguerite's concealed weapon was convincing evidence that she had to be isolated from Marina and the children. When Howard confronted Marguerite, she became belligerent. Of course, a helpless woman like herself needed the protection of a weapon, she offered in her defense.

The concealed bayonet could be used, if necessary, to place a restraining order on Marguerite. For the time being, the Secret Service placed her under constant surveillance, and they told Marina that, henceforth, she did not have to see or talk with Marguerite.

Marina and the children were moved into one of the bedrooms. Marguerite was not allowed to enter. The Secret Service ordered the maids to put sheets and blankets on the sofa bed for Marina, who slept alongside the baby beds. Marguerite had the second bedroom to herself. In protest, she spent the night in a chair in the living room. She did not mind, she would say; as a nurse, she was used to going without sleep.

Marguerite sensed that something was up. She confronted Robert, Pete, and the Secret Service, complaining, "Something is wrong with Marina. She won't have anything to do with me." When Robert replied that Marina had been offered a home, the incensed Marguerite demanded to know why Robert had not told her. Robert explained that he had kept quiet because he knew how she would react. Marguerite shot back: "What, do you mean the way I am acting now? I am acting in a normal fashion. You are telling me that you are taking my daughter-in-law and my grandchildren away from me, and I have lost my son, and my grandchildren and daughter are going to live with strangers. This is a normal reaction."

Robert responded: "Well, that is why we didn't tell you. We knew you would take it that way."

To add insult to injury, no one would disclose to Marguerite the location of Marina's new refuge, leaving Marguerite guessing. As Marguerite later declared to the Warren Commission: "In fact, at the time I thought she was going to live in Mr. Gregory's home. I just thought that. I did not ask. I was so hurt. I did not ask."

Marguerite turned the blame on the Secret Service agents whom she now despised. Surely, they, not Robert, had arranged all this. Unlike Lee, Robert, she felt, was too easily influenced by others. He would go along with anything the Secret Service told him. She blamed Pete, too: "Now, Mr. Gregory is involved. Mr. Gregory did all the Russian talking. They all knew better but me." Marguerite saw the decision as mean-spirited revenge on her. Howard and Kunkel were "gloating" at her humiliation.

From that point on, Marina Oswald refused to talk with or see her mother-in-law.

Marguerite left Six Flags on November 29. As she departed, she knocked on the door to say goodbye to Marina. Leo Gopadze opened it, saying that Marina was being questioned and could not come to the door. The Secret Service drove the fuming Marguerite back to her apartment in Fort Worth. For her protection, the Secret Service would stand guard over her for the next few weeks. Marguerite Oswald would never again see her daughter-in-law and grandchildren.

36

WIRETAPS AND WINDING DOWN

Americans had less to be thankful for on Thanksgiving Day, 1963. Their young president had been assassinated. The events in Dallas left them with a sense of shock and trauma. Nothing seemed to be as it had been.

The torment of the Oswald family was not over. The day after Thanksgiving, Robert Oswald had to deal with another bit of unpleasantness. The funeral home complained that families whose loved ones were buried in Rose Hill objected to a presidential assassin being interred next to their departed, much less the crowds of thrill seekers wanting to see the Oswald grave. Robert ignored their requests that he find another burial place. As time passed, fewer visitors came and the pressure from Rose Hill families diminished.

In a strange twist, Lee's body would be exhumed in October 1981 at the behest of a conspiracy theorist, convinced the body buried was that of a Soviet look-alike substituted for the real Oswald. Marina agreed after consulting with Mike Howard, who advised her to take the fool's money. Marina already knew the answer: a wife could detect a double for her real husband. Indeed, dental records and a full-scale autopsy proved the body was that of Lee Harvey Oswald—who was then reinterred at Rose Hill. Marina watched the proceedings with Mike Howard, the last time they would meet. Lee had been buried wearing his golden wedding ring. It was retrieved at Marina's request. The ring was sold at auction in 2013 for more than $100,000.

• • •

As Marina and her children took up residence in the Martin household, their host's charitable intentions came under question. As contributions to Marina continued to pour in, James Martin drew up a contract appointing him as Marina's business manager for a ten-year period. The contract was signed by both Robert and Marina. Martin would later testify that he had to quit his job at the Six Flags Inn to take care of media and film offers. Marina, he claimed, earned a considerable amount from his efforts, and he was dismayed when Robert and Marina canceled his business-manager contract, and Robert moved Marina out of his house.

Financial dealings aside, Mrs. Martin grew increasingly disenchanted with her house guests, especially when rumors began to circulate that Marina and Martin were having an affair. In his own testimony before the Warren Commission, Martin complained that the "lazy" Marina was less than an ideal house guest and that the "real Marina" was far from the image of the grieving widow that he, as her business manager, had carefully cultivated.

James Martin's remarks underscore some sad facts of life. As the widow of Lee Harvey Oswald, Marina was deluged with lucrative offers from media vultures to cash in on her misfortune. It is no wonder that she eventually settled on a life of seclusion.

• • •

Unknown to Marina and Robert, the FBI decided to wiretap them as they tried to resume a normal life. Marina had moved from the Martins into her own home, purchased from contributions, sales of Lee Harvey Oswald memorabilia, and the earnings from other deals, arranged by Marina's "business manager." The FBI hoped to capture candid conversations involving Marina and possible Oswald conspirators. They were duty bound to check out every possibility.

To the FBI's disappointment, the wiretaps picked up mostly routine exchanges, but they did pick up Marina's sexual encounters with Martin during her stay in the Martin household. Among the collection of wiretaps was a tape of their night together at the exclusive Willard Hotel on the eve of testimony before the Warren Commission. FBI agents eavesdropped from the adjoining room. The incensed Robert interpreted Marina's liaison with Martin as coerced, but the FBI agents did not intercede. The matter calmed down when Marina revealed the encounter was consensual. FBI wiretaps also captured a gossip session between Marina and Ruth Paine in which Marina recounted an erotic dream about Martin and volunteered that Lee was "not a real man."

Rumors of Marina's sexual adventures circulated within the local Russian community, which brought forth a warning from the prim George Bouhe. Marina should behave. Bouhe would not visit Marina alone, which would be improper. Martin, meanwhile, told his wife to look the other way because he was earning good money from Marina.

After Robert terminated Martin's contract, Martin threatened to go to Chief Justice Warren with the story of their affair. Warren waived him off; such untoward matters were not relevant to the assassination inquiry.

With Martin out of the way, arguments broke out within the Russian community as to who would represent the cash-cow Marina. Threats of lawsuits followed, and collapse threatened the formerly tight Russian community.

37

DEFENDING "THE BOY"

I t is not possible to understand Lee Harvey Oswald without delving into his mother. Those privy to Marguerite Oswald's testimony on February 10 and 12 of 1964 could have concluded they were seeing a reincarnated older version of Lee Harvey Oswald. A high-school dropout scraping by with assorted odd jobs, in her mind, Marguerite Oswald had spent her life taking on the powers that be that had held her and her talented son down.

The parallels between the biographies of Lee and Marguerite Oswald are striking. They both were convinced they had been dealt a bad hand in the cards of life. Both exhibited a tenuous relationship with reality. Both were underdogs, through no fault of their own. Both craved the limelight, which Marguerite refused to share with others. Both had a loose relationship with the truth. When caught in a lie, Marguerite dug in her heels and insisted she had told the truth. Her life had been a series of slights and mistreatments by those positioned above her.

. . .

Marguerite Oswald left the Six Flags Inn on Monday, November 25 with a chip on her shoulder. She was the grieving mother of Lee Harvey Oswald. Marina, the grieving widow, really knew nothing of the "boy." Yet all eyes were on Marina, who, under James Martin's tutelage, was being transformed from a frumpy scarecrow into a chic model. As deals were monetized, Marguerite felt she, herself a destitute widow, was lagging behind Marina in the spoils. (She estimated Marina's earnings at $38,000.) Marguerite relished speaking engagements and was always game for interviews. Once the word was out that she was unhinged, invitations became rare. She could, however, look forward to her testimony before the Warren Commission on February 10 and 12, 1964, with the Supreme Court chief justice, Earl Warren, himself presiding to hear Marguerite's account of "the boy's" life.

Warren's staff would have alerted him to the bizarre testimony to expect from the dowdy, bespectacled fifty-seven-year-old nurse. Marguerite had begun to formulate her story of "the boy" within hours of the assassination.

In her first encounter with the FBI at the Dallas police headquarters just hours after the shooting, she told them: "For the security of my country, I want this kept perfectly quiet until you investigate. I happen to know that the State Department furnished the money for my son to return back to the United States, and I don't know if that would be made public what that would involve, and so, please, will you investigate this and keep this quiet?"

Within twenty-four hours, Marguerite had further refined her narrative. Her "boy" had transformed into "a hero," a secret agent for the United States. He loved his country, as did his mother. He deserved to be buried in Arlington National Cemetery.

Marguerite claimed to anyone who would listen that she possessed "all the records" to prove "the boy's" innocence. A government conspiracy had prevented her from telling her story. Already at Six Flags, Secret

Service agents Howard and Kunkel refused to "put her on tape," other than for five to ten minutes. As she testified later before the Warren Commission: "I will state now emphatically that I have never been questioned by the FBI or the Secret Service. Never, gentlemen. If they have more, they should produce my voice."

Chief Justice Warren had been alerted that Marguerite had procedural demands to be clarified before she "told her story." Her first demand was addressed directly to Chief Justice Warren, presiding: "I implore you, in the name of justice, to let my son Lee Harvey Oswald, who is accused of assassinating the president, and I, the mother of this man, who is the accused's mother, be represented by counsel. We have information pertinent to this case. . . . And I think that my son should be considered in this. He is dead. But we can show cause that my son is not the assassin of President Kennedy. And so I would like my son [to be represented]—he is the main object of the Presidential Commission, is he not, sir?"

Marguerite already had a lawyer, and she had picked out Lee's advocate in advance—Mark Lane, a New York lawyer, among the first to dispute the Warren Commission's lone gunman finding. Lane believed that JFK was killed by a CIA plot.

Chief Justice Warren emphatically shot down Marguerite's first request: "The commission is not here to prosecute your dead son. It is not here and it was not established to prosecute anyone. It is the purpose and the provenance of the commission to obtain all the facts that it can obtain, and then make an impartial report—not as a prosecutor, but as an impartial commission—on the manner in which the president came to his death."

Marguerite was not buying what Justice Warren was selling: "We do not know the questions that you are asking of myself or Marina or the other witnesses. And I contend that you cannot ask them the pertinent questions because you don't know what I know, and what Mr. Lane knows."

In effect, Marguerite was demanding that Mark Lane be present to challenge all testimony relating to Lee Harvey Oswald and his presumed role in the assassination.

As Warren continued to refuse Lee's counsel, Marguerite grudgingly conceded that "I will have to accept your verdict, but I don't do it graciously. I want that for record."

Marguerite and Justice Warren then turned to her heralded "documents" that she claimed would answer all questions of the assassination. In her back-and-forth with the chief justice, Marguerite plays the innocent and destitute victim, even claiming that the Secret Service had stolen some of her precious documents. She states to Warren: "And so the documents stay with me. I make the statement perfectly plain. And so the documents stay with me." Any documents photocopied must be done in her presence, Marguerite demanded. Marguerite clearly had money on her mind with respect to her papers: "I need to protect myself financially, because I am a widow, and do not have the money."

Marguerite's most bizarre request came next; namely, she be granted subpoena power: "When I tell my story, I will be including people in my story that possibly you don't know of. I request that I have the privilege, through you, of course, to subpoena these people that are in connection with the story that I tell."

Marguerite, it seems, had her sights on Marina, whose testimony implicated "the boy." Per Marguerite: "I also request that after my testimony, that Marina Oswald will be subpoenaed—not subpoenaed but will then testify again, if you see fit. And I believe that I have contrary testimony to her testimony that would make it necessary for her to be recalled."

The chief justice quashed Marguerite's demand for subpoena power with dispatch: "Well, Mrs. Oswald, of course you have no power of subpoena, and we have no power to give you the power of subpoena. But you may be sure that if your evidence produces anything that is critical to this investigation, that we will pursue it to the end."

Marguerite was still not ready to give in on subpoena power for herself. Marguerite to Justice Warren: "You will give me the assurance that these people I name, regardless of title—I am liable to name some very important people—"

Warren (interrupting): "No, we cannot give you any assurance, because we don't know—"

Marguerite interrupting defiantly: "I see no reason, then, for my testimony."

Justice Warren explained the trap that Marguerite was setting as he declared to the assembly: "But the only thing—I would not want Mrs. Oswald to leave here and say, 'I gave the commission a list of witnesses and they did not call all of them.'"

. . .

As the commission turned to its afternoon session, Marguerite was far from exhausting her litany of complaints. Now her villains were the two Secret Service agents, Howard and Kunkel, tasked by LBJ to protect the Oswald family. Their original sin, according to Marguerite, was their deference to Marina and Robert at the Six Flags Inn. The agents, in Marguerite's mind, were wasting their time on Marina and Robert, who knew nothing. She, on the other hand, had all the records—documents that somehow would exonerate "the boy."

By the time Marguerite testified before the Warren Commission more than ten weeks after Six Flags, she had come to the conclusion that Howard and Kunkel were out to murder her. Why? In her mind, the Secret Service had to suppress the fact that Lee was an American secret agent and innocent of killing the president. When Mike Howard knocked on her door in Fort Worth to announce her protective detail, she called the local newspaper to be on the alert if she disappeared. Similarly, Marguerite enlisted another newsman to ride to the airport with her and Howard as protection against an assassination.

Although the chief justice and general counsel remained polite, I imagine they wondered why they were wasting time on this woman who appeared to live in her own fantasy world.

Marguerite continued her testimony on February 12, running through an exhausting account of her marriages, sons, divorces, and her battles with adversity as a single mother, whose combative nature made it difficult to hold jobs. Her account of Lee growing up trailing behind a vagabond mother follows her script—a heroic mother fighting for her rights and those of her son against the obstacles that society places in her way. In her testimony, she brushes off Lee's chronic truancies and incidents of violence. In the Bronx, living with the family of Lee's half-brother, John Pic, Lee threatened his sister-in-law with a knife. By Marguerite's account, no big deal. Lee only pulled out a small pocketknife. They did not deserve to be thrown out of the house by Pic's "hysterical" wife. Lee was portrayed as a loving son, who bought his mother a $35 coat with his first Marine paycheck. She notes that he also paid his room and board—to her.

Still to be addressed by the commission was Marguerite's complaint that no one had bothered to interrogate her—most specifically Howard and Kunkel at Six Flags—although she claimed that she alone had the key information on Lee's innocence.

Marguerite's claim was patently false. Pete Gregory and Robert Oswald had witnessed Agent Howard "putting Marguerite on tape." The tape recording and its transcript, labeled "November 25, 1963, an interview by J. M. Howard," was introduced as a thirty-eight-page transcribed exhibit while the general counsel played the actual tape—which Marguerite claimed did not exist—for an attentive audience. As the tape played, it became apparent that these were Marguerite's and Howard's voices. In the background, crying infants (June and Rachel) could be heard:

JUSTICE WARREN: And that is your voice?

MARGUERITE: That is my voice.

JUSTICE WARREN: Yes.

MARGUERITE: But I am not going to vary from my story.

Indeed, Marguerite stubbornly continued to challenge the existence of the taped interview with Howard: "I have stated previously, if I was taped it was during a conversation going on that they taped me. I have never sat down and been taped, sir. I don't think I am out of my mind."

The chief justice was incredulous: "It would hardly seem possible, Mrs. Oswald, that unless this is a complete fabrication that anyone could have given these answers but you . . . so many of these questions and answers are exactly what you have told us."

When challenged to explain her obvious lie, Marguerite maintained that someone had doctored the tapes and substituted recorded voices and sounds of infants. She then went back to her litany of complaints about Mike Howard. He was the one on the tape; so he could have manipulated it. Exasperated, General Counsel Rankin put an end to the clown show: "She does identify the voices as being hers and all we have is her word, and this tape, and the transcription at the present time. So, for the moment, I suppose we will just have to leave it where it is. I don't see any other answer to it."

• • •

The Warren Commission did not devote a specific section of Marguerite's testimony to her "proof" that Lee Harvey Oswald was indeed a secret agent somehow caught in a dark plot against the president. Her "proof" trickled out in the form of episodes and anecdotes in her rambling statement: That the State Department "paid" for Lee's return proved he was a secret agent (Marguerite failed to mention that this was a loan Lee repaid). Lee always walked ahead of his wife—according to Marguerite a typical practice of secret agents to protect their wives. The flood of contributions to Officer Tippit's widow, Marguerite contended, proved that this money had been prepared in advance. Marguerite claimed to have a picture of Lee at the book depository purportedly after the shots were fired. When marked as an exhibit, no one could find Oswald in the picture.

Marguerite's claim that she was shown a photo of Jack Ruby before he shot Lee attracted the most attention. Her story runs like this: As she and Marina were confined in the Executive Inn on Saturday (one day after the shooting), an FBI agent, Bardwell Odum, knocked on the door with a photo he wanted Marina to see. Marguerite did not admit him, but she was briefly shown the photo of a man she did not recognize. Later, at the Six Flags Inn, she saw a newspaper picture of Ruby. She claimed that this was the same person she had seen in the Executive Inn photo.

In a sworn affidavit, Agent Odum testified that the photograph (attached to the affidavit) was of an unidentified man—not Jack Ruby. (Recent releases by the CIA explain the photo was an unidentified man, clearly not Jack Ruby, entering the Soviet Embassy in Mexico City.)

. . .

Marguerite Oswald's testimony before the Warren Commission discredited her claim to have proof that her son was innocent. Her testimony instead established that she was on the borderline of mental incapacity. We do not know if this was the "normal" Marguerite or whether her behavior was brought on by the trauma of the assassination. Her own description of herself as she ran through her life story—aggressive, combative, self-pitying, and with delusional images of grandeur—appear to be lifelong characteristics.

Despite her gentle handling by the chief justice and general counsel, Marguerite added the Warren Commission to her list of enemies. Consider her closing remarks:

Mrs. OSWALD: I think you are making a very big mistake not pursuing this further because I have told important people about this particular incident and I say it is correct and I hope you will continue while I am gone not just to ignore what I have said.

The CHAIRMAN: Mrs. Oswald, you misjudge the Commission when you say we will not pursue it further.

Mrs. OSWALD: Fine, I don't know, I am asking.

The CHAIRMAN: You may be sure we will pursue it further.

Mrs. OSWALD: Thank you, and I have more people that I could call. I have told Mr. Doyle [her lawyer], the people—Would you like me to name the people on the record for you? Mr. Lane, I called Mr. Lane—

The CHAIRMAN: To what purpose are you naming these people?

The chief justice's question seemed to hit the mark, as Marguerite hemmed and hawed about the "important people" who would back her up.

38

THE GREGORYS' CHRISTMAS

The Gregorys looked forward to Christmas to mark a return to their normal lives. They felt themselves fortunate that their involvement with Lee and Marina Oswald had been largely overlooked by the press. Marina had disappeared into obscurity. Pete had returned to his engineering work and golf. I had returned to my studies, sharing my experience with only a few close friends.

Christmas was supposed to be special. My sister Anita (three years older than I) and her husband, Carter, had been married in August of 1963 and were planning to come for the holiday from St. Louis. With the exception of my older brother, Don, who was working as an engineer in Connecticut, the whole family would be together.

Little did Pete and my mother know that they had not seen the last of Marguerite Oswald.

There was still no escaping news related to the assassination. Older sister Edith and brother-in-law Joe, driving the short distance from Arlington, had to turn off the news that Robert Oswald, brother of the assassin, was rumored to be spending his Christmas Day with Marina. They turned the radio to a music station. Like the rest of us Gregorys, they had had enough.

Marguerite Oswald, meanwhile, continued to harbor her grudges. She telephoned Robert repeatedly, but he wanted nothing to do with her. He refused to tell her where Marina and the children were staying. All he would say was that Marina and the children were doing well.

Marguerite attempted to figure out for herself Marina's whereabouts. It was, she suspected, at the home of that Mr. Gregory who did "all the Russian talking." Marguerite's Secret Service guards had left. Although she still did some interviews and television appearances, in which she asserted Lee's innocence and recounted what a wonderful son he was, Marguerite's limelight was fading, and she was mad about that.

The final insult came when she, too, learned through the Christmas Day radio broadcast that her son Robert and his family were spending Christmas with Marina—and had obviously not invited her. She suspected that this was not the first time that Robert had seen Marina. Even worse, the radio announced that Mrs. Marguerite Oswald was unavailable for news interviews. Marguerite did not welcome that bit of misinformation. She was always ready to talk to the press, but they had realized she had nothing sensible to say.

As Marguerite later complained to the Warren Commission:

"Gentlemen, I stayed home crying, hoping against hope that the Secret Service would come and let me be with my family for Christmas time, waiting there patiently. I was available for news. I had blasted this in the paper over and over. I waited for them to come get me. But there again, I am excluded."

Back at the Gregory house, my sister Anita and brother-in-law Carter set out in late morning to make some social calls. Pete and Joe sat down for a chat. The telephone rang. Pete answered it, expecting a neighbor or relative on the other end of the line. It was Marguerite. Crying, she savagely tore into Pete. It was his fault that she wasn't having a Christmas this year and that she was not going to see her grandchildren. It was *all* his fault. She did not, however, ask the question most on her mind: Were the Gregorys sheltering Marina and her precious grandchildren?

Pete's response was measured: "Mrs. Oswald, I do not want to talk to you, and I would appreciate it if you would leave us alone." He hung up the phone and reported the content of the call to the assembled family. Joe, who took to heart such insults to his family, had to retreat to another room so as not to disturb the festive mood.

PART VI

LONE ASSASSIN?

Although *losers should not change history*, I had no trouble accepting that the Lee Harvey Oswald I knew was up to killing the president. Obscured by dyslexia and little formal schooling, Oswald was indeed a dedicated Marxist (not communist, as he stated), although that fact would not explain his choice of JFK as his target.

Yes, he himself was among Marx's oppressed, and it was his chosen task to tell the world and, remarkably, do something about it.

Oswald's street smarts were plain for all to see, including myself. He outmaneuvered a brittle Soviet officialdom into granting him resident status. He pestered U.S. diplomats into renewing his passport he threw on their desk. He lived off the charity of others, while feigning insult.

We disparage Lee Harvey Oswald as a dreamer, a loser, and a psycho but in his absurd way he did spectacularly succeed in "becoming someone." Here we are, decades later, grubbing for every scrap of information about him, performing our own amateur psychoanalysis.

We cannot unravel the events of November 22, 1963, without unlocking the mystery of Lee Harvey Oswald himself. My portrait of Oswald—his marriage to Marina, and his relationship with Marguerite—aims to solve this mystery.

I am not going to engage in forensic analysis of an extra bullet and shots fired, directives to kill from Castro or Khrushchev, right-wing fanatics, or deep-state cabals.

The Warren Report itself is not expansive as to Oswald's motives, such as resentment toward authority, his obsession to occupy a place in history, his propensity for violence, and his pronounced antagonism toward the United States. Notably, the Warren Report does touch on Oswald's stormy relationship with Marina—her belittling of him as a spouse, breadwinner, sexual partner, and dreamer. As stated in the Warren Report: "The relations between Lee and Marina Oswald are of great importance in any attempt to understand Oswald's possible motivation."

I begin my extraction of conclusions from my Lee Harvey Oswald portrait with the two questions that underlie all conspiracy theories: Did he do it and was he alone?

39

DID OSWALD ACT ALONE?

There's a problem with accepting Oswald as the lone assassin. And it's that we want to believe that things happen for a reason. There must be a hand or hands that guide events. The Warren Commission's lone-assassin verdict rests on a seemingly implausible series of coincidences: our introducing Lee and Marina to the Dallas Russians; a friend of Marina finding Lee a job that would later place him on the motorcade route; Lee being denied a Cuban visa; Lee's rifle shot barely missing General Edwin Walker. We are conditioned to believe that what appear to be random events are actually guided by higher forces.

The Warren Commission's lone-shooter conclusion also confronts us with an uncomfortable asymmetry—or lack of balance, if you will. With Kennedy, would we have had a Vietnam? A Great Society? We do not want to believe that the course of history itself changed because of a loser like Oswald.

We began with the fact that two-thirds of the American public believe that the Kennedy assassination must have been a conspiracy. Big events must have big causes. Conspiracies are more exciting than the fact-filled and plodding Warren Commission report—an exhaustive investigation that few, if any, have read through. Those who attack the commission's findings spin fascinating and sinister tales of rightist or leftist cabals, black helicopters, Cuban assassination squads, and the like. These accounts attract more attention than the hundreds of thousands of words of testimony that conclude the president was killed by a "lone nut."

Understanding the Kennedy assassination and Lee Harvey Oswald's role in it requires answering seven questions:

> Did Oswald shoot President Kennedy from the sixth floor of the Texas School Book Depository?
>
> If so, was he a lone gunman or part of a conspiracy?
>
> Did Oswald have a motive—be it rational or crazy—for killing a major political figure, not necessarily Kennedy?
>
> Did Oswald have the intellectual wherewithal to kill a high-level target?
>
> Did Oswald have means to carry out the assassination?
>
> Did Oswald possess "the soul of a killer"?
>
> Did Oswald have a compelling reason—again, rational or crazy—to pick John F. Kennedy as his target?

On the first question—Did Oswald pull the trigger?—the answer is a resounding yes, disputed by almost no one. Convincing evidence places Oswald at the sixth-floor window of the Texas School Book Depository. Co-workers saw him arrive at work with a package suited to conceal a rifle. Oswald abandoned his rifle behind boxes, fled the scene of the crime, and with his mail-order pistol shot dead the police officer who stopped him for questioning.

Although clever nitpickers may claim otherwise, these facts are firmly established. Those who dispute them should reread the relevant sections of the Warren Report itself or Priscilla McMillan's account in *Marina and Lee* of Lee's symbolic farewell gift of his wedding ring to Marina the night before November 22. He did not intend to return. He was going to Dallas to shoot the president.

The main controversy, addressed in the second question, is not whether Oswald fired at the president. Rather it is whether he planned and executed the killing of the president *alone* or as part of a *conspiracy*. Some two-thirds of Americans come down on the side of the latter.

Like any investigative body, the Warren Commission could not prove a negative; namely, the absence of a conspiracy involving Oswald. Instead, the Warren Commission's summary report lists a string of entities—Cuba, the Soviet government, organized crime, ultra-right groups, anti-Castro elements, the FBI, the Secret Service, the CIA—that it concluded did *not* conspire to kill the president. Notably, the Warren Commission extended their "no conspiracy" finding to Jack Ruby. They could find no evidence that another "loner"—Jack Ruby—also did not act alone. But Ruby is another story.

The conspiracy verdict has been slow to die. Marina Oswald first accepted that her husband killed Kennedy and acted alone. Yet, in her November 22, 1996, interview with Oprah Winfrey, thirty-three years after the assassination, Marina declared that she now thought Lee innocent, a patsy set up by the U.S. government. She provided little concrete evidence. And, still speaking in broken English, she admitted that she had told June and Rachel that their father was guilty. Now she thought differently.

But wait. The House Select Committee on Assassinations, established in 1976 to investigate the Kennedy and Martin Luther King assassinations, reached a sensational conclusion that "on the basis of the evidence available to it, that President John F. Kennedy was *probably assassinated* [my italics] as a result of a *conspiracy*. The committee is unable to identify the other gunman or the extent of the conspiracy."

It turns out that the House committee's sensational conclusion of a second shooter was based on a faulty acoustic analysis of a police motorcycle backfire captured on a police channel Dictabelt recording. Subsequent technical analysis by the FBI and the National Academy of Sciences concluded that "reliable acoustic data do not support a conclusion that there was a second gunman." On the basis of this information, the Justice Department concluded "that no persuasive evidence can be identified to support the theory of a conspiracy in . . . the assassination of President Kennedy."

I first had to confront the conspiracy theory in the course of my interview by the Secret Service the day after the assassination. When asked directly in the car headed to Oklahoma City, I rejected out of hand that Lee Harvey Oswald would have been part of a conspiratorial group. I said (and I remember my words distinctly): "If I were to organize a conspiracy, the last person I would have wanted in it would be Lee Harvey Oswald. He would have been too difficult and too unreliable." That summarized my conviction then and it remains so now.

Virtually all who knew Lee Harvey Oswald used the term "loner" to describe him. To engage in a conspiracy, the conspirators must know one another. They must share a common bond of memberships or philosophy. They must divide into followers and leaders. The leaders must have powers of persuasion and a plan. Lee Harvey Oswald would definitely not be a follower; this would be against every bone in his body. Nor would he be a leader because he would not be able to recruit any followers. In his campaign to recruit for the Fair Play for Cuba committee, Oswald brought in one potential new member—A. J. Hidell, his fictional alias.

Most likely, Oswald would not even want to be part of a gang. He did things on his own, including not joining organizations that shared his political beliefs. True, he did subscribe to radical periodicals, but he belonged to no communist or Marxist cells. He did have a membership card in Fair Play for Cuba, but he joined to enhance his credentials for a Cuban visa.

The Warren Commission identified and interviewed hundreds of individuals who crossed paths with Lee and Marina Oswald. The dragnet extended down to casual neighbors or even to persons who shared a bus ride with Oswald to Mexico City. In no case could Warren Commission investigators identify a person or persons who showed any sign of conspiring with Oswald.

Vincent Bugliosi, in his *Reclaiming History*, assigned a zero probability that participants in a successful conspiracy to kill the president would keep their mouths shut for over fifty years, despite the fact that uncovering the plot is the Holy Grail for conspiracy theorists. To demonstrate his point, Bugliosi points out that this complex conspiracy would have had to be hatched in four short days. The motorcade route was set only on November 18. On September 18, when it was announced that the president would visit Dallas, Lee Harvey Oswald was on his way to Mexico City focused on getting a visa for Cuba, where he and Marina would live.

More than a half century has passed since the assassination. We have a former U.S. intelligence director, elderly Cuban intelligence officers, an errant former KGB agent or two, CIA officers (including members of Richard Nixon's "plumbers" team), and Mafia bosses elaborating on a conspiracy. Yet none of the conspiracy enthusiasts have been able to explain how the conspiracy worked. No one can explain where, when, and by whom it was hatched. Where were Oswald's co-conspirators when the shots were fired? Did they intend for Oswald to be caught? If so, how were they to ensure that he would not implicate them during his first interrogation? If Jack Ruby's job was to prevent Oswald from "singing," he did not kill Oswald for two days, during which time his interrogators could have uncovered the conspiracy.

. . .

I do not rule out two types of quasi conspiracies. Lee Harvey Oswald could have decided on his own to act in what *he considered* the interests of a communist regime, such as Cuba. He might have harbored an undisclosed thirst to avenge the Bay of Pigs or the purported CIA/ Mafia attempts to poison Fidel Castro. But Oswald would have assigned *himself* the task of wreaking vengeance on those responsible. We have no evidence of Oswald's animus toward our thirty-fifth president. In fact, the few signs we have point to a favorable attitude toward JFK.

The other possibility is that, say, an official in Mexico City's Cuban Embassy could have told Oswald that they appreciate his work on their behalf in New Orleans and that the world would be better off without John F. Kennedy. They would have supplied no resources, no plans. They simply would set Oswald loose in the hostile waters of America like a drifting mine that could conceivably strike its target, but most likely would not. From what we know about Oswald's visit to the Mexico City Cuban Embassy, the meeting ended in verbal fisticuffs with the Cuba counsel. Not a promising start of a plot to kill the U.S. president.

Oswald's three years behind the Iron Curtain would have offered the Soviet KGB an opportunity to train an Oswald-Manchurian candidate. The opening of formerly secret archives in Minsk and Moscow revealed that Oswald's KGB handlers concluded, after extensive surveillance, that Oswald was "uninteresting." The feeling was: let this odd guy have fun chasing girls. The "uninteresting" label was also confirmed by one of the highest KGB defectors (Yuri Nosenko, who was held for three years in detention before his testimony was accepted). The KGB consensus held that Oswald was trouble, best isolated far from Moscow where he could cause little grief.

As someone who has worked intensively with such documents, the Oswald KGB file is genuine, and they show that "uninteresting" Lee Harvey Oswald was regarded as being in need of psychiatric evaluation. He did not have the makings of a James Bond counter spy.

The Oswald files were classified as top secret. Remember, the Soviet leaders expected their system to last, and their secrets to be maintained. By the end of the Yeltsin government, there would have been little incentive to forge exculpatory documents for a regime that no longer existed.

40

OSWALD'S MOTIVE

Let's consider our third question: Lee Harvey Oswald's ideological and personal motives to shoot the president of the United States.

. . .

Oswald was a real Marxist, not a poseur dabbling in radical chic. He was never to be satisfied—disappointed with both the Soviet version of Marxism and the capitalism that preyed on the downtrodden like himself.

Marxist ideology is an unlikely motive for Oswald to kill a U.S. president.

Marx believed in the inevitability of socialist revolution pitting the working class against the bourgeoisie. Marx himself was not an advocate of political assassination. Deep underlying forces would birth the socialist revolution, not organized assassinations. As a Marxist, Oswald would have felt the same way.

Oswald's attempt on the life of General Walker was another matter. His disappointment at missing the "fascist" General Walker confirms that he did indeed have the "soul of a killer." He was capable of killing a public figure so opposed to his beliefs. I imagine Oswald would have joined a crowd of leftists who would welcome Walker's demise. Oswald told the unconvinced Marina that killing Walker would be akin to assassinating Hitler. *Just think how many lives could have been saved. Killing Walker would be a good thing to do.*

Killing JFK was an entirely different matter. In the era of peaceful coexistence, it is hard to make the case that Oswald saw in the youthful Kennedy a class enemy of such danger that he needed to be eliminated.

Oswald did not kill Kennedy out of ideological motives. We must look to the personal—to his life story of underestimation, slights, and degradations by society at large and his wife in particular. From his unstable mother, he learned that he was oppressed and that he had to personally correct the wrong.

I met Lee and Marina as they returned to one of his many "hometowns," Fort Worth, Texas, in June of 1962. Lee's troubled biography shows him to have been an introverted bookworm and mediocre student. As a seventeen-year-old Marine, he was mercilessly teased as "OzzieBugs." His tortured spelling and punctuation stemmed from dyslexia, supplemented by laziness and/or rebellion.

Deep in his heart, Lee was convinced that he was brighter, had bigger ideas, and was meant for better things. His mother, Marguerite, agreed with her youngest son's self-assessment. He was meant for greatness, unlike Lee's brother Robert, who let himself be pushed around.

Starting at age fifteen, Lee Harvey Oswald sought to demonstrate exceptionality through his professed communist or Marxist (as he preferred to say) convictions. What better way, at least in his mind, for the student in the back row to stand out?

Desertion to the citadel of Marxism, the Soviet Union, was a logical step. Lee's pledge to fight on behalf of the Soviet worker state earned him an unfavorable discharge, but it freed him to pursue a new life in a worker's paradise that would recognize his talents and genius.

Then, what disappointment! In Moscow, he encountered the same sorts of dull bureaucrats. Instead of a hero's welcome, only his suicide attempt prevented them from sending him back home. He was put out to pasture in backwater Minsk, Belorussia, where he found himself working as a mechanic on the factory floor. The double salary and his own apartment were insufficient compensation for the indignities he was suffering.

Although Lee did not realize it then, his time in Minsk was the best in his short life. He made friends (some of them sent his way by the KGB). He was invited to parties, picnics, and holiday celebrations. He married a beautiful Russian girl, and they had a child together.

Still, he felt Russia was a dead end for him. If he were to accomplish great things, it must be in America, after all. Nothing better symbolizes Oswald's disappointment on his arrival at Dallas's Love Field as his unsuccessful search for a swarm of reporters. He had left his native country as a nonentity and returned as one.

When at this point I came into Lee and Marina's life, I witnessed firsthand this small man's attempt to prove to the world and to his young wife that he was indeed exceptional. In some sense, Oswald was already a tinderbox waiting to be engulfed in flames.

Back in Texas, Lee fostered the persona of a Marxist intellectual—a notable person who would one day change the world. Lee felt that he had two trump cards. First, he was fluent in Russian. Second, the publishing world would fight over his *Historic Diary*. These two assets would buy his way out of the factory floor. This wasn't happening. He had to camp out at his brother's house and even tolerate living with his despised mother as she drove him around looking for a job. Again, a nine-to-five dead end, manning a welding torch for miserly pay.

In returning to Texas, Oswald had reversed positions with Marina. The small Russian émigré community wanted to meet, befriend, and help his wife. He was an unwanted and unpleasant appendage. He had to keep Marina isolated. If not, she would understand he was an insignificant poseur striving for recognition in a world that was wholly indifferent and stacked against him.

Indeed, our invitation to meet the Dallas Russians, under the patronage of George Bouhe, opened a Pandora's box of visits, English lessons, material assistance, and conversations with Russian women older and wiser than Marina. Lee again found himself at a dead end. It was time either to do something of consequence or move on, in this case to Castro's Cuba.

• • •

I believe that despite the lack of signs of affection and despite the awful spousal abuse, Lee deeply loved Marina, and her view of him mattered to him, perhaps to the extreme. The couple had violent arguments. After they moved to Dallas and then to New Orleans and back, they more often lived separated than together. But this was a love affair that endured through thick and thin, and it was oddly reciprocal.

As Lee fell back on his leftist fantasies, Marina made it increasingly clear that she considered his Marxist ideas silly and vacuous. She understood that back in Minsk only fools and careerists could be or pretend to be communist believers. For Marina, Lee's vaunted Cuba was a leech that sucked out the resources of the poor Russians.

Shortly before the assassination, Lee, dressed in black, with a rifle in his hand and a pistol at his side holding a FAIR PLAY FOR CUBA sign, asked Marina to take his photo in their backyard. She burst out laughing at his silliness. After the assassination, the same picture was no longer a laughing matter.

How would a husband of Lee's fragile disposition respond to his wife's scorn? Not only by showing the world he was *someone* but by showing his wife as well.

The attempt on General Walker, Lee's mysterious trip to Mexico City, and a threatening visit from the FBI brought home to Marina that Lee was serious about committing a deed that would earn him a place in the history books. Given Oswald's psychological and emotional backdrop, what better way to prove to his wife that he was a person who could change history than to kill the president of the United States?

It is notable that when the newsflash came in that the president had been shot in downtown Dallas, Marina instinctively ran to the Paine family's garage. When she saw there was no rifle under the blanket, she knew.

. . .

In her testimony before the Warren Commission, Marina Oswald showed deep insight into her husband's psyche. She described Lee's state of mind in the clearest of terms, as only a spouse could:

"At least his imagination, his fantasy, which was quite unfounded, as to the fact that he was an *outstanding man*. And then the fact that he was very much interested, exceedingly so, in autobiographical works of outstanding statesmen of the United States and others . . . I think that he *compared himself* to these people whose autobiographies he read. That seems strange to me, because it is necessary to have an education in order to achieve success of that kind. . . . You see, when *I would make fun of him*, of his activity to some extent, in the sense that it didn't help anyone really, he said that I didn't understand him. . . . He said that after twenty years he would be prime minister."

Marina went on to say: "I think that he had *a sick imagination*—at least at that time I already considered him to be not quite normal—not always, but at times. I always tried to point out to him that *he was a man like any others* who were around us. But he simply could not understand that. I tried to tell him that it would be better to direct his energies to some more practical matters, and not something like that."

The serial failures of which Marina spoke created in Lee "a sick imagination," made worse by the fact that his wife made fun of his ambitions. His unstable mother had already done her damage. In Marguerite's mind, Lee was indeed exceptional, destined for greatness. She clung to this illusion even after her son killed the president of the United States. Lee's hatred of her could have been a form of self-loathing: he saw too much of himself in her.

. . .

To make matters worse, Lee and Marina's marriage suffered from sexual problems from day one. Marina was left unsatisfied by her husband's lovemaking, and she was ashamed that they had to resort to "unnatural" means for her to climax. In Minsk, Marina kept such problems to herself, but as their marriage threatened to break up, she vocalized her sexual frustration to members of the Russian community. In one case, "right in front" of Oswald, Marina complained about his inadequacy as a husband. She told others that they very seldom had sexual relations and that her husband "was not a man."

Marina, therefore, ridiculed her husband not only for his politics but for his performance in bed. What better way for Oswald to kill two birds with one stone than by the "manly" act of killing the most powerful man on earth?

. . .

Lee Harvey Oswald had a powerful motive to kill a high political official. He did it to prove to a doubting world, and to a doubting wife, that he was *someone*. From an early age, he had been taught by his mother that he would be exceptional. At last, he would have his revenge on those who doubted him. It is as simple as that.

41

INTELLIGENCE AND MEANS?

My fifth question is whether Lee Harvey Oswald had the intellectual and material wherewithal to kill a major political figure. Some doubt sociopath Oswald's guilt on the grounds that such a loser could not do what he did. Others use his loser status as proof that he was part of a conspiracy. He could not have assassinated a president of the United States without help, the thinking goes: How could such a small man arrange to be at the site of the motorcade, with a rifle he had purchased by mail order, and get off three shots as the president's car passed directly below him?

For those, like me, who are convinced that Lee Harvey Oswald killed Kennedy through his own devices, the question answers itself. If you succeed in doing something, clearly you possess the means of doing it.

Skepticism that an insignificant nobody could kill the president is a snobbish reaction. How could a young guy, earning a low income, without much education change history? Surely it would take someone with more going for him than Lee Harvey Oswald. At most, he could have been a minor cog in some grand conspiracy—a simple patsy lured into pulling the trigger but not planning it. Maybe he received some training in the arts of political assassination, perhaps from the KGB, Castro's agents, the Mafia, or even the CIA or FBI? The conviction that such a negligible man could not have accomplished this alone opens an endless variety of conspiracy theories that could occupy us without end.

My take on Lee Harvey Oswald is that, despite his many deficiencies, he had what it takes to assassinate a major political figure. Of course, he needed a string of luck to have the president of the United States in his sight.

Having known Lee, I believe he had the intellect, wiles, cunning, and manipulative skills to pull it off. To be sure, he was aided by a remarkable sequence of coincidences, such as getting a job—well before there was any thought of Kennedy coming to Dallas—at a workplace that would fall on the motorcade route. That he narrowly missed assassinating General Walker meant that he was still around to shoot JFK.

Let me remind you of the things that Oswald managed, using his own devices. With little money and self-taught language training, he traveled to Moscow. He thwarted the efforts of Soviet authorities to kick him out by attempting suicide. Sent to remote Minsk to minimize the trouble he could cause, he kept his options open and bullied, bluffed, and cajoled U.S. authorities to return him to the United States, with his wife and child, at U.S. government expense. He even got free sharpshooter training as a Marine. After moving to Dallas, he managed to live off the charity of others (the Dallas Russians) while feigning displeasure toward them. He was able to dump his wife and children on others at will so that he could pursue his intrigues.

Lee Harvey Oswald's preparation for the assassination of a major political figure was simple and low-cost. He rented a post office box under an assumed name and ordered from a mail order catalog a sharpshooter's rifle with a telescopic lens, which he hid among his things in a convenient garage.

Lee knew how to plan. He spent a couple of weeks plotting the shooting of General Edwin Walker. He took pictures of Walker's house, cased the layout, identified the best location from which to shoot, and he plotted his escape route by foot and bus with care. In the case of Walker, he missed narrowly but he made his escape as planned. He apparently left behind no useful clues for the Dallas police.

In the case of the Kennedy assassination, Oswald gleaned from the local press the president's motorcade route. He had a neighbor drive him to work at the Texas School Book Depository with this rifle wrapped in the shape of curtain rods. He needed no special permit to enter the building as an employee, and the Secret Service did not have the resources to sweep every building along the route. As an employee, he could pick out a window that gave him a clear view of the motorcade and in a room that would be empty as the motorcade passed below. After he shot the president, he exited the building while a supervisor identified him as a regular employee. He then took a city bus and then a taxi to his boardinghouse.

What Lee Harvey Oswald did on November 22, 1963, was a low-tech political assassination. His sharpshooter rifle ordered by mail cost $19.95 and his Smith & Wesson .38 caliber cost $29.95. In today's prices, Oswald spent about $500 for the weapons he needed to kill the president.

We misjudge Oswald by focusing on his working-class attire and simple manner of speech, all the while not noticing his street-smart intelligence, craftiness, and wiliness. As a teenager, he scored reasonably high on what were then called achievement tests. He had potent manipulative skills with respect to other people, including his wife. Many wives would have left Lee after his abuse. Marina escaped periodically to sympathetic Russian-speaking friends, but she stayed with him as he played the role of penitent husband who promised never to strike her again. Marina even stayed with him after she discovered that he actually had tried to assassinate General Walker.

My father noted from his ordeal at the Six Flags Inn that Lee and his mother had much in common. Marguerite went through a number of husbands, made her way in life via part-time jobs by cajoling, whining, and manipulating, and making bizarre demands that showed her fragile grasp of reality. The most ridiculous instance was her demand that her "hero" son should be buried in Arlington National Cemetery. Marguerite pushed and prodded until she got her way (of course, she didn't get her way about Arlington). It did not matter to her if she drove people up the wall. She knew what she wanted, and no one would stand in the way. Lee acted in the same way.

Pete Gregory, in his testimony before the Warren Commission, captured Marguerite perfectly: "She impressed me as being not necessarily rational. She is *quite clever,* but she certainly is *most peculiar.* She demands public attention. She wants to be at the center of attention." Pete Gregory's words also fit Lee Oswald to a T: not entirely rational but clever and must be the center of attention.

Marguerite understood that Lee was like her. She held it against her successful son, Robert, that—unlike Lee—he was easygoing, influenced by others, and did not know how to bully his way. Unlike Robert and half-brother John, Lee was not shunted off to orphanages and military academies. He was raised by Marguerite, became Marguerite, and despised her.

One of Lee's most valuable conspiratorial skills was his knack of talking without disclosing much. He left questions about himself unanswered in a deliberate silence, replying not with words but a gesture or a shake of his head. He had a way of letting you draw false impressions, which you then believed to be true. In this regard, Lee was a natural conspirator. Other people should not know his business. What he did was for him alone, not even for his wife to know.

How many conspiracies have been exposed by conspirators bragging or saying too much? Lee Harvey Oswald did none of that. He said nothing, hinted at nothing. Besides, there was no one to tell. He did things alone.

There is no doubt that Lee Harvey Oswald had the financial resources to do what he did. The Oswald budget reconstructed by the Warren Commission shows that he had enough to travel to Mexico by bus, relocate frequently, buy a sharpshooter rifle, and keep a family of a wife and two children barely above water. There was no sinister financier funneling the money that Lee needed to shoot at General Edwin Walker or the president.

I know from personal observation that Lee and Marina's shopping trips yielded a small bag of groceries to last a whole week. From jobs that paid $1.25 per hour, Oswald rented an apartment, fed a family, moved locations, and paid back his debts. He gave Marina pocket money of $2 per week, and she rarely spent all of it. He did not smoke or drink. He traveled by city bus or on foot.

Investigative journalist Gerald Posner agreed that Lee Harvey Oswald had the capabilities of killing a high-profile target. Writes Posner: "The real Oswald . . . is anything but the credulous neophyte, too simple to understand the intricate affairs about him. Rather, he is wily and adept at creating the very dramas that populate the JFK case, from his defection to the Soviet Union at the height of the Cold War, to his pro-Castro advocacy on the sweltering streets of New Orleans only months before the president was killed."

42

SOUL OF A KILLER

We are poor judges of whether someone has the soul of a killer. After every mass killing, for example, people who knew the murderers describe them as good neighbors—a quiet person who kept mainly to himself but was always pleasant. If we could detect those with souls of killers, there would be fewer shootings in schools, movie theaters, naval yards, and on the political campaign trail. If anyone had asked me in August 1962 whether Lee Harvey Oswald had the soul of a killer, I would have considered the question crazy. But when they brought Lee into the Dallas police station, I immediately did not doubt that he could be the killer.

In the case of Oswald, we already know that he had the soul of a killer. He took a shot at General Walker that barely missed his head. Lee had a clear intent to kill and was quite disappointed when his shot missed.

Oswald shot at two prominent political figures. One was a right-wing true believer, whom he could justify shooting as a political enemy of his cause. The same could not be said of his ultimate victim, JFK. The choice of such disparate targets discloses his real objective: to commit a heinous and notorious political crime that would make him a part of history. Oswald's killer soul was also evident in his murder of the police officer who stopped him.

The irony is that Lee Harvey Oswald would have settled for killing General Walker. The murder of Walker would make Oswald a tiny footnote. He failed, only to be rewarded with the highest profile target of all. Then, Jack Ruby denied Lee Oswald his most desired glory: his day in court, where he could display his greatness with the whole world watching.

Oswald's biography reveals that he was a violent person. As a child, he and Marguerite were expelled from his half-brother's home because of his violent threats. His brother Robert Oswald noted a sadistic streak in twelve-year-old Lee when he took him rabbit hunting outside of Fort Worth. After bagging a few rabbits, which Robert intended to skin and cook, they spied another, some twenty feet away. Robert let Lee take the shot with his pump action .22 caliber. Lee's first shot killed the rabbit, but Lee ran toward the dead rabbit needlessly firing shot after shot into the carcass. At that point, Robert began to worry about the mental state of his brother. As Robert remarked to Secret Service Agent Mike Howard while they were holed up at the Six Flags Inn: "I should have seen it coming."

Robert Oswald reports another incident of Lee's violent behavior in his early teens. When Lee and Marguerite were living with half-brother John Pic and his wife in New York, Pic's wife claimed that the twelve-year-old Lee threatened her with a knife. When Marguerite intervened, Lee hit her. When this evidence was brought before the Warren Commission, various experts concluded that Lee Harvey Oswald, even in his youth, had a violent personality.

I have recollections of bruises on Marina's face. Later, Marina said openly to her Dallas Russian friends that Lee was an abusive husband.

True or feigned, expressions of guilt followed episodes of abuse, and Marina played the role of an abused wife in its classic form.

She later testified before the Warren Commission that others saw bruises only because she had such sensitive skin. Also, she said, she sometimes deserved a beating when she tried to make Lee jealous. These things I did not see, other than a blue bruise under her eye. Most importantly, I witnessed the incident when Marina's backward tumble from their front porch sent Lee into a rage that constituted spousal abuse.

In the Marines, Lee smuggled a pistol into the barracks. Such an offense was punished by court martial. He was court martialed a second time for assaulting a fellow Marine. In the service he spent more than a month in the brig. Contrary to practice, he was not given a private-first-class insignia to wear on his uniform. In New Orleans he was briefly jailed for a fight with an anti-Castro foe. Although many are prone to violence without having the soul of a killer, a violent streak is a warning sign of serious bad deeds to come.

43

WHY JFK?

Lee Harvey Oswald did not assassinate Kennedy according to a plan hatched long before the event. Other than the city bus and Greyhound, Oswald was limited in his geographical mobility. The president must come to him, not he to the president. JFK's plans to visit Texas were not finalized until the last moment, and there was some talk of canceling them due to the possibility of a hostile reception in the purported home of America's right wing. In fact, the president first planned to limit his visit to Houston; the other cities—Fort Worth, Dallas, and Austin—were added only after slighted Texas politicians intervened.

Oswald got his job in the Texas School Book Depository long before there was any thought of the president coming to Dallas, much less of a motorcade that would pass by the building. He would not have attempted to shoot General Walker if his real goal was to assassinate the president. He was clearly intent on killing Walker. This was no warm-up exercise for bigger things. Had he succeeded, the police would eventually have found him, and Kennedy would not have been assassinated.

Oswald was not overcome with any dislike of JFK. In my presence he hinted at a favorable view of the president and his family. Marina clearly admired the Kennedys, especially Jackie. Lee would have known that his killing of Kennedy would strike his wife a devastating blow. Indeed, Marina felt extreme remorse, sorrow, and guilt toward Jackie Kennedy after the assassination. Despite Secret Service agents' pleas, she insisted on watching JFK's funeral and was badly shaken by pictures of the grieving widow with her children.

Whether Oswald liked or disliked Kennedy is not the point. As Norman Mailer put it: "[Oswald] probably did like Kennedy as much as he could approve of any conventional politician . . . such sentiments had very little to do with his act. He would not be shooting at Kennedy because he liked him or disliked him—that would be irrelevant to the depth of his deed." Instead, Kennedy "was the largest opportunity he had ever been offered. . . . The assassination of a president would be seismographic in its effect."

Priscilla McMillan also underscores the attraction and even symbolism of the opportunity to kill the president: "The uncanny selection of a route that would carry the president right under his window could mean only one thing. Fate had singled him out to do the dangerous and necessary task, which had been his destiny all along and which would cause him to go down in history."

The answer to "Why Kennedy?" could not be simpler: an eerie set of circumstances gave Oswald the opportunity to fulfill his dreams far beyond anything he had ever hoped for. Instead of passing out pro-Castro leaflets, publishing the story of his life, or shooting General Walker, he could now perform on the grand stage of history, and he was being offered this chance in a remarkably easy fashion. His rifle was ready. His shooting site was ready. The president would pass at a time when he could be alone at the sixth-floor window. The Secret Service did not check rooftops and upper floors. This sequence of events could not be luck; Lee Harvey Oswald would have concluded that it must have been preordained.

Oswald left the Irving home where Marina was living on the morning of November 22; he did not wake her. He picked up his rifle, concealed by a paper covering, and was driven to downtown Dallas by a neighbor. He knew he was not coming back. He was going to meet his destiny. His logic must have told him that he could not escape; he would be captured. He probably even hoped for that. If he shot the president and miraculously escaped, he would not go down in the history books. Instead, an unknown assassin would get the credit.

His logic told him that he must be captured. However, his instincts told him to escape. After firing the shots, he left the building and fled on a city bus and then taxi to his rooming house. He entered the rooming house, departing shortly thereafter carrying a loaded Smith and Wesson .38 caliber pistol. A logical plan would have been to behave in a normal way. But in his panic, he cut a suspicious figure. An alert policeman, officer J.D. Tippit, stopped Oswald, who shot the officer dead in a panic and was soon captured in a movie theater and hauled to the Dallas police station.

Entering police headquarters, Oswald knew that his place in history was blemished. In a heroic and almost nihilistic act, he had single-handedly changed history, but why would a great figure of history execute a fellow workingman—a police officer with a wife and children?

Despite his bravado, Oswald was not without fear. When Marina last saw him behind a glass wall at the Dallas police station, he was clearly frightened. He knew that he would be sentenced to death or to life in prison. His impending ordeal would be worth it, however. He planned that his stunning deed would be his crowning glory. He already had the name of a well-known ACLU attorney. He would have his day in court as the whole world hung on his every word. He would impress those listening with his Marxist erudition. He would explain that American society is corrupt and unfair. He would show the world that he was someone.

Jack Ruby deprived him of the opportunity.

EPILOGUE

I can look back on the more than half century that has passed since that fateful day in November 1963 with some pride of accomplishment. The succeeding years took me to study in Berlin, where I met my late wife, Annemarie. We had been married fifty-four years when she passed on. I have two sons, who grew up well, and one has given me four granddaughters. I earned a Ph.D. in economics from Harvard, and I taught at my alma mater, the University of Oklahoma, and then at the University of Houston. I have been for more than a decade a Research Fellow at the Hoover Institution at Stanford University. I was fortunate to be an eyewitness to the collapse of the Soviet Union, the homeland that Lee Harvey Oswald briefly adopted after renouncing his own country for its enemy.

Virtually all of the people mentioned in my account have passed away—including my father and the Dallas Russians. Marina herself has stayed out of the limelight in isolation in a small community not far from Dallas. She has granted few interviews. One was to thank the American people for their kindness shortly after the assassination. The other was to state that she now had doubts that Lee did it. Her daughters with Lee, and her son with her second husband, are grown.

Our family's effort to remain beneath the radar after the assassination was successful. Although Pete's and my involvement with the Oswalds was immediately known to the FBI and Secret Service, our names did not appear in the press, either local or national. Our lying low was instinctively aimed at friends, neighbors, and business associates, who would ask: What kind of people would have associated with a communist and a deserter?

We did not anticipate that we would become fodder for the conspiracy theory industry, which could turn minor events and peripheral players into key conspirators. All that was required would be a minor discrepancy here, a misspoken word there, and Pete and Paul Gregory would suddenly become sinister players in a dark conspiracy.

One potential avenue of attack would be Pete Gregory's oil consulting business, which brought him into contact with Texas oil barons, who were somehow to gain from JFK's assassination. One of the purveyors of this theory, a reporter from the defunct *Fort Worth Post* ("Homer" something or other), used to pester Pete with unwanted telephone calls urging him to come clean about the assassination. My gracious father would plead with "Homer" to leave him alone, but to no avail.

• • •

I last saw Marina on November 22, 1962. On the eve of the fiftieth anniversary of November 22, 1963, I obtained from Priscilla McMillan her phone number and address. I sent Marina an early draft of this book, and I spoke with her husband, who protects her from those who wish to exploit her. It was clear that he did not want me to speak with Marina. I respected his wishes. Marina has been wise to drop out of public view.

Instead, I decided to write Marina the following letter, to which I have received no response:

Dear Marina,

I talked by phone to your husband, Ken. He said he would pass along my greetings. It has been more than fifty years since we last saw each other (Thanksgiving 1962). Your last contact with the Gregory family would have been with my father from November 24–28, 1963. This is my second letter to you. The first was to Elsbeth Street, when I thought the postcard that Lee had written to me had been written by you.

I went on to become a university professor specializing in Russia. I have taught for almost fifty years at the University of Houston and have served as a fellow at the Hoover Institution of Stanford University for fifteen years. I have written quite a few books about Russia, some of which have been well received.

My historian colleagues convinced me that I should write about my time together with you and Lee to help complete the historical record. I was one of the few who knew the two of you when you arrived, and we spent a considerable amount of time together, which I remember fondly.

Trying to remember things that occurred more than fifty years ago is difficult, but I have tried to put together a description of this time, as I remember it. After November 22, 1963, I pretty much kept quiet about what had happened as did my whole family. My father passed in 1982. My mother in 1987.

I hope that you have had a good life in America after such a tragic start.

My regards,
Paul Gregory

ACKNOWLEDGMENTS

I am indebted to Priscilla McMillan for her encouragement to write this book. She has claimed that for the period from June to November 1962, I knew Lee and Marina Oswald better than anyone and had an obligation to add what I know to the historical record. My colleague at the Hoover Institution, the late Richard Burress, himself an expert on the Lincoln assassination, pestered me for a number of years to write about my experiences. I should have taken his advice earlier. Roger Williams, my colleague, kept reminding me that it was time to start writing this memoir. My late brother-in-law, Joe Padgett, interviewed my father and me and wrote his own account, which he did not release to the family until after my father's death. I am indebted to former Secret Service Agent Mike Howard, who shared with me his account of that turbulent time as he and other agents tried to determine whether Lee was part of a conspiracy and, if so, whether Marina was an accomplice. I also owe a debt of gratitude to Robert Oswald, who answered specific questions about the events at the Six Flags Inn. (I was gratified that Robert remembered my father, Pete Gregory, as a "good guy.") The greatest debt of all would be to my late father, Peter Gregory, who handled himself with calm, courage, dignity, and patriotism throughout this ordeal and had the good sense to keep this story within the family.

SELECTED SOURCES

CHAPTER 1

4. **When the Pew Research Center:** Deane, Claudia and Maeve Duggan, Rich Morin. "Americans Name the 10 Most Significant Historic Events of Their Lifetimes." *Pew Research Center*, December 15, 2016. https://www.pewresearch .org/politics/2016/12/15/americans-name-the-10-most-significant-historic -events-of-their-lifetimes/.

5. **two-thirds believe "others were involved.":** Enten, Harry. "Most People Believe in JFK Conspiracy Theories." FiveThirtyEight, October 23, 2017. https://fivethirtyeight.com/features/the-one-thing-in-politics-most -americans-believe-in-jfk-conspiracies/.

8. **Priscilla McMillan, author of the memorable** *Marina and Lee*: McMillan, Priscilla Johnson. *Marina and Lee: The Tormented Love and Fatal Obsession Behind Lee Harvey Oswald's Assassination of John F. Kennedy*. New York: Harper & Row Publishers, 1977.

8. **an essay I wrote for the** *New York Times*: Gregory, Paul. "Lee Harvey Oswald Was My Friend." *New York Times Magazine*, November 7, 2013. https://www .nytimes.com/2013/11/10/magazine/lee-harvey-oswald-was-my-friend.html.

8. **"I dislike everybody.":** Warren Commission, *Report of the President's Commission on the Assassination of President Kennedy*, p. 380. Washington, DC: United States Government Printing Office, 1964. https://www.archives .gov/research/jfk/warren-commission-report.

9. **". . . which was definitely radical":** *Hearings before the President's Commission on the Assassination of President Kennedy*, 88th Cong., 1st sess., Vol. XXIII, Commission Exhibit No. 1792, p. 407 (1964). https://www.history-matters .com/archive/jfk/wc/wcvols/wh23/pdf/WH23_CE_1792.pdf.

9. **Fort Worth telephone number (Pershing 1 1639):** *Hearings before the President's Commission* (1964), Vol. XVI, Commission Exhibit No. 18, p. 48–49. https://www.history-matters.com/archive/jfk/wc/wcvols/wh16/html /WH_Vol16_0036b.htm, https://www.history-matters.com/archive/jfk/wc /wcvols/wh16/html/WH_Vol16_0037a.htm.

CHAPTER 2

17. **questioning Elizabeth Gregory about Oswald:** Blakey, Robert G. House Select Committee on Assassinations Letter to Attorney General Keuch, Robert L., 1978. National Archives, Washington, DC https://www.archives.gov/files /research/jfk/releases/docid-32247845.pdf.

20. **Marina's comings and goings:** *Hearings before the President's Commission* (1964), Vol. I (statement of Marguerite Oswald). https://www.govinfo .gov/content/pkg/GPO-WARRENCOMMISSIONHEARINGS-1/pdf /GPO-WARRENCOMMISSIONHEARINGS-1.pdf, http://jfk-archives .blogspot.com/2010/09/marguerite-oswald.html.

21. **under constant surveillance:** Warren Commission, *Report of the President's Commission on the Assassination of President Kennedy.* Washington, DC: United States Government Printing Office, 1964. https://www.archives.gov/research /jfk/warren-commission-report/chapter-7.html#early.

22. **visited the Mexico City Embassy:** *Hearings before the President's Commission* (1964), Vol. XVI, Commission Exhibit No. 18, p. 61. https://www.govinfo .gov/content/pkg/GPO-WARRENCOMMISSIONHEARINGS-16/pdf /GPO-WARRENCOMMISSIONHEARINGS-16.pdf, https://www.archives .gov/files/research/jfk/releases/104-10067-10413.pdf.

25. **"needs to have a black eye":** *Hearings before the President's Commission* (1964), Vol. I, p. 139 (statement of Marguerite Oswald). https://www.govinfo .gov/content/pkg/GPO-WARRENCOMMISSIONHEARINGS-1 /pdf/GPO-WARRENCOMMISSIONHEARINGS-1.pdf, https://www .jfk-assassination.net/russ/testimony/2_10_64_AM.htm.

25. **to shower naked with other boys:** Warren Commission, *Report of the President's Commission on the Assassination of President Kennedy,* p. 379. Washington, DC: United States Government Printing Office, 1964. https://www.archives.gov /research/jfk/warren-commission-report/chapter-7.html#early.

25–26. **FBI agents monitoring from the next room:** Hoover, J. Edgar. FBI Memorandum for Attorney General, Mr. Tolson, February 24, 1964. Mary Ferrell Foundation, Assassination Archives and Research Center. https://www .maryferrell.org/showDoc.html?docId=10098#relPageId=76.

CHAPTER 3

29. **standing by in the basement garage:** *Hearings before the President's Commission* (1964), Vol. XIX, Decker Exhibit No. 5323, pp. 466–478. https://www.govinfo .gov/content/pkg/GPO-WARRENCOMMISSIONHEARINGS-19/pdf /GPO-WARRENCOMMISSIONHEARINGS-19.pdf.

31. **"show the world that a Jew had guts":** *Hearings before the President's Commission* (1964), Vol. XIII, p. 68 (statement of Forrest V. Sorrels). https://

www.history-matters.com/archive/jfk/wc/wcvols/wh13/pdf/WH13_Sorrels
.pdf.

CHAPTER 4

32. **the group met nonstop to plan strategy:** John Kennedy Assassination, Lee
Harvey Oswald KGB Files, Yeltsin-Clinton 1999 Exchange. https://www
.jfk-assassination.net/pdf/OswaldKGB.pdf.

33. **"for some purposes of our own":** "Russians Wary of '63 Oswald Letter
Soviet Embassy Officials Believed Note Was Forgery." *Deseret News*, August 7,
1999. https://www.deseret.com/1999/8/7/19459349/russians-wary-of-63
-oswald-letter-br-soviet-embassy-officials-believed-note-was-forgery.

33. **"organizers of this shameful crime":** https://aarclibrary.org/publib/jfk/other
/yeltsin/pdf/Yeltsin_NewsFabrications.pdf.

34. **informant at a high level in Soviet intelligence:** Neuman, Scott. "Documents
Offer Insight into Soviet View of JFK Assassination." NPR, October 27,
2017. https://www.npr.org/sections/thetwo-way/2017/10/27/560345132
/documents-offer-insights-into-soviet-view-of-jfks-assassination.

34. **medications to dampen her sex drive:** Newsom, Milton L. FBI Lee Harvey
Oswald Report, March 23, 1964. Mary Ferrell Foundation, Assassination
Archives and Research Center. https://www.maryferrell.org/showDoc
.html?docId=10098#relPageId=67.

35. **why he went to Russia:** *Hearings before the President's Commission* (1964),
Vol. VIII, p. 379 (statement of Anna N. Meller). https://www.govinfo
.gov/content/pkg/GPO-WARRENCOMMISSIONHEARINGS-8/pdf
/GPO-WARRENCOMMISSIONHEARINGS-8.pdf, pp.380–385.

35. **ordering Oswald to assassinate Kennedy:** Woolsey, James R., and Pacepa,
Ion. *Operation Dragon: Inside the Kremlin's Secret War on America*. New York:
Encounter, 2021.

35. **in the history of the country:** Mathis, James, and Murphy, Martha Wagner.
"Documenting the Death of a President." *Prologue Magazine*, Vol. 49, No.
3 (Fall 2017). https://www.archives.gov/publications/prologue/2017/fall
/jfk-records.

CHAPTER 5

39. **unjustly oppresses the little guy:** *Hearings before the President's Commission*
(1964), Vol. XVI, Commission Exhibit 24, p. 94. https://www.govinfo
.gov/content/pkg/GPO-WARRENCOMMISSIONHEARINGS-16/pdf
/GPO-WARRENCOMMISSIONHEARINGS-16.pdf.

39. new life in a real-life Marxist state: Parnell, W. Tracy. "Timeline of the Life of Lee Harvey Oswald." The Lee Harvey Oswald Research Page. https://jfkassassination.net/parnell/chrono.htm.

39. visit from a young American: Warren Commission, *Report of the President's Commission on the Assassination of President Kennedy,* p. 747. Washington, DC: United States Government Printing Office, 1964. https://www.archives.gov /research/jfk/warren-commission-report/appendix-15.html#attempts.

41. "tonight at. 8 .oo as visa expire": *Hearings before the President's Commission* (1964), Vol. XVI, Commission Exhibit 24, p. 94. https://www.history-matters .com/archive/jfk/wc/wcvols/wh16/pdf/WH16_CE_24.pdf.

43. 700 rubles monthly for one year: Warren Commission, *Report of the President's Commission on the Assassination of President Kennedy,* p. 269. Washington, DC: United States Government Printing Office, 1964. https://www.archives.gov /research/jfk/warren-commission-report/chapter-6.html#contacts.

43. interviewed Oswald in his hotel room at the Metropole: McMillan, Priscilla Johnson. *Marina and Lee: The Tormented Love and Fatal Obsession Behind Lee Harvey Oswald's Assassination of John F. Kennedy.* New York: Harper & Row Publishers, 1977, pp. 68–72.

43. not revealed any of himself to her: *Hearings before the President's Commission* (1964), Vol. XIX, Cadigan Exhibit No. 29, p. 302. https://www.govinfo .gov/content/pkg/GPO-WARRENCOMMISSIONHEARINGS-19/pdf /GPO-WARRENCOMMISSIONHEARINGS-19.pdf.

43. personal space was to remain private: Smith, Nicola. "Writer Worked for a Future President, and Interviewed a Future Assassin." *Valley News,* November 22, 2013. https://www.vnews.com/Archives/2013/11 /LeeandMarinaOswald-ns-vn-112213.

44. denunciation of the United States: *Hearings before the President's Commission* (1964), Vol. XVI, Commission Exhibit No. 25, p. 121. https://www .history-matters.com/archive/jfk/wc/wcvols/wh16/html/WH_Vol16_0073a .htm.

CHAPTER 6

45. to reciprocate his feelings: *Hearings before the President's Commission* (1964), Vol. XVI, Commission Exhibit 24, p. 95. https://www.history-matters.com /archive/jfk/wc/wcvols/wh16/pdf/WH16_CE_24.pdf.

45. to stay in Hotel Minsk: *Hearings before the President's Commission* (1964), Vol. XVI, Commission Exhibit 24, p. 98. https://www.history-matters.com /archive/jfk/wc/wcvols/wh16/pdf/WH16_CE_24.pdf.

46. Belarus's first head of state: http://www.mzk1.ru/2018/04/li-xarvi-osvald -%E2%94%80-zagadka-veka/.

46. **red-brick structure with a corrugated metal roof:** Wronski, Peter. "Minsk Part 3: Oswald at Word I: The Experiment Shop – Radio & TV." Lee Harvey Oswald in Russia: An Unauthorized History from the Kennedy Assassination, website. http://www.russianbooks.org/oswald/minsk3.htm.

47. **Lee affected a credible Shakespearian voice:** Titovets, Ernst. "Excerpt from Tape #1." Lee Oswald reading a piece from *Othello* by William Shakespeare in December 1960. Ernst Titovets, website, 2011. http://www.etitovets.com /Recorded%20_voices.html.

47. **lyrics of folk songs that he liked:** *Hearings before the President's Commission* (1964), Vol. XVI, Commission Exhibit 108, p. 467. https://www .history-matters.com/archive/jfk/wc/wcvols/wh16/html/WH_Vol16_0250b .htm.

47. **a love letter to Marina:** *Hearings before the President's Commission* (1964), Vol. XVI, Commission Exhibit 53, p. 191. https://www.govinfo.gov /content/pkg/GPO-WARRENCOMMISSIONHEARINGS-16/pdf /GPO-WARRENCOMMISSIONHEARINGS-16.pdf.

49. **entitled *The Collective* (*kollektiv* in Russian):** Warren Commission, *Report of the President's Commission on the Assassination of President Kennedy,* p. 395. Washington, DC: United States Government Printing Office, 1964. https://www.archives.gov/research/jfk/warren-commission-report/chapter-7 .html#defection.

52. **proved to be extremely jealous:** McMillan, Priscilla Johnson. *Marina and Lee: The Tormented Love and Fatal Obsession Behind Lee Harvey Oswald's Assassination of John F. Kennedy.* New York: Harper & Row Publishers, 1977, p. 95.

53. **less than he should be as a man:** McMillan, Priscilla Johnson. *Marina and Lee: The Tormented Love and Fatal Obsession Behind Lee Harvey Oswald's Assassination of John F. Kennedy.* New York: Harper & Row Publishers, 1977, pp. 120–122.

53. **at two o'clock in the morning:** Ibid.

54. **vanished with this letter:** *Hearings before the President's Commission* (1964), Vol. XVI, Commission Exhibit 72, p. 234. https://www.history-matters.com /archive/jfk/wc/wcvols/wh16/html/WH_Vol16_0129b.htm.

59. **of the Soviet enterprise:** http://jfk.hood.edu/Collection/FBI%20Records %20Files/105-82555/105-82555%20Section%20063/Section%2063C.pdf.

CHAPTER 7

57. **called "a police state":** From Oswald's notes written on board the SS *Maasdam.* https://www.history-matters.com/archive/jfk/wc/wcvols/wh16 /html/WH_Vol16_0066a.htm.

58. **"constructive and practical people can live in peace":** *Hearings before the President's Commission* (1964), Vol. XVI, Commission Exhibit 25, pp. 113–121. https://www.history-matters.com/archive/jfk/wc/wcvols/wh16/html/WH_Vol16_0069a.htm.

60. **"cannot be judged as being fair or impartial":** *Hearings before the President's Commission* (1964), Vol. XIX, Cadigan Exhibit No. 14, p. 287. https://www.govinfo.gov/content/pkg/GPO-WARRENCOMMISSIONHEARINGS-19/pdf/GPO-WARRENCOMMISSIONHEARINGS-19.pdf.

61. **Revenge for the undesirable discharge:** Reston, James Jr. *The Accidental Victim: JFK, Lee Harvey Oswald, and the Real Target in Dallas.* Zola Books, 2013. https://www.amazon.com/Accidental-Victim-Harvey-Oswald-Target/dp/1624908705.

61. **who served as his personal assistant:** *Hearings before the President's Commission* (1964), Vol. XVI, Commission Exhibit 180-202, pp. 530–583. https://www.govinfo.gov/content/pkg/GPO-WARRENCOMMISSIONHEARINGS-16/pdf/GPO-WARRENCOMMISSIONHEARINGS-16.pdf.

63. **"absence of any real family life":** Warren Commission, *Report of the President's Commission on the Assassination of President Kennedy,* p. 380. Washington, DC: United States Government Printing Office, 1964. https://www.archives.gov/research/jfk/warren-commission-report/chapter-7.html#newyork.

CHAPTER 9

73. **to his credit that Robert did not:** *Hearings before the President's Commission* (1964), Vol. I, pp. 264–469 (statement of Robert Edward Lee Oswald).

73. **"a fair statement, yes":** *Hearings before the President's Commission* (1964), Vol. II, p. 347 (statement of Peter Paul Gregory). https://www.govinfo.gov/content/pkg/GPO-WARRENCOMMISSIONHEARINGS-2/pdf/GPO-WARRENCOMMISSIONHEARINGS-2.pdf.

CHAPTER 11

81. **She did not let him in:** *Hearings before the President's Commission* (1964), Vol. X, pp. 229–231 (statement of Chester Allen Riggs Jr.). https://www.govinfo.gov/content/pkg/GPO-WARRENCOMMISSIONHEARINGS-10/pdf/GPO-WARRENCOMMISSIONHEARINGS-10.pdf.

CHAPTER 12

86. **send him in Minsk copies of *Time* Magazine:** McMillan, Priscilla Johnson. *Marina and Lee: The Tormented Love and Fatal Obsession Behind Lee Harvey Oswald's Assassination of John F. Kennedy.* New York: Harper & Row Publishers, 1977, p. 130.

CHAPTER 13

100. **and some of his books were Russian:** Smikin, John. *"Lee Harvey Oswald: Primary Sources."* Spartacus Educational, website, last modified 2021. https://spartacus-educational.com/JFKoswald.htm#source. *Time.* February 21, 1964. Vol. 56, No. 8.

100. **how much Russian Oswald knew:** Norwood, James. *"Oswald's Proficiency in the Russian Language."* Harvey and Lee. https://harveyandlee.net/Russian.html.

101. **he or she were out of Minsk:** *Hearings before the President's Commission* (1964), Vol. XVI, Commission Exhibit 62, 65-Continued, p. 211. https://www.govinfo.gov/content/pkg/GPO-WARRENCOMMISSIONHEARINGS-16/pdf/GPO-WARRENCOMMISSIONHEARINGS-16.pdf.

CHAPTER 16

113. **misspellings and grammatical errors:** Warren Commission, *Report of the President's Commission on the Assassination of President Kennedy,* pp. 395–399. Washington, DC: United States Government Printing Office, 1964. https://www.archives.gov/research/jfk/warren-commission-report/chapter-7.html#defection.

113. **are confusing and rambling:** *Hearings before the President's Commission* (1964), Vol. XVI, Commission Exhibit 25, pp. 113–121. https://www.history-matters.com/archive/jfk/wc/wcvols/wh16/html/WH_Vol16_0069a.htm.

CHAPTER 17

118. **"I went, and I came back":** *Hearings before the President's Commission* (1964), Vol. IV, p. 403 (statement of John W. Fain). http://jfkassassination.net/russ/testimony/fain.htm.

CHAPTER 18

123. **wanted me to read it (I declined, thinking it was none of my business):** *Hearings before the President's Commission* (1964), Vol. XVI, Commission Exhibit 49, p. 183. https://www.history-matters.com/archive/jfk/wc/wcvols/wh16/html/WH_Vol16_0266b.htm. *Hearings before the President's Commission* (1964), Vol. XVI, Commission Exhibit 132, pp. 507–508. https://www.history-matters.com/archive/jfk/wc/wcvols/wh16/html/WH_Vol16_0104a.htm https://www.history-matters.com/archive/jfk/wc/wcvols/wh16/html/WH_Vol16_0266a.htm.

124. **inaccessible to the outside world:** *"KGB Files on Lee Harvey Oswald Offer Peek Into Accused Assassin's Time as Defector in Russia."* *Dallas Morning News,* November 10, 2012. https://www.dallasnews.com/news/2012/11/11

/kgb-files-on-lee-harvey-oswald-offer-peek-into-accused-assassins-time-as
-defector-in-russia/.

124. **relatives left behind in Minsk:** *Hearings before the President's Commission*
(1964), Vol. XVI, Commission Exhibit 57, p. 199. https://www
.history-matters.com/archive/jfk/wc/wcvols/wh16/html/WH_Vol16_0112a
.htm.

124. **Lee's portion in English:** *Hearings before the President's Commission* (1964),
Vol. XVI, Commission Exhibit 50, p. 185. https://www.history-matters.com
/archive/jfk/wc/wcvols/wh16/html/WH_Vol16_0105a.htm.

124. **return where she belonged:** *Hearings before the President's Commission* (1964),
Vol. XVI, Commission Exhibit 75, p. 238. https://www.history-matters.com
/archive/jfk/wc/wcvols/wh16/html/WH_Vol16_0131b.htm.

CHAPTER 23

145. **Marina had even less:** Boehe testimony. Image 8. https://catalog.archives.gov
/id/7460379/8/public?contributionType=transcription.

146. **"he would take care of his own child":** Boehe testimony. Image 77. https://
catalog.archives.gov/id/7460379/77/public?contributionType=transcription.

146. **"a $1.25 per hour job?":** Gannaway, Captain W.P. Correspondence
to Lieutenant Jack Revill, Special Services Bureau, Dallas Police
Department, February 17, 1964. Records of the John F. Kennedy
Assassination Collection: Key Persons Files: Bouhe, George, National
Archives, Washington, DC https://catalog.archives.gov/id/7460379/89
/public?contributionType=transcription.

146. **while all of this was going on:** *Hearings before the President's Commission*
(1964), Vol. VII, p. 355 (statement of George A. Bouhe). http://aarclibrary
.org/publib/jfk/wc/wcvols/wh8/pdf/WH8_Bouhe.pdf.

146. **Lee should go back to Russia:** Image 18. https://catalog.archives.gov
/id/7460379.

148. **telling him to come over:** McMillan, Priscilla Johnson. *Marina and Lee: The
Tormented Love and Fatal Obsession Behind Lee Harvey Oswald's Assassination
of John F. Kennedy.* New York: Harper & Row Publishers, 1977, p. 229.

CHAPTER 26

158. **she answered through a translator:** *Hearings before the President's Commission*
(1964), Vol. I, p. 1 (statement of Marina Oswald). https://www.govinfo
.gov/content/pkg/GPO-WARRENCOMMISSIONHEARINGS-1/pdf
/GPO-WARRENCOMMISSIONHEARINGS-1.pdf.

163. Kennedy was not: Titovets, Ernst. *Oswald: Russian Episode*. Minsk: Mon Litera Publishing House, 2010. https://www.amazon.com/Oswald-Russian-Episode-Ernst-Titovets/dp/1501011316.

163. information on his command of Russian: *Hearings before the President's Commission* (1964), Vol. I, Commission Exhibit I, pp. 1–2. https://www.govinfo.gov/content/pkg/GPO-WARRENCOMMISSIONHEARINGS-16/pdf/GPO-WARRENCOMMISSIONHEARINGS-16.pdf.

CHAPTER 27

164. using his legs: McMillan, Priscilla Johnson. *Marina and Lee: The Tormented Love and Fatal Obsession Behind Lee Harvey Oswald's Assassination of John F. Kennedy*. New York: Harper & Row Publishers, 1977, p. 287.

164. "fighter for peace": *Hearings before the President's Commission* (1964), Vol. XIX, Cadigan Exhibit No. 9, p. 281. https://www.govinfo.gov/content/pkg/GPO-WARRENCOMMISSIONHEARINGS-19/pdf/GPO-WARRENCOMMISSIONHEARINGS-19.pdf.

165. their journal, *The Militant*: Dobbs, Ferrell. Letter to Lee Harvey Oswald, November 5, 1962. John F. Kennedy, Dallas Police Department Collection, University of North Texas Libraries. https://texashistory.unt.edu/ark:/67531/metapth339995/m1/1/.

165. forming a new chapter: Fair Play for Cuba Committee. Letter to Lee Harvey Oswald, May 29, 1963. John F. Kennedy, Dallas Police Department Collection, University of North Texas Libraries. https://texashistory.unt.edu/ark:/67531/metapth337534/.

165. "considerable attendance" at his demonstrations: *Hearings before the President's Commission* (1964), Vol. XIX, De Mohrenschildt Exhibit No. 8, p. 552. https://www.govinfo.gov/content/pkg/GPO-WARRENCOMMISSIONHEARINGS-19/pdf/GPO-WARRENCOMMISSIONHEARINGS-19.pdf.

167. identifying himself as Lee Oswald: Warren Commission, *Report of the President's Commission on the Assassination of President Kennedy*, p. 301. Washington, DC: United States Government Printing Office, 1964. https://www.archives.gov/research/jfk/warren-commission-report/chapter-6.html#contacts.

167. "Cuban Revolution rather than helping it": Warren Commission, *Report of the President's Commission on the Assassination of President Kennedy*, p. 302. Washington, DC: United States Government Printing Office, 1964. https://www.archives.gov/research/jfk/warren-commission-report/chapter-6.html#contacts. See also https://www.archives.gov/files/research/jfk/releases/180-10142-10302.pdf.

167. sexual relationship between Oswald and Duran: Scott, Peter Dale. "Deep Politics III: Overview: The CIA, the Drug Traffic, and Oswald in Mexico." History Matters, last modified December 2000. https://history-matters.com /pds/DP3_Overview.htm.

168. disappointed by his failure to reach Cuba: Warren Commission, *Report of the President's Commission on the Assassination of President Kennedy,* p. 538. Washington, DC: United States Government Printing Office, 1964. https://www.archives.gov/research/jfk/warren-commission-report/chapter-6 .html#contacts.

168. Hosty flushed down the toilet: "Agent Tells Fate of Oswald Note." *New York Times,* December 13, 1975. https://www.nytimes.com/1975/12/13 /archives/agent-tells-fate-of-oswald-note-says-he-flushed-it-down-drain-on .html.

168. at the Texas School Book Depository: Warren Commission, *Report of the President's Commission on the Assassination of President Kennedy,* p. 32. Washington, DC: United States Government Printing Office, 1964. https:// www.archives.gov/research/jfk/warren-commission-report/chapter-2.html #motorcade.

169. ten times because of repeated mistakes: Scott, Paul. "Oswald's Last Letter." *The Review of The NEWS,* December 16, 1970. http://jfk.hood.edu/Collection /Weisberg%20Subject%20Index%20Files/A%20Disk/Allen-Scott%20 Columns/Item%2003.pdf.

169. as well as nonexistent punctuation: *Hearings before the President's Commission* (1964), Vol. XVI, Commission Exhibit No. 15, p. 33. https://www .history-matters.com/archive/jfk/wc/wcvols/wh16/html/WH_Vol16_0029a .htm.

170. Oswald as their Manchurian candidate: Woolsey, James R., and Pacepa, Ion. *Operation Dragon: Inside the Kremlin's Secret War on America.* New York: Encounter, 2021. https://www.amazon.com/Operation-Dragon-Inside -Kremlins-America/dp/1641771453.

170. cover in embassies and consulates worldwide: https://www.archives.gov /files/research/jfk/releases/docid-32364160.pdf.

170. organized by ultra-right plotters: Hoover, J. Edgar. "Reaction of Soviet and Communist Party Officials to JFK Assassination," 1966. Report. National Archives, Washington, DC https://www.archives.gov/files/research/jfk/releases /docid-32204484.pdf.

170. less than $15: "Oswald's Act Held Consistent with Personality." *New York Times.* September 28, 1964, p. 15. https://www.nytimes.com/1964/09/28 /archives/oswalds-act-held-consistent-with-personality.html.

CHAPTER 30

181. ACLU work on behalf of American communists: *Hearings before the President's Commission* (1964), Vol. X, p. 116 (statement of John J. Abt). https://www.jfk-assassination.net/russ/testimony/abt.htm.

182. what a good father her Lee was: *Hearings before the President's Commission* (1964), Vol. I, p. 150 (statement of Marguerite Oswald). https://www.govinfo .gov/content/pkg/GPO-WARRENCOMMISSIONHEARINGS-1/pdf /GPO-WARRENCOMMISSIONHEARINGS-1.pdf, http://jfk-archives .blogspot.com/2010/09/marguerite-oswald.html.

182. photo of a man he hoped Marina could identify: *Hearings before the President's Commission* (1964), Vol. XI, p. 468 (statement of Bardwell Odum). https://www.history-matters.com/archive/jfk/wc/wcvols/wh11/pdf/WH11 _Odum_aff.pdf.

183. to protect Oswald's family: DeLeón, Jessica. "Remembering the Assassination of President John F. Kennedy 50 Years Ago." University of North Texas website. https://northtexan.unt.edu/issues/2013-fall/living-history.

183. ready to make their move in the morning: Phone conversations with Mike Howard, September 2013 and January 23, 2021.

CHAPTER 31

185. some forty-five minutes from Dallas: *Hearings before the President's Commission* (1964), Vol. II, pp. 344 (statement of Peter Paul Gregory). https://www.govinfo .gov/content/pkg/GPO-WARRENCOMMISSIONHEARINGS-2/pdf /GPO-WARRENCOMMISSIONHEARINGS-2.pdf.

There is a second Secret Service report drafted by Charles Kunkel (SS) that covers the events from leaving the Executive Inn to Parkland Hospital, to the Six Flags Inn. There are just a few minor discrepancies. http://jfk.hood.edu /Collection/Weisberg%20Subject%20Index%20Files/O%20Disk/Oswald%20 Marina%20Custody/Item%2001.pdf. For Gregory's testimony before the Warren Commission, see: https://www.history-matters.com/archive /jfk/wc/wcvols/wh2/pdf/WH2_Gregory.pdf.

185. the right thing in calling "Mr. Gregory": *Hearings before the President's Commission* (1964), Vol. I, p. 155 (statement of Marguerite Oswald). https:// www.jfk-assassination.net/russ/testimony/2_10_64_AM.htm.

186. "just wanted to get us out of there": *Hearings before the President's Commission* (1964), Vol. I, p. 156 (statement of Marguerite Oswald). https://www .jfk-assassination.net/russ/testimony/2_10_64_AM.htm.

186. "out in the sticks": Ibid.

186. $50 from *Life* magazine to settle the bill: Ibid.

188. "Your son has expired": Ibid.

188. allowed to see her dead son: Ibid.

188. "it was you at that moment": Padgett, Joseph T., *Of Assassin's Bullets, a Bayonet, and Christmas Dinner,* 1982, typesript (Library of Congress, Txu 111.768).

189. "He cry. He eye wet.": *Hearings before the President's Commission* (1964), Vol. I, p. 161 (statement of Marguerite Oswald). https://www.jfk-assassination.net /russ/testimony/2_10_64_AM.htm.

189. separated from the other guests: Telephone interview of Mike Howard, January 24, 2022.

CHAPTER 32

191. occupied the two rooms on either side: *Hearings before the President's Commission* (1964), Vol. II. https://www.govinfo.gov/content/pkg/GPO -WARRENCOMMISSIONHEARINGS-2/pdf/GPO -WARRENCOMMISSIONHEARINGS-2.pdf.

192. "Mr. Gregory did all the Russian talking": *Investigation of the Assassination of President John F. Kennedy: Hearings before the Select Committee on Assassinations of the U.S. House of Representatives,* Ninety-fifth Congress, Second Session: 11 Paperback—August 24, 2017. https://www.amazon.com /Investigation-Assassination-President-John-Kennedy/dp/1376161362 P.171.

192. custom for breastfeeding mothers to drink beer: Conversation with Mike Howard, October 11, 2013.

193. no one wanted to hear her story: *Hearings before the President's Commission* (1964), Vol. I, p. 129 (statement of Marguerite Oswald). https://history-matters.com/archive/jfk/wc/wcvols/wh1/pdf/WH1 _MargueriteOswald_3rd.pdf.

194. was young and beautiful, she claimed: *Hearings before the President's Commission* (1964), Vol. I (statement of Marguerite Oswald).

194. "get it out of her system": *Hearings before the President's Commission* (1964), Vol. I (statement of Robert Edward Lee Oswald).

194. listening in during her Washington testimony: *Hearings before the President's Commission* (1964), Vol. I, p. 166 (statement of Marguerite Oswald). https://history-matters.com/archive/jfk/wc/wcvols/wh1/pdf /WH1_MargueriteOswald_3rd.pdf.

195. "would scratch my eyes out": *Hearings before the President's Commission* (1964), Vol. I, p. 82 (statement of Marina Oswald). https://www.govinfo .gov/content/pkg/GPO-WARRENCOMMISSIONHEARINGS-1/pdf /GPO-WARRENCOMMISSIONHEARINGS-1.pdf.

196. "we should be concerned about": *Hearings before the President's Commission* (1964), Vol. I, p. 167 (statement of Marguerite Oswald). https://www.govinfo

.gov/content/pkg/GPO-WARRENCOMMISSIONHEARINGS-1/pdf
/GPO-WARRENCOMMISSIONHEARINGS-1.pdf.

CHAPTER 33

198. left for the funeral on time: *Hearings before the President's Commission* (1964), Vol. I (statement of Marguerite Oswald). https://www.govinfo .gov/content/pkg/GPO-WARRENCOMMISSIONHEARINGS-1/pdf /GPO-WARRENCOMMISSIONHEARINGS-1.pdf.

199. "and we are with you": McMillan, Priscilla Johnson. *Marina and Lee: The Tormented Love and Fatal Obsession Behind Lee Harvey Oswald's Assassination of John F. Kennedy.* New York: Harper & Row Publishers, 1977, p. 444.

CHAPTER 34

202. less appealing participant in a conspiracy: https://www.history-matters .com/archive/jfk/wc/wcvols/wh23/pdf/WH23_CE_1792.pdf, https:// reopenkennedycase.forumotion.net/t565-lost-in-translation, and https://www .maryferrell.org/pages/Essay_-_Oswald_Legend_7.html.

202. "faultless without deviation": *Hearings before the President's Commission* (1964), Vol. XXIII, Commission Exhibit No. 1792, p. 405. https://www .history-matters.com/archive/jfk/wc/wcvols/wh23/pdf/WH23_CE_1792.pdf.

202. not examined the rifle, only its butt: *Hearings before the President's Commission* (1964), Vol. XXIII, Commission Exhibit No. 1792, p. 408. https://www .history-matters.com/archive/jfk/wc/wcvols/wh23/pdf/WH23_CE_1792.pdf.

203. been a while since he had used his Russian: *Hearings before the President's Commission* (1964), Vol. XXIII, Commission Exhibit No. 1792, p. 405. https://www.history-matters.com/archive/jfk/wc/wcvols/wh23/pdf/WH23 _CE_1792.pdf.

204. translator was to occupy Pete's place: *Hearings before the President's Commission* (1964), Vol. XXIII, Commission Exhibit No. 1792, p. 406. https://www.history-matters.com/archive/jfk/wc/wcvols/wh23/pdf/WH23 _CE_1792.pdf.

205. enough to cement Marina's suspicions: *Hearings before the President's Commission* (1964), Vol. I (statement of Marina Oswald). https://www .govinfo.gov/content/pkg/GPO-WARRENCOMMISSIONHEARINGS-1 /pdf/GPO-WARRENCOMMISSIONHEARINGS-1.pdf.

Pete Gregory's account of the Gopadze incident is confirmed by Marina Oswald's testimony before the Warren Commission. In her account, she feared that Gopadze was FBI. (He was not. He was Secret Service.) https://www .govinfo.gov/content/pkg/GPO-WARRENCOMMISSIONHEARINGS-1 /pdf/GPO-WARRENCOMMISSIONHEARINGS-1.pdf.

207. identified as the lone gunman: Simpich, Bill. "The Twelve Who Built the Oswald Legend." Essay from the Mary Ferrell Foundation, June 3, 2012. https://www.maryferrell.org/pages/Essay_-_Oswald_Legend_7.html.

CHAPTER 35

212. Howard removed the bayonet: Conversation with Mike Howard, September 2013. Joe Padgett essay.

213. "you would take it that way": *Hearings before the President's Commission* (1964), Vol. I (statement of Marguerite Oswald).

213. "I did not ask": *Hearings before the President's Commission* (1964), Vol. I (statement of Marguerite Oswald).

CHAPTER 36

214. look-alike substituted for the real Oswald: Balz, Dan. "Body Exhumed, Ruled Oswald's." *Washington Post*, October 5, 1981. https://www.washingtonpost.com/archive/politics/1981/10/05/body-exhumed-ruled-oswalds/44af8a52-d830-419d-b742-fa5976a02cf5/.

215. as her business manager, had carefully cultivated: *Hearings before the President's Commission* (1964), Vol. I, p. 498 (statement of James Martin). http://jfkassassination.net/russ/testimony/martin_jh.htm.

216. tried to resume a normal life: Memorandum for Mr. Tolson, February 24, 1964. Mary Ferrell Foundation, Assassination Archives and Research Center. https://www.maryferrell.org/showDoc.html?docId=10098#relPageId=25.

216. her stay in the Martin household: Memorandum for Mr. Tolson, February 24, 1964. Mary Ferrell Foundation, Assassination Archives and Research Center. https://www.maryferrell.org/showDoc.html?docId=10098#relPageId=25.

216. eve of testimony before the Warren Commission: Lee Harvey Oswald Memorandum for FBI Director, February 20, 1964. Mary Ferrell Foundation, Assassination Archives and Research Center. https://www.maryferrell.org/showDoc.html?docId=10098#relPageId=45.

216. the FBI agents did not intercede: Hoover, J. Edgar. Memorandum for Mr. Tolson, February 24, 1964. Mary Ferrell Foundation, Assassination Archives and Research Center. https://www.maryferrell.org/showDoc.html?docId=10098#relPageId=76. Hoover, J. Edgar. Letter to J. Lee Rankin, General Counsel, The President's Commission, February 17, 1964. Mary Ferrell Foundation, Assassination Archives and Research Center. https://www.maryferrell.org/showDoc.html?docId=10098#relPageId=82.

216. Marina should behave: Newsom, Milton L. FBI Lee Harvey Oswald Report, March 23, 1964. Mary Ferrell Foundation, Assassination

Archives and Research Center. https://www.maryferrell.org/showDoc
.html?docId=10098#relPageId=64.

216. the story of their affair: Newsom, Milton L. FBI Lee Harvey Oswald
Report, March 23, 1964. Mary Ferrell Foundation, Assassination
Archives and Research Center. https://www.maryferrell.org/showDoc
.html?docId=10098#relPageId=56.

216. not relevant to the assassination inquiry: Newsom, Milton L. FBI
Lee Harvey Oswald Report, March 23, 1964. Mary Ferrell Foundation,
Assassination Archives and Research Center. https://www.maryferrell.org
/showDoc.html?docId=10098#relPageId=56.

216. Threats of lawsuits followed: Newsom, Milton L. FBI Lee Harvey
Oswald Report, March 23, 1964. Mary Ferrell Foundation, Assassination
Archives and Research Center. https://www.maryferrell.org/showDoc
.html?docId=10098#relPageId=60.

CHAPTER 37

218. bespectacled fifty-seven-year-old nurse: *Hearings before the President's
Commission* (1964), Vol. I, p. 230 (statement of Marguerite Oswald).
https://history-matters.com/archive/jfk/wc/wcvols/wh1/pdf/WH1
_MargueriteOswald_3rd.pdf.

220. necessary for her to be recalled: *Hearings before the President's
Commission* (1964), Vol. I, p. 129 (statement of Marguerite Oswald).
https://history-matters.com/archive/jfk/wc/wcvols/wh1/pdf/WH1
_MargueriteOswald_3rd.pdf.

224. photo of a man she did not recognize: *Hearings before the President's
Commission* (1964), Vol. XI, p. 468 (statement of Bardwell D. Odum). https://
www.history-matters.com/archive/jfk/wc/wcvols/wh11/pdf/WH11_Odum
_aff.pdf.

225. "you naming these people?": *Hearings before the President's Commission* (1964),
Vol. I, p. 264 (statement of Marguerite Oswald). https://history-matters.com
/archive/jfk/wc/wcvols/wh1/pdf/WH1_MargueriteOswald_3rd.pdf.

230. antagonism toward the United States: Warren Commission, *Report of
the President's Commission on the Assassination of President Kennedy,* p. 23.
Washington, DC: United States Government Printing Office, 1964. https://
www.archives.gov/research/jfk/warren-commission-report/chapter-1.

230. "understand Oswald's possible motivation": Warren Commission, *Report
of the President's Commission on the Assassination of President Kennedy,* p.
416. Washington, DC: United States Government Printing Office, 1964.
https://www.archives.gov/research/jfk/warren-commission-report/chapter-7
.html#relationship.

CHAPTER 39

231. **must have been a conspiracy:** Bugliosi, Vincent. *Reclaiming History: The Assassination of President John F. Kennedy.* New York: W.W. Norton & Company, 2007. https://www.amazon.com/Reclaiming-History -Assassination-President-Kennedy/dp/0393045250.

232. **the president was killed by a "lone nut":** Ibid, xxvi–xxvii.

233. **going to Dallas to shoot the president:** McMillan, Priscilla Johnson. *Marina and Lee: The Tormented Love and Fatal Obsession Behind Lee Harvey Oswald's Assassination of John F. Kennedy.* New York: Harper & Row Publishers, 1977.

233. **did *not* conspire to kill the president:** Warren Commission, *Report of the President's Commission on the Assassination of President Kennedy,* p. 1. Washington, DC: United States Government Printing Office, 1964. https://www .archives.gov/research/jfk/warren-commission-report/chapter-1 summary.

233. **that their father was guilty:** Transcript of Marina Oswald Porter's appearance on *Oprah Winfrey Show*, November 22, 1996. Transcribed by R. J. DellaRosa. November Days 1963, Tumblr.com. http://novemberdays1963.tumblr.com /page/2.

234. **"the extent of the conspiracy":** *Report of the Select Committee on Assassinations of the U.S. House of Representatives on the assassination of President John F. Kennedy,* Washington, DC: United States Government Printing Office, 1979. https://www.archives.gov/research/jfk/select-committee-report/summary .html.

234. **"the assassination of President Kennedy":** Weld, William F. Letter from Office of the Attorney General to Chairman of Committee on the Judiciary, Peter W. Rodino, Jr., n.d., p. 5. http://jfk.hood.edu/Collection/Weisberg%20 Subject%20Index%20Files/J%20Disk/Justice%20Department%20of /Justice%20Department%20of%20JFK-King%20Reinvestigation /Item%2014.pdf.

CHAPTER 40

242. **insight into her husband's psyche:** *Hearings before the President's Commission* (1964), Vol. I, p. 23 (statement of Marina Oswald). https://www.govinfo .gov/content/pkg/GPO-WARRENCOMMISSIONHEARINGS-1/pdf /GPO-WARRENCOMMISSIONHEARINGS-1.pdf.

243. **to members of the Russian community:** Warren Commission, *Report of the President's Commission on the Assassination of President Kennedy,* pp. 435–437. Washington, DC: United States Government Printing Office, 1964. https://www.archives.gov/research/jfk/warren-commission-report/chapter-7 .html#relationship.

CHAPTER 41

244. **as the president's car passed directly below him?:** Epstein, Edward. *Legend: The Secret World of Lee Harvey Oswald.* New York: Ballantine, 1978.

246. **Smith & Wesson .38 caliber cost $29.95:** Jura, Jackie. "Oswald Handgun JFK .38 Revolver." Orwell Today website. https://www.orwelltoday.com/jfkoswaldgunplanted.shtml.

248. **needed to shoot at General Edwin Walker or the president:** Warren Commission, *Report of the President's Commission on the Assassination of President Kennedy,* appendix 14. Washington, DC: United States Government Printing Office, 1964. https://www.archives.gov/research/jfk/warren-commission-report/appendix-14.html.

248. **"months before the president was killed":** Bailey, Sam. "Oswald: Myth, Mystery and Meaning." *PBS Thirteen*, November 19, 2013. https://www.pbs.org/wgbh/frontline/article/oswald_myth_mystery_meaning/.

CHAPTER 42

250. **"I should have seen it coming":** Interview with Mike Howard, Secret Service retired. This conversation took place one night at the Six Flags Inn.

250. **had a violent personality:** Oswald, Robert, with Myrick and Barbara Land. *Lee: A Portrait of Lee Harvey Oswald.* New York: Coward-McCann, 1967. pp. 51–53.

CHAPTER 43

252. **after slighted Texas politicians intervened:** Interview of Mike Howard, Secret Service retired, https://www.youtube.com/watch?v=t2wvG6Yi71Y&t=793s.

INDEX

Communist Party of the Soviet Union, 45, 78

communists and communism
anti-communism of 1950s and 1960s, 112–13
Dallas Russians and, 104, 105, 108, 158
LHO's interest in and subsequent disenchantment with, 58, 114, 132, 164–65, 169, 203, 207, 229, 235, 236, 239
Marina Oswald and, 241
in Mexico, 167
in Soviet Union, 36, 50, 89
See also American Communist Party
Communist Youth League, 140
Connally, John, 60–61, 180
Continental Life Building (Fort Worth), 69, 177, 178
Convair, 135–36
Cronkite, Walter, 6, 7
Cuba and Cubans
in assassination conspiracies, 9, 36, 232, 235
LHO's admiration for and plans related to, 59, 82, 115–16, 157, 164–70, 236, 241
Marina Oswald's opinion of, 115–16
suspected role of, in assassination, 33, 34, 166
Warren Commission's absolving of role of, 35, 233
See also Fair Play for Cuba Committee (FPCC)
Cuban Embassy (Mexico City), 33, 118, 157, 166, 169, 236
Cuban Missile Crisis, 6
Cunningham Drugs (Fort Worth), 126
Cutter, Tom, 117

Daily Worker, 112
Dallas, Tex., 3–4, 6–8, 10, 11, 14–17, 19, 22, 26, 28–31, 33,
35–37, 56, 62, 63, 67, 73, 74, 99, 120, 121, 128–30, 136, 139, 145, 149, 150, 154–58, 161, 164–65, 168–69, 171–73, 178–82, 185–87, 192, 201–3, 206, 210–11, 214, 218, 233, 235, 240–42, 245–46, 249, 252, 254. See also Dallas Russians; Dealey Plaza; Love Field
Dallas-Forth Worth Turnpike, 185
Dallas Russians, 8, 18, 19, 21, 33, 35, 65, 73, 87, 104–9, 111, 117, 121, 128, 131, 133–34, 139, 143, 145–48, 150, 151, 156, 157, 200, 208, 213, 216, 231, 241, 243, 245, 250, 255
Daniels, Price, 113
Das Kapital (Marx), 146
Davis, Cullin, 97
Davis, "Stinky," 97
Dealey Plaza, 4, 6–7, 168, 172–73
Democratic Party, 113
Denton, Tex., 185
Denver, Bob, 97
DFW airport, 136
Dictabelt recordings, 234
Dobrynin, Anatoly, 32
Dorothy Lane (Dallas), 65, 129, 133, 155, 185, photo section
Duran, Silvia, 167

Eisenhower, Dwight D., 113, 207
Elm Street (Dallas), 173
Elsbeth Street (Dallas), 145–51, 153, 155, 256
Engels, Friedrich, 87
English language, 8, 24, 27, 32, 41, 46–47, 58, 61, 77, 80, 81, 90, 91, 96, 101, 105–7, 116, 122, 124, 126–27, 132–33, 139, 146, 148, 153, 156, 181, 185, 189, 192, 208, 233, 241
Executive Inn (Dallas), 183, 203, 224

ABOUT THE AUTHOR

Paul R. Gregory is a Research Fellow at Stanford's Hoover Institution and a pioneer in the study of Soviet and Russian economics. A student of the fabled Harvard Russian Research Center, he received his PhD from Harvard in 1969. His textbook on the Russian economy was used to teach more than two generations of students. In addition to his scholarly work, he has been an active blogger on Russian affairs for *Forbes*, *The Hill*, and other media platforms.

Author photo: Hoover Institution on War, Revolution, and Peace, Stanford University.